THE GLORY
OF THE SUN

THE GLORY
OF THE SUN

by

STERLING W. SILL

BOOKCRAFT, INC.
SALT LAKE CITY, UTAH

Copyright
Bookcraft, Inc.
1961

STERLING W. SILL

FOREWORD

Some time ago the writer was asked to give a series of gospel messages on the weekly radio program of the Church, called "Sunday Evening from Temple Square." The first fifty-two of these messages making up the speaking portion of these radio broadcasts are presented in this volume.

When writing to the Corinthians the Apostle Paul referred to the important fact that in the resurrection there will be three general degrees of glory. They will differ from each other, all the way from the twinkle of the tiniest star up to the blaze of the noonday sun, thereby corresponding to the differences in the excellence of our individual lives. This fact has the greatest possible present significance to us. The mission of Jesus in the world and his purpose in organizing the Church was to make available detailed instruction and direction as to how everyone might qualify for the celestial kingdom.

Celestial glory is the order in which God himself dwells. It "excels in all things"—glory, might, dominion, and power. To the members of the Church at Philippi the Apostle Paul pointed out that through obedience to the commandments, God would "change" their bodies that they may be "fashioned like unto his glorious body." (Phil. 3:21) Our minds and hearts may also become like God, and every principle of the gospel is designed to qualify us for the highest glory. There are no commandments directing us to the lower kingdoms. We fall into the lesser degrees by the amount of our default from the celestial. It was this highest order to which Jesus referred when he said, "Strait is the gate, and narrow is the way which leadeth unto life, and few there be that find it."

It is the greatest of tragedies that only a comparative few will ever reach this goal, though it is easily available to everyone. This is the most important of all of life's objectives and a more powerful incentive to accomplishment cannot be conceived. Neither could any course in life be more personally profitable than to follow faithfully the program designed by our eternal Father to qualify us for "The Glory of the Sun." How enthusiastically we should work and how anxiously we should assist each other in this tremendous project of exaltation.

President David O. McKay recently said that the purpose of the gospel is to change people. That was also the mission of Jesus. That is also the intended function of the stimulating ideas and ennobling ideals of the scriptures. That is the purpose of all of the work of the Church. The work of God himself is to exalt his children to their greatest possible maximum on the basis of their own free agency. It is hoped that these weekly radio messages may encourage someone in the right direction, and in the process bring some pleasure to those who read them.

Each chapter suggests an opportunity for the reader to make a personal decision on some important point bearing on this general objective. Wise decisions lead to wise actions, and wise actions in spiritual and religious matters can bring about our eternal welfare and happiness. As we get older and as we think more seriously about the issues of life, we become increasingly aware that the most important part of our existence lies beyond the boundaries of mortality. To assist us in qualifying for eternal life we need an intimate knowledge of gospel principles, as "no man can be saved in ignorance." But we also need to be inspired in our faith, ideals, and ambitions must be put in actual operation, proper standards of conduct must be adopted and lived, and it is thought that to hold up stimulating gospel ideas regularly before our minds will help us in the attainment of life's most important **goals.**

On one occasion Abraham Lincoln said that, "Most people are about as happy as they make up their minds to be." Without losing any of the truth of this helpful suggestion, we might paraphrase it to say that, "Most people are about as righteous, or about as religious, or about as successful as they make up their minds to be." What could be more important to the success of our lives than to firmly make up our minds to qualify for this tremendous objective, "The Glory of the Sun." This requires that our minds must be constantly fed and vitalized.

In general there are two kinds of literature. There is a literature of knowledge, and there is a literature of power. The function of the first is to teach; the function of the second is to move. It is hoped that these chapters may help to provide the necessary "nudge" to help someone move a little more steadily and happily in the right direction.

In preparing these messages an attempt has been made to supplement the foundation truths of the scriptures with some of the inspirational ideas of great and good men. The rich deposits of wisdom left for us the weaknesses within ourselves that may cause our failure. Indecision, procrastination, indifference, and lack of understanding are among the soft spots in our projected success and must have our constant attention.

When one spends a substantial part of his time attempting to counsel others in regard to the various problems that trouble human lives, he is impressed with the fact that we all need as much help as we can get from the right sources outside ourselves. Otherwise, we may fail to deal as successfully as is possible with our daily problems. It is also probable that no one ever undertakes to direct a series of messages aimed at the unseen needs of unseen people, without being impressed with his own incompetence. Most of us struggle along far below the level of perfection, and more or less we are all bothered by rather severe personal limitations.

In a general truth, Martin Luther once said, "Only a

few of the first fruits of wisdom, only small fragments of the boundless heights, breadths, and depths of truth have I been able to gather." However, we should not allow our personal imperfections to deter our effort nor relax our industry. Rather we should seek more vigorously to understand those basic principles of truth, and then make whatever personal applications are necessary to best serve our individual needs.

I am very grateful for the privilege of appearing on the "Sunday Evening from Temple Square" program with Albert Fallows, Jessie Evans Smith, Alexander Schreiner, Frank Asper, and others. I only wish their inspiring music could be made a part of these pages. I am also personally very grateful to the Church for this interesting assignment and for the members of the radio staff who have conducted the program.

May God be with us all, as we make our earnest way toward "The Glory of the Sun."

CONTENTS

There is one glory of the sun. . . .   Paul
(I Corinthians 15:41)

These are they whose bodies are celestial, whose glory is that of the sun, even the glory of God, the highest of all, whose glory the sun of the firmament is written of as being typical. (D & C 76:70)

God and You

ONE OF THE biggest businesses in the world is the business of holding conventions. Every day in every part of this country and other countries, men and women are meeting together to exchange ideas, solve problems, and develop more effective techniques for accomplishment. Helpful ideas and attitudes are also made available to us over radio networks, through our study, and by many other means.

But the place where our world probably feels the need for great ideas most urgently is in the field of religion. For example, how helpful it would be in solving the problems of the world as well as our personal problems if everyone in the world knew that above the dictators and above chance and and above circumstance, there is God to whom every human being must finally render an account of his life. To know God is not only to know that he lives, but it is also to know the kind of being that he is and what our relationship to him ought to be. Then probably next in importance to understanding God and making ourselves worthy of his confidence, we need to understand ourselves and be deserving of our own respect.

As I go about the country a little bit I find a great many people depressed and discouraged, because they don't really understand or believe in themselves. Probably the most widespread disease in the world is the inferiority complex. We are tainted with too much of the old sectarian doctrine of man's natural depravity and inherent weakness. There is nothing depraved about the man God has made except that which man brings upon himself.

Some time ago a stranger came to me and indicated that

he would like to talk about his troubles. He had the usual problems of discouragement, and of course a discouraged man is always a weak man. Such a man usually acts according to how he feels rather than by what the facts are. Consequently, such a one seldom knows the real causes of his trouble. We tend to look outside ourselves for the answers to our problems that can only be found in us. This man told me that in his opinion most of his problems, marital, spiritual, and material, stemmed from the fact that he lacked capital in his business. After discussing his circumstances with him at some length I was impressed that the reason he lacked capital in his business was because he wasn't using the capital he had in himself. Every man carries within himself the very things that he seeks. If he needs faith God has already implanted in his own heart the seeds of faith waiting only for him to make them grow. If he needs courage he can find it within himself.

In trying to restimulate my friend's efforts I told him the story of Fred Douglas, the Negro journalist and statesman of American slave days, who six months before his birth was pledged by his white master to a creditor in payment for a debt. And until he was older than my friend he did not even own his own body. Finally some friends of his took up a collection of $750 and purchased Fred Douglas and made him a present of himself. That is about what someone needs to do for us, for what good does it do to have great personal resources if we bury our talents in the ground because we disbelieve in ourselves.

I made a suggestion to my discouraged friend that he go to the library and get some good books on physiology, psychology and religion and read about the tremendous capital which God had invested in his hands, his brain, and his immortal spirit.

One of the most prominent teachings of Jesus had to do with the great worth of human personality. All of us are included in his appraisal. Jesus taught that we are all the actual children of God. When we fail to believe in ourselves we are in a sense denying God, for we are the greatest of his creations. He indicated our possibilities and what our standard of accomplishment should be when he said, "Be ye therefore perfect, even as your Father which is in heaven is perfect." That does not sound as if he intended that we should be weaklings and failures. The one business of life is to succeed. We were not placed here to waste our lives in failure.

Looking toward our eternal success and happiness everyone of us has been equipped as only the great God of the universe could equip us. Yet with the exception of God we probably know less about ourselves than any other thing in the world. We can ask a man questions about science, invention, or history and he will answer us. But if we ask him to write out an analysis of himself and tell us about his mind and soul qualities, we may not get a very good answer. Or ask him the purpose of his life or what he conceives his eternal destiny to be. The wisdom of the ancients advised, "Know thyself." That is still one of our most urgent assignments, and we should first understand who we are—that we are the children of God, and that the offspring has the potentiality of the parent.

Think of the capital God has given us in this great instrument called the brain. It is made up of 14 billion cells. It can contain more knowledge and more helpful ideas than can be stored in a dozen libraries.

A prominent neuro-physicist recently said that it would cost over three billion dollars to construct an electronic computer which could anywhere near compare to the human brain. But how much would it cost to endow an electronic computer with perception, insight, foresight, faith, and the powers of reason? If our brain represents an investment of three billion dollars, we should see to it that a more adequate return is obtained on the Lord's money.

Or, think of the resources and the possibilities of a pair of willing human hands. A man who had gone blind when a child, later had an operation performed on his eyes, and the first thing that his newly restored vision rested upon was his own hand. And he said he could not conceive anything so wonderful as his own hand, with its marvelous little boney levers, its circulation system, its communication network, its temperature control, its self-healing powers, its wonderful covering of skin and its ability to do the most difficult tasks.

Or, think of the wonders of the human voice and what we can do with it. The intellect sits enthroned in all of its powers, and yet it manifests itself mainly through the voice. Some time ago I attended a meeting where some of the audience were deaf mutes. For their benefit one of their number translated what was said by finger signs. Then the congregation stood up to sing and these fine deaf mutes followed their leader by singing with their fingers. I have never thought of my voice for its musical ability but that night coming home, I closed my car windows so that I would not frighten anyone unduly and I sang to the top of my voice all of the way, and I thought that I had never heard anything quite so wonderful as my own voice. We should thank God every day of our lives for these great gifts and abilities which are patterned after, and contain the possibilities of God's own abilities.

Or, think of the great capital asset of human personality. Personality is probably the most amazing fact in the universe. It is one of our most useful instruments of achievement and happiness, and we ourselves determine what it will be. With it we may serve others and make them happy. Not only have we been created in God's image, but we have been endowed with his attributes, and has bestowed upon us the endless possibilities of personality. Unlike the other parts of creation we may to a large degree determine our own destiny, and one of the ingredients of strength is not discouragement but enthusiasm. The thing that we probably need more than anything else is a good dose of inspiration occasionally. Edward Everett Hale said that the best education is to be perpetually thrilled by life. We need to be thrilled by our possibilities and by the progress that one may make even within the narrow limits of this life.

Think of a human being as he lies in the lap of his mother, a helpless babe. He has eyes perfectly fashioned but as yet they cannot discern objects. He has ears that cannot distinguish sounds, and yet within the span of a few short years what a change may be wrought. From such a beginning have come the great orators, generals, artists and workers to perform the wonders of our age. If such marvels can be brought about in one short life, what may we not expect in eternity from one of these God-men. Grant immortality to man with God for his guide, what is there in the way of mental, moral, or spiritual accomplishment that he may not aspire to? What a tragedy then when we lose heart and become weary and discouraged and weak. In some ways man is like a self-winding watch. He winds himself up by his own motion. It is very important that you believe in yourself. You are "God's greatest miracle." "The world is God's *handiwork* but *man* is his son."

We should cling to our inheritance. There is everything in knowing our origin and constantly reaffirming it in our lives. Only by the inspiration of knowing who we are and what our potential is can we reach our highest possibility as children of God.

On May 20, 1927, a young man by the name of Charles A. Lindbergh climbed into the cockpit of a little one-engined airplane and pointed its nose out across the great Atlantic. Thirty-three hours and thirty minutes later he set down at LeBourget Field in Paris. Then the newspapers around the world wrote great headlines saying, "Lindbergh Flies the Atlantic Alone." Then the New York *Sun* published an editorial and said, "Alone? Is he alone at whose right side rides courage? Who has skill sitting within the cockpit and faith upon his left hand? What is solitude to him who has self-reliance to show the way and ambition to read the dials? Does he lack for company for whom the air is cleft by daring, and darkness is made light by enterprise? True, the bodies of other men are absent from his crowded cabin. But as his aircraft keeps its course, he holds communion with those rarer spirits whose sustaining potency gives strength to his arm, resourcefulness to his mind, and contentment to his soul. Alone? With what more inspiring companions could he fly?"

And with what more inspiring companions could you fly? You are not alone. You are a child of God, created in his image, endowed with his attributes, entitled to his inspiration. And one of your greatest privileges is to seek him whom you resemble. It is important that you believe in God. It is even more important that God believes in you and that you believe in yourself. Real education is to learn more and more about each of the two most important beings in the world—God and you.

May you so live as to be continually entitled to his inspiration and guidance, giving you great faith in God and great confidence in yourself.

An Accursed Thing

BEFORE the children of Israel could be established in their promised land, it was first necessary to drive out the land's present occupants. The first city in the path of the invading Israelites was the strong and well-fortified city of Jericho. The Lord told Joshua exactly how to proceed to take the city, and at the same time he pointed out that the city and all that was therein had been accursed and must be destroyed. He also said that the Israelites must not defile themselves by taking possession of any of these "accursed things." But there is always someone who cannot follow instructions. Joshua had such a soldier by the name of Achan who as the city was being destroyed gathered up some of the gold of Jericho and hid it in his tent.

The next city in the path of the oncoming Israelites was the small and comparatively insignificant city of Ai, against which the Israelites marched with great confidence. But Joshua and his soldiers were shocked and humiliated to find that they could not stand before the soldiers of Ai. The military force that had been all-powerful at Jericho crumbled at Ai, and the soldiers turned their backs and fled in confusion and many of them were slain. Joshua describes his beaten and demoralized fellow soldiers by saying, "Their hearts became as water."

Then Joshua fell upon his face and put dust on his head and rent his clothes and he said, "Oh, God, why hast thou brought us over Jordan to destroy us. Would to God we had been content to dwell on the other side of Jordan." Then he said, "What shall I *say* when Israel turneth their backs before their enemies?" Then the Lord gave one of the important

fundamental laws of both individual and national success
which has come ringing down across 3400 years. The Lord
said to Joshua, "Get thee up. Why liest thou thus upon thy
face? Israel hath sinned and they have also transgressed my
covenant. And they have taken of the accursed thing, and
have put it among their own stuff. Therefore, the children of
Israel could not stand before their enemies but turned their
backs before their enemies because they are accursed. Neither will I be with you any more except you destroy the accursed from among you." So Joshua sought out the guilty
Achan, and the record says that Achan was "stoned with
stones" and "burned with fire." When the army had thus
cleansed itself, it marched again against Ai, this time with
immediate and complete success. (See Joshua 7 & 8)

Every one of the great nations of the past has fallen for
this same reason. They have taken some "accursed thing"
into their tents and allowed it to bring destruction upon
them. In *their* experience and in the experience of Joshua's
army we see an instructive lesson for our own day. For
whether it be a nation, a group or an individual, life is always trying to cleanse itself, and it is merciless in punishing
those who make it impure.

Certainly the greatest danger confronting twentieth century America is not the threat of nuclear devastation. The
most destructive threat of our day is the sin that hides inside
our tents. It is our own moral disintegration and willingness
to transgress the laws of God. Aristotle once said to Alexander the Great that the greatest enemy that ever confronted
an army was never in the ranks of the foe but always in
its own camp. If America is ever destroyed, the fundamental
reason will be the enemy within, and it will *not* be because
of any shortage of manpower or inferior armaments or lagging
industrial production or inadequate food supply. We have
all of these in great abundance. In fact, it has been said that
our national *problem* is surplus. Our national disease is over-
weight, and our national sin is forgetfulness. We forget God

who is the source of our strength and prosperity. One does not need to know very much about early American history to realize that special providential favor has attended this nation from its very beginning and has been the source of our national greatness.

This was understood and frequently discussed by the founding fathers. Benjamin Franklin said, "If a sparrow cannot fall to the ground without his notice, neither can a nation rise without his aid." Mr. Franklin pointed to the Bible admonition that "Unless God shall build the house, they labour in vain who build it."

These basic principles of success were also understood by Abraham Lincoln who in his Thanksgiving Day proclamation of 1863 to the people of his war-torn nation said, "Inasmuch as we know that nations, like individuals, are subjected to the punishments and chastisements in this world, may we not justly fear that the awful calamity of Civil War that now desolates our land may be but a punishment inflicted upon us for our presumptuous sins to the needful end of our national reformation as a whole people. We have been the recipients of the choicest bounties of heaven. We have been preserved these many years in peace and prosperity. We have grown in numbers, wealth and power as no other nation has ever grown. But we have forgotten God. We have forgotten the gracious hand that preserved us in peace and multiplied and enriched and strengthened us and we have vainly imagined in the deceitfulness of our hearts that all of these blessings were produced by some superior wisdom or virtue of our own. Intoxicated with unbroken success we have become too self-sufficient to feel the necessity of redeeming and preserving grace, too proud to pray to the God who made us. It behooves us then," said the president, "to humble ourselves before the offended power to confess our national sins and pray for clemency and forgiveness."

When our nation *may* be approaching the hour of its

greatest need, we are experiencing among us a great increase in crime and unrighteousness. Many forms of immorality are rapidly gaining ground among us. Religion is taking second place in our lives to many less worthy interests.

Under these conditions we are reminded of the warning of Daniel Webster before the New York Historical Society on February 22, 1852 just before his death. He pointed out some of the dangers which are now gathering about *us*. He said, "If we and our posterity shall be true to the Christian religion, if we and they shall live always in the fear of God and shall respect his commandments, we may have the highest hopes for the future fortunes of our country. It will have no decline and fall, but it will go on prospering and to prosper. But if we or our posterity reject religious instruction and authority, violate the rules of eternal justice, trifle with the injunctions of morality, and recklessly destroy the political constitution which holds us together, no man can tell how sudden a catastrophe may overwhelm us, that shall bury all of our glory in profound obscurity. Should that catastrophe happen let it have no history. Let the horrible narrative never be written. Let its fate be that of the lost books of Livy which no human eye shall ever read, or the missing Pleiad of which no man can ever know more than that it is lost, and lost forever."

Twenty years before Daniel Webster spoke these lines the Lord had warned Joseph Smith of the wars and destruction that our sins would bring upon us if we did not cleanse ourselves. The Lord said, "And thus, with the sword and by bloodshed the inhabitants of the earth shall mourn; and with famine, and plague, and earthquake, and the thunder of heaven, and the fierce and vivid lightning also, shall the inhabitants of the earth be made to feel the wrath, and indignation, and chastening hand of an Almighty God, until the consumption decreed hath made a full end of all nations." (D&C 87:6)

In other words God is saying to us again under more critical circumstances what he said to Joshua, "There is an accursed thing in thee, O Israel, therefore thou couldst not stand before thine enemies. Neither will I be with you any more except you repent." (See Joshua 7:13) As it is with our nation so it is with us as individuals, except that our individual sins are more important because we have full responsibility. The nation is made up of many people whose decisions we cannot make, whereas we have full control of our own lives. Our own conduct is our primary responsibility. The first soul that everyone should bring to God is his own soul, and the most common cause of our personal failure is that we get "an accursed thing" in our individual lives. We may think of it as just a little dishonesty, a little immorality, a little disobedience to God and a little unwillingness to do our full duty, just as Achan took just a little of the gold of Jericho. But ere we are aware in our failure we hear a repetition of the judgment that befell the Israelites at Ai. Then God says in substance, to them and to us, "There is an accursed thing in thee, O Israel, therefore thou canst not stand before thine enemies. Neither will I be with you any more except you destroy the accursed thing from among you." This is a natural unchanging law of success, applying to our nation and to us individually.

A roadside billboard of an oil company says, "A clean engine produces power." And so does a clean mind, a clear conscience, and an uncontaminated spirit. If a nation or an individual wants to be strong, it must keep a clean, vigorous heart. When we think we can hide evil in our lives and mix deceit and unrighteousness in our hearts, then we had better look out, for some disaster like that which destroyed the Israelites at Ai, is just around the corner. If we put off the cleansing of ourselves too long, the evil may extend its cancerous growth until like Achan we must be completely eliminated in this necessary process of purification.

If we desire to be strong, we must houseclean our lives as Joshua housecleaned the tent of Achan by destroying the "accursed thing" that was responsible for the defeat and humiliation of the body of which he was a part. Jesus gave effective expression to this law of success when he said, " . . . if thy right hand offend thee, cut it off, and cast it from thee: for it is profitable for thee that one of thy members should perish, and not that thy whole body should be cast into hell." (Matt. 5:30)

There is no such thing as "accidental failure." All failure is suicide. There is no such thing as "accidental success." All success is based on our worthiness and our obedience to the laws of success.

When men or nations are weakened by sin then like a tree that is rotten at its heart, they will sooner or later fall before the most trivial enemy. The natural consequence of sin is always weakness. As the armies of Israel could not stand at Ai because of the "accursed thing" in their midst, so we are threatened by every unclean thing to which we offer an asylum in our lives. The crisis at Ai did not cause the weakness of the Israelites, it only revealed it to their view. So it is with us. Day by day we build our lives and wait for some crisis to show us what we have become. Day by day we may nurse some "accursed thing" under the protecting cover of our tents "until we march against Ai." And then we find our success undermined, and we fall in defeat and disgrace with the poisoned arrows of the foe sticking from our backs.

We should never permit in our minds or in our activities that which God has called "accursed." For the laws of God go on unrepealed, and unrepealable, and any offender must hear for himself those terrible words of judgment; saying, "There is an accursed thing in thee, O Israel, therefore thou canst not stand before thine enemies, neither will I be with thee anymore except ye destroy the accursed thing from among you.".

May God help us in this great responsibility to cleanse our lives of evil.

The Big Three

IT IS A very interesting experience to have the privilege of meeting with a number of different occupational groups and listen to them talk about their ambitions, and objectives as they try to develop more effective means of occupational accomplishment. After a number of such experiences, one is likely to be impressed with how much more interesting and how much more important are the things making up the field of religion.

In the Church we talk about God and eternal life and building character and Godliness in ourselves and our children. Of course, all education is primarily about ourselves. We study medicine to learn to keep ourselves well physically. Through psychology, psychiatry, and other studies of the mind, we learn how to keep ourselves well mentally. Agriculture is how we feed ourselves. The social studies teach us how to live in an orderly way together. Then we study religion to learn how to keep ourselves well spiritually.

The biggest problems that we ever encounter center in ourselves. Isn't it interesting that the one subject that people know less about than anything else in the world is our own individual selves? That is, you can ask a man questions about science, invention, or history and he will answer you. But if you ask him to write out an analysis of himself to tell you about his mind and soul qualities, you may not get a very good answer. Or suppose you ask him where he came from or what the purpose of his life is, or where he is going—what kind of an answer would you be likely to get? Certainly the big three among life's questions are whence? why? whither? The old Persian philosopher, Omar Khayyam, wrestled long and hard with these questions without finding any answers that were very satisfactory. He says:

> I came like water and like the wind I go.
> Into this universe and why not knowing,
> Nor whence like water willy nilly flowing.
> And out of it as wind along the waste,
> I know not whether willy nilly blowing.
>
> Up from earth's center through the seventh gate,
> I rose and on the throne of Saturn sate.
> And many a knot unraveled by the way,
> But not the Master knot of human fate.
> There was a door to which I found no key.
> There was a veil through which I could not see.
>
> *Rubaiyat*, Stanza 28, 29, 31-32.

Shakespeare's Macbeth gave his opinion of the purpose of life by saying, "Life is a tale told by an idiot full of sound and fury signifying nothing." (*Macbeth*, Act IV, Scene 5.) And Hamlet's contribution was "how weary, stale, flat and unprofitable seem to me all the uses of this world. . . . 'Tis like an unweeded garden that goes to seed, things rank and gross in nature possess it merely." (*Hamlet*, Act I, Scene 2.)

One of the most stimulating of all possible experiences is to study that challenging set of scriptural ideas containing God's answers to the big three. The Lord has revealed that there are three great general divisions of life which someone had compared to the three acts of a play. Our pre-existence was the first act; our short mortality is the second act; our everlasting eternity will be the third act. It has been pointed out that if one went into the theater after the first act had been finished and left before the third act began, he might not have a very good understanding of the play.

For the same reason life just didn't make sense to Hamlet or Macbeth or Omar Khayyam because their perspective was too restricted. Each of these departments of our lives gives the others significance, and each has an important influence upon those that follow it. This influence was indi-

cated by the Lord when he said, "And they who keep their
first estate shall be added upon; and they who keep not their
first estate shall not have glory in the same kingdom with
those who keep their first estate; and they who keep their
second estate shall have glory added upon their heads for ever
and ever." (Abraham 3:26)

It helps us to make a more intelligent blueprint for success in this life if we know what happened in our first estate
and what its relationship is to our present and future situation. We also need to know what to look forward to in the
final act. I have a relative who when she reads a book always reads the last chapter first. That is, she wants to know
where she is going before she starts out. That is also a pretty
sensible procedure for attaining success in the three divisions
of our lives. Success in life is like making a road map. We
need to know where we are going and the best possible means
of getting there. Suppose then that we review briefly some
of the things that happened in our own first act.

Jesus has been given as the pattern for our own lives,
so suppose we start with him. Nothing in the scriptures could
be plainer than the fact that the life of Christ did not begin
at Bethlehem, nor did it end on Calvary. He himself said,

"I come forth from the Father, and am come into the
world: again, I leave the world, and go unto the Father."
(John 16:28) In praying to his Father he said, "I have glorified thee on the earth: I have finished the work which thou
gavest me to do. And now, O Father, glorify thou me with
thine own self with the glory which I had with thee before
the world was." (John 17:4-5)

But it is just as certain that *our* lives do not begin or end
within the narrow limits of mortality. We were all literally
begotten sons and daughters unto God in the spirit before
this world began. There we laid the foundation for our future progress. The scriptures tell us of a great council that
was held in heaven where the plans for our mortality were

discussed. We had come to a place in our progress where young people always come when it is desirable for them to move away from the homes of their parents. It was necessary in our eternal development to see good and evil side by side. This was not possible in the presence of God, for no sin is permitted to remain in his presence. During our pre-existence we walked by sight. We knew God. He is our Father. We lived with him. But it was also necessary for us to learn to walk a little way by faith. There were certain things that we must learn to do on our own account to prepare us for eternal life.

Most of life is but a preparation for something greater that is to follow. We prepare for school; we prepare for marriage; we prepare for our life's work; we prepare for death; we prepare for eternal life. Our pre-existence was the childhood of our immortality. Mortal life is the period when we learn to exercise our free agency properly and stand on our own feet and become sovereign souls. This is the place where we are to be tested and proved and tried. Here we learn to accept good and reject evil. In our first estate we learned that a wonderful new earth was to be created on which we were to be permitted to live. We were to be "added upon" by the gift of these wonderful, beautiful mortal bodies without which we could never receive "a fulness of joy." (D & C 93:33)

For a brief period we were to be endowed with the miraculous power of procreation and were to have the privilege of organizing a family and having it sealed together by the authority of the priesthood, and if we were obedient to God this family unit would continue throughout eternity and be the basis for a large part of our happiness.

We were to learn obedience to God, and to pattern our lives after the example of his only Begotten Son in the flesh. We knew that because of our free agency, this would be a world of sin and suffering, war and bloodshed, disease and death, and what must have been most important of all we knew that straight would be the gate and narrow would be the way leading to the highest degree of glory and only a few would ever get into the presence of God in the celestial kingdom.   Yet we were so delighted with our wonderful opportunities that "all the sons of God shouted for joy."   (Job 38:7)

Abraham was given a vision of our pre-existence about which he says, "Now the Lord had shown unto me, Abraham, the intelligences that were organized before the world was; and among all these there were many of the noble and great ones; And God saw these souls that they were good, and he stood in the midst of them and he said, These I will make my rulers; for he stood among those that were spirits, and he saw that they were good; and he said unto me, Abraham, thou art one of them; thou was chosen before thou were born.   And there stood one among them that was like unto God, and he said unto those who were with him; We will go down, for there is space there, and we will take of these materials, and we will make an earth whereon these may dwell; And we will prove them herewith, to see if they will do all things whatsoever the Lord their God shall command them."   (Abraham 3:22-25)

But many of us were also chosen for leadership in that Grand Council. The Prophet Joseph Smith has said that every man who has the calling to administer to the inhabitants of this earth was ordained to that purpose in the grand council in heaven before the world was. (*D.H.C.* 364) That is, many of us were among the noble and great in the spirit world and were high in the councils of heaven before this earth was formed. And I am sure that if we now understood the tremendous importance of our lives as we understood it then, that we would be willing to crawl on our hands and knees through life for the wonderful opportunity which is presently ours.

Then we entered our second estate through the miracle of birth. There are those who claim difficulty believing in their own immortality including the literal resurrection of the body. It seems that this should not be difficult for anyone who can believe in his own birth. That is, if you can believe in creation, if you can believe that two microscopic bits of protoplasm can come together and by a process of subdivision form other cells completely unlike themselves to make this great masterpiece of bone and sinew, vision and energy, intelligence and light, personality and will, that we call a human being. If you can believe in your own physical birth, it should not be difficult to believe in any one of the other miracles that God has promised for our eternal life.

Someone has put this idea into verse and said:

> Impossible you say that man survives the grave,
> That there are other lives
> More strange, oh friend;
> That we should ever rise
> From out the dark,
> To walk beneath the skies.

> But having risen to life and light,
> We need not wonder at our deathless flight.
> Life is the unbelievable,
> But now that this incredible has taught us how
> We can believe the all imagining power
> That breathed the cosmos forth as golden flower,
> Had potence in his breath.

> And plants us new surprises beyond death,
> New spaces and new goals
> For the adventure of ascending souls.
> Be brave, O heart, be brave.

> It is not strange that man survives the grave,
> 'Twould be a stranger thing were he destroyed,
> Than that he ever vaulted from the void.

We have been wonderfully "added upon" in our second estate. We know that even greater wonders await us in the final act, when glory will be added upon our heads forever and ever. Jesus came into this world just as we did through physical birth. He left this existence as each of us must leave it through physical death.

In the meantime we should follow the example of his life as closely as possible. One of the most thrilling lines in all of the scripture so far as I know was spoken by the mother of Jesus to the servants at the marriage feast in Cana. She said to them, "Whatsoever he saith unto you, do it." (John 2:5) What a wonderful motto for our lives.

What a great satisfaction there will be in such a life when we pass through the miracle of death into our final estate. Most of the rewards come in the last act. That's where "the happy endings" are. That is where God is. That is also where many of the tragedies are discovered if we have not lived Godly lives. Probably the most important experience in life is death. Death is the gateway to immortality. We live to die, and then we die to live. Someone has said that if the death of the body forever ended all there was of human life and personality then the universe would be throwing away with utter heedlessness its most precious possession.

A reasonable person does not build a violin with infinite care gathering the materials and shaping the body of it so that it can play the compositions of the masters and then by some whim of chance caprice smash it to bits. Neither does God build the great masterpiece of human life and then when it has just begun to live throw it utterly away. God holds securely in his hands the keys of eternal life. Every mortal being living upon this earth is a child of God begotten in heaven in God's own image. Everyone living upon the earth has been added upon and granted the blessings of mortality, including this wonderful body fashioned in the likeness of the spirit. We are now undergoing the final test, and if we are successful God will add glory upon our heads forever and ever.

Jesus said of all who obey, "Then all that my Father hath shall be given unto them." We all like to inherit from

STERLING W. SILL

Printed by

DESERET NEWS PRESS

in the United States of America

THE GLORY
OF THE SUN

by

STERLING W. SILL

B O O K C R A F T ,   I N C .
SALT LAKE CITY, UTAH

THE GLORY
OF THE SUN

a wealthy father. What could be more satisfactory than to inherit from God? But to live at our best we first need to know God's answers to the big three of life, which are, whence? why? whither?

Christians

THOMAS CARLYLE once said that a man's religion is the most important thing about him. That is what he believes in and lives by and stands for and devotes his life to. God himself is the author of religion. Religion is God's plan for our development. Every human being is also a human becoming, and God desires that we become as he is.

However, the history of man's acceptance of religion presents a rather dismal spectacle. Religion is based on man's free agency and the plan contemplates that both good and evil should be in the world, side by side. In the very beginning God taught the people the gospel, but Satan came among them and said, "Believe it not," and they believed it not and men have tended to love darkness more than light.

Before the world was very old, God decided to send the flood and cleanse it of its unrighteousness. But soon after the flood, wickedness again took over the minds of people and we had the confusion of tongues at Babel. Then the Lord started over again and established a new people from the seed of Abraham, the father of the faithful; but even the history of this chosen race presents a rather spotty picture of wickedness, bondage, idolatry, and difficulty.

Finally in the meridian of time the Son of God himself was sent into the world to atone for our sins and to organize his church upon the earth. But Jesus was mocked, crowned with thorns, and crucified. It was not very long before all of the apostles chosen by Jesus had suffered a violent death except John who was exiled to the Isle of Patmos. Then without inspired leadership the church sank to the level of a purely human institution. Many of the original Christian doctrines were changed, some were lost, some new ones were added and because of the unrighteousness of people the world slipped into that long, dark night of apostasy.

But one of the signs that should precede the glorious second coming of Christ was that "this gospel of the kingdom shall be preached in all the world as a witness unto all nations and then shall the end come." Never before has the world had a greater need of the authorized religion of Jesus Christ than now, and one of our most important problems is to identify it.

The religion that Christ taught was called Christianity. Those who followed him were called Christians. But today a large number of sects with unauthorized ministers have sprung up, each teaching a different doctrine. But the word "Christian" is still generally applied to this wide variety of contending systems with teachings and practices that are antagonistic to each other. It is probable that no other single term may now have so many opposite meanings as the once highly significant name, "Christian."

In fact Albert N. Whitehead once said that it would be impossible to imagine anything more unchristian than present Christian theology. He said that Christ himself would probably not understand it. Certainly Christ would not accept the authorship of the confusion in which present-day Christianity lives. Mr. Whitehead has pointed out that modern Christianity teaches a theology that has very little in common with the teachings of Jesus except a few words. Many modernists no longer hold the Christian faith, and certainly modernism can no longer properly be called Christian. The term Christian is far too fine a word to be misrepresented and abused as it presently is.

Socrates had a very helpful procedure when as he went around Athens he kept asking people to define their terms. Before he entered into any serious discussion he wanted to know that everyone understood what he was talking about and that all were discussing the same thing. Because Christianity in its original meaning is so tremendously important to us, it might also be a very helpful process to define our Christian terms. Certainly when many modern men confess their faith in God many of them have in mind something entirely different from the God of the Bible whom Jesus addressed as "our Father which art in heaven"! Some people regard God as living entirely in the past. Some diffuse him into the vapor of nothingness; some think of him only in such indefinite terms as nature or force or intelligence or law! One great minister said that, "God was an eternal principle." Another described the nature of God as a circle whose center was everywhere and whose circumference was nowhere. Some people describe God as Almighty, eternal, immense, incomprehensible and infinite, which is merely another way for saying there is no God. Of what use is a doctrine that cannot be understood and was never intended to be understood.

With something as important as Christianity, why should we allow it to lose its meaning because we tolerate every conceivable interpretation of doctrine that comes under this venerable title of Christianity. Tolerance itself ceases to be a virtue when it covers up grossly misleading falsehood and leads to confusion. We might ask ourselves what kind of definition of Christianity would be acceptable to Christ?

One dictionary says that originally a Christian was one who followed Christ, who believed in his doctrine, and who practiced his teachings. In the best sense a Christian would be one who believed in all of the teachings of Christ, as the most seriously anti-Christian would hold some beliefs in common with Christianity.

An old deacon was once asked whether or not he was a Christian, and he said that he was in spots. We can imagine that a fractional Christianity would never be very popular with Christ. How then could Christ possibly tolerate the present-day confusion originating with uninspired and irresponsible men who minister in his name? Certainly Paul was speaking for the Master when he said, "One Lord, one faith, one baptism, One God and Father of all. . . . " (Eph. 4:5) Paul warned the members of the church at Galatia of the seriousness of tampering with the word of the Lord when he said, "Though we, or an angel from heaven, preach any other gospel unto you than that which we have preached unto you, let him be accursed." (Gal. 1:8)

No one could be more particular about the truth than the Lord himself. Speaking through John the Revelator, he said, "If any man shall add unto these things, God shall add unto him the plagues that are written in this book: And if any man shall take away from the words of the book of this prophecy, God shall take away his part out of the book of life, and out of the holy city, and from the things which are written in this book." (Rev. 22:18-19)

The Lord had used almost the identical words in speaking to the people through Moses. He said, "Ye shall not add unto the word which I command you, neither shall ye diminish ought from it." (Deut. 4:2)

Inasmuch as the Lord is the same yesterday, today, and forever we would not expect him to change his position now merely to accommodate our confusion. In fact, in our own day the Lord said to the Prophet Joseph Smith that these conflicting creeds were *all* wrong, that they were an abomination in his sight. He said, "They teach for doctrines the commandments of men, having a form of godliness, but they deny the power thereof." (Joseph Smith 2:19) That is pretty strong language, but it is the language of the Lord himself, and we had better give it pretty serious attention.

Not only should the doctrines be true to qualify under the great name of Christ, but true Christianity must also be complete. It must not be spotty. There must be no gaps in its doctrines and there must be nothing left over. If merely to hold a few beliefs in common with Christ would qualify one as a Christian, then every heathen and every atheist and every criminal would be a Christian. We would not like to think of Peter as accepting just *part* of the teachings of Jesus. If Jesus is divine, then *all* of his doctrines are true.

Suppose that we examine some of the doctrines of original Christianity and make our own comparisons.

No. 1. In the days of Jesus, Christ's ministers did not choose themselves. Jesus said to these selected for service, "Come follow me." And they left their nets and their tax gathering to do his work. Jesus said to them distinctly, "Ye have not chosen me, but I have chosen you, and ordained you, that ye should go and bring forth fruit. (John 15:16)

Paul cautioned the Hebrews against any other course. He said, "And no man taketh this honour unto himself, but he that is called of God, as was Aaron." (Heb. 5:4) Yet most ministers of today select the ministry in much the same way as others select law or medicine or business, and for much the same reasons.

No. 2. The original ministers of Christianity did not teach their own doctrine. Even Jesus said, "My doctrine is not mine, but his that sent me." (John 7:16) In his letter to Timothy Paul was greatly concerned about those who went "contrary to sound doctrine." (I Tim. 1:10) Paul foretold to Timothy that the time would come when people would not endure sound doctrine. Many people in our day are not even concerned about whether the doctrine is sound or not. Some say that all roads lead to the same place and it doesn't matter what one believes or what he practices.

No. 3. Jesus taught that everyone who reaches the age of accountability must repent and be baptized if he would be saved. But there are many who have never heard the gospel. Certainly it would be unfair to condemn people for something they had never had the privilege of knowing. In Jesus' day these people were given a chance to hear it beyond the grave and their baptism was performed for them by an earthly representative. For this purpose Jesus visited the spirits in prison and preached the gospel to those who had been disobedient in the days of Noah. Referring to this doctrine Peter, the chief apostle said, "For Christ also hath once suffered for sins, the just for the unjust, that he might bring us to God, being put to death in the flesh but quickened by the Spirit: By which also he went and preached unto the spirits in prison; Which sometime were disobedient, when once the longsuffering of God waited in the days of Noah, while the ark was a preparing, wherein few, that is, eight souls were saved by water." (I Peter 3:18)

Peter makes perfectly clear that this doctrine of salvation for the dead was clearly taught in his day. He said, "For for this cause was the gospel preached also to them that are dead, that they might be judged according to men in the flesh, but live according to God in the spirit." (I Peter 4:6)

Paul also makes clear that the people of his day were performing these ordinances of vicarious baptism for the dead. He said, "Else what shall they do which are baptized for the dead, if the dead rise not at all? why are they then baptized for the dead?" (I Cor. 15:29) This doctrine is tremendously important as it involves the eternal salvation of a large percentage of all of God's children. This doctrine is a part of the Bible. It is a part of the doctrine of Jesus. It is a part of the gospel of Christ. Whatever *we* may think, *Christ* thought that it was absolutely necessary, or he never would have instituted it in the first place. Salvation for the dead is clearly a doctrine of the New Testament. If the doctrine is not good, then we had better throw the New Testament away. But if the New Testament is the word of God, then the doctrine must be acknowledged. If any church or any individual does not believe this doctrine, that church or that individual does not believe the New Testament. The work of salvation is not finished, and we have no right nor authority for discarding this or any other of the great Christian doctrines. We should remember that the Lord himself has pre-scribed a very severe penalty for those who add to or take from his doctrine.

No. 4. In First Corinthians Paul mentions the three de-grees of glory to which people are assigned after the resur-rection. These Paul likens to the glory of the sun, the moon and the stars. Paul gives us the names of two of these glories as the celestial and the terrestrial. But Paul doesn't tell us very much about who will go there or under what conditions.

On February 16, 1832 the Lord himself gave a vision of the degrees of glory to Joseph Smith and Sidney Rigdon, giv-ing much additional information not given in the Bible. The Bible gives enough information on many subjects to let us know that these doctrines were taught as a part of original Christianity. But many of these truths are now found in the Bible only in incomplete form. Therefore in our own day the Lord has given us three great volumes of new scripture making the great doctrines complete and outlining in con-siderable detail all of these tremendously important Christian doctrines so necessary to our eternal exaltation.

May God so direct us by his Spirit that we may take the time to learn what these important doctrines are, and then be good Christians in the best meaning of that great term is my humble prayer.

Death

MOST PEOPLE have the rather frequent experience of attending the funeral of some friend or relative. This serves one of our important needs inasmuch as it is about the only time that some of us think very seriously about death. One of our interesting human traits is that we don't like to think about those things that are unpleasant, even to avoid them. From unpleasant situations we have a natural tendency to turn away. We frequently follow the procedure credited to the ostrich, and bury our heads in the sand when any danger or unpleasant thing approaches.

We see evidence of this tendency manifest in the movies. When people become terrified by fear, or some unpleasant sight, the usual thing is to put their hands over the eyes. With a little more courage they may peek through their fingers. We do about the same thing mentally when an idea that seems to us to be unpleasant tries to get into our minds.

But unpleasant things do not cease to exist just because they are ignored. Death continues to walk among us with apparent unconcern for any slights or dislikes of ours. And death will probably not postpone any of its functions merely because we hold our hands tightly over our eyes. The ancient Egyptians had an interesting and a much more logical way of dealing with this situation. It is reported that at their great festive state occasions they kept constantly on display before the revelers, the skeleton of a dead man. That is, they wanted to keep everyone constantly reminded of the fact that someday he would die.

Now I don't want to frighten anyone unduly except to

suggest that some day you are going to die. At least, it has
been pointed out that judging from the past, there will be
very few of us get out of this world alive. Inasmuch then as
death is certain, suppose that we do as the ancient Egyptians did and hold it up to view, with our eyes wide open. We
often think of a death as a very unfortunate experience, but
that may not always be so. Death is probably the most important experience in life. Death is the gateway to immortality. We live to die, and then we die to live. If we were
to get a little better acquainted with death, we may find out
some good things about it, especially if we don't look at it
through the misty vision of our prejudice or tears. But rather
we should give some thoughtful consideration to death when
our personal feelings are not so heavily involved.

There is an old Greek play written around the fall of
ancient Athens. It tells of an Athenian philosopher who was
captured by a Roman general. The Roman told the Athenian
that he was about to be put to death. The Athenian didn't
seem very disturbed about it, and the Roman thought that
probably he hadn't understood, and so he suggested that
maybe the Athenian didn't know what it meant to die. The
Athenian replied that on the contrary he thought he understood death better than the Roman did. Then he said to the
Roman, "Thou dost not know what it is to die for thou dost
not know what it is to live. To die is to begin to live. It is
to end all stale and weary work to begin a newer and a
better. It is to leave deceitful knaves for the society of gods
and goodness."

I am satisfied that beyond death we will find more pleasant experiences than we have ever before imagined. When
James M. Barrie's little character Peter Pan thought he was
drowning he cried out in his extremity. Death will be an
awfully big experience and so it will be for all of us. Inasmuch therefore as death is so extremely important to everyone, we should understand as much about it as possible.

Our lives have been compared to a three-act play. Our

ante-mortal existence is the first act. Our mortality is the second act. Eternity is the third act. It has been pointed out that if one were to go into the theatre after the first act had been finished and leave before the third act began he may not get much out of the play, and for exactly the same reason life just doesn't make sense to some people.

Before we can get the most out of the second act we must know something about what went on in the first act, and we must believe in and look forward to the third act. Nothing could be plainer from the scripture than that the life of Christ did not begin at Bethlehem, nor did it end on Calvary. Jesus said plainly, "I came forth from the Father and am come into the world, again I leave the world and go unto the Father." Just before his death he said in his prayer, "And now, O Father, glorify thou me with thine own self with the glory which I had with thee before the world was." (John 17:5)

Twenty-two hundred years before his birth in Bethlehem the Lord showed himself to the great prophet of the Jaredites who was known as the brother of Jared. By way of introduction the Lord said, "Behold, I am he who was prepared from the foundation of the world to redeem my people." Then he said, "Seest thou that ye are created after mine own image?" The brother of Jared expressed surprise that the Lord was so much like himself in appearance. Then the Lord said, "Behold, this body, which ye now behold, is the body of my spirit; and man have I created after the body of my spirit; and even as I appear unto thee to be in the spirit will I appear unto my people in the flesh." (Ether 3:14-16)

Then some twenty-two centuries later the Lord was born a baby in the manger at Bethlehem. And for thirty-three years he trod the dusty roads of this earth. When his time was fulfilled, he was put to death upon the cross. His spirit and his body were again separated. And while his body lay in the tomb of Joseph of Arimathea, his spirit was ministering in the spirit world among those who were disobedient in the days of Noah. Then his spirit and body were united again through the resurrection, never again to be separated.

The life of Jesus is our pattern, and we will follow his course of birth, death, and resurrection. But of one thing we may be sure, and that is that death is a good thing, otherwise it would not have been included in the universal plan of salvation to include even the Son of God. Nothing that God does is superfluous or unnecessary. And we probably receive more blessings in consequence of our death than we do in consequence of our birth.

The Lord has not made known to us every detail of his work or how he will proceed in every instance, nor has he told us all his reasons for doing things exactly as he does. But we can be sure that God holds firmly in his hands the secrets of eternal life, and is able to fulfill to us his every promise. In the first Article of Faith we say, "We believe in God." That means that we believe that he exists and that we understand something about the kind of person that he is, but it also means that we trust him and that we believe that he knows his business.

One of his great prophets has said that, "There must needs be a space betwixt the time of death and the time of the resurrection." (Alma 40:6) This period is necessary in which to cleanse and purify and educate the spirit before the body and spirit are again reunited for eternity. It is logical that part of this process could best be done during the time the spirit and body were separated. Sometimes when an automobile is being rebuilt, it is necessary that it should be disassembled as it was in the beginning.

It is very interesting to read in the holy scriptures of the conditions that will exist during this period when the spirit is disembodied. The Prophet Alma says: "Now, concerning the state of the soul between death and the resurrection— Behold, it has been made known unto me by an angel, that the spirits of all men, as soon as they are departed from this mortal body, yea, the spirits of all men, whether they be good or evil, are taken home to that God who gave them life.

"And then shall it come to pass, that the spirits of those who are righteous are received into a state of happiness, which is called paradise, a state of rest, a state of peace, where they shall rest from all their troubles and from all care, and sorrow.

"And then shall it come to pass, that the spirits of the wicked, yea, who are evil—for behold, they have no part nor portion of the Spirit of the Lord; for behold, they chose evil works rather than good; therefore the spirit of the devil did enter into them, and take possession of their house—and these shall be cast out into outer darkness; there shall be weeping, and wailing, and gnashing of teeth, and this because of their own iniquity, being led captive by the will of the devil.

"Now this is the state of the souls of the wicked, yea, in darkness, and a state of awful, fearful looking for the fiery indignation of the wrath of God upon them; thus they remain in this state, as well as the righteous in paradise, until the time of their resurrection." (Alma 40:11-14)

The Savior himself takes us behind the scenes and tells us of the conditions that will exist during this period. He illustrates his instruction by giving an account of two men who died. One was a rich man who had apparently lived unrighteously. The other was a poor man named Lazarus. The Savior said, "And it came to pass, that the beggar died, and was carried by the angels into Abraham's bosom: the rich man also died, and was buried; And in hell he lifted up his eyes, being in torments, and seeth Abraham afar off, and Lazarus in his bosom. And he cried and said, Father Abraham, have mercy on me, and send Lazarus, that he may dip the tip of his finger in water, and cool my tongue; for I am tormented in this flame. But Abraham said, Son, remember that thou in thy lifetime receivedst thy good things, and likewise Lazarus evil things: but now he is comforted, and thou art tormented. And beside all this, between us and you there is a great gulf fixed: so that they which would pass from hence to you cannot; neither can they pass to us, that would come from thence.

"Then he said, I pray thee therefore, father, that thou wouldest send him to my father's house: For I have five brethren; that he may testify unto them, lest they also come into this place of torment. Abraham saith unto him, They have Moses and the prophets; let them hear them. And he said, Nay, father Abraham: but if one went unto them from the dead, they will repent. And he said unto him, If they hear not Moses and the prophets, neither will they be per-suaded, though one rose from the dead." (Luke 16:22-31)

We can understand something about our own future by understanding the state of these three men. They were carry-ing on a conversation. They recognized each other just as they had done while in mortality. They could speak and hear and understand. They could remember the events of their earth life. They could feel pleasure and pain, happiness and unhappiness. And when the rich man learned that there was nothing that he could do to relieve his own present suffering, the next thing that he thought about was the wel-fare of his family on the earth, and he wanted Lazarus to be sent to teach them the gospel so that they would not make the same mistakes that he had made. These same conditions will prevail for us. That is, you will be yourself, and I will be myself, throughout all eternity not only before but also after the resurrection.

When as the Prophet Nephi says, ". . . and the spirit and the body is restored to itself again, and all men become incor-ruptible, and immortal, and they are living souls, having a perfect knowledge like unto us in the flesh, save it be that our knowledge shall be perfect." (II Nephi 9:13) But in the best sense there are no dead. Jesus was not more dead after Calvary than he was before Bethlehem or at any point in be-tween. The poet has said:

He is not dead, my friend's not dead
But in the paths we mortals tread
Has gone some few trifling steps ahead.
And nearer to the end.

But we when round the bend
Face to face shall meet again our friend,
We thought was dead.

And someone else has given us another interesting perspective of our third act by saying:

I am standing upon the seashore. A ship at my side spreads her white sails to the morning breeze and starts for the blue ocean. She is an object of beauty and strength, and I stand and watch her until at length she hangs like a speck of white cloud where the sea and sky come down to mingle with each other. Then someone at my side says, "There, she is gone."

Gone where? Gone from my sight, that is all. She is just as large in mast and hull and spar as she was when she left my side, and is just as able to bear her load of living weight to the place of destination. Her diminished size is in me, not in her; and just at the moment when someone at my side says, "There, she is gone," there are other eyes watching her coming, and other voices ready to take up the glad shout saying, "Here she comes." And such is dying.

In 1822 John Howard Payne wrote his great musical masterpiece, "Home, Sweet Home." When this song was written, John Howard Payne was in Paris far away from the old homestead that he knew and loved so well. But John Howard Payne was going home for a holiday. He knew that the happiest holidays are those that we go home for. Home is where mother and father are. Home is where we grew up, and John Howard Payne was going home. But within a very few years everyone of us will be going home. We will be going back to where we grew up. We will be going back to where God is. We will be going back to where our parents and family and friends are.

May God so prosper our lives that we may all be able to sing with John Howard Payne, "There's no place like home."

The Dimensions of Life

IN THE DAYS of Job it was said, "All that a man hath, will he give for his life." (Job 2:4) We cling to life with every ounce of our strength. There is no inconvenience that we would not suffer. There is no hardship that we would not endure. There is no expense that we would not involve ourselves in to prolong life even for a week or a month, even though we knew that that period would be filled with pain and unhappiness. God himself has planted this love of life in the human soul, designed to encourage us to preserve this precious gift at all costs and live it at its best. How this should be done presents us with the most stimulating of all challenges.

Henry Thoreau, an early-day American philosopher, suggested that we should begin by thanking God every day of our lives for the privilege of having been born. And then he went on to speculate on the rather unique supposition of what it might have been like if we had not been born, and he pointed out many of the benefits that we would have missed as a consequence.

What this great philosopher may not have known was that as pointed out in the scriptures, one-third of all the spirit children of God were never born and never will be born because of disobedience in their pre-existence, and yet every spirit child of God hungers for a body. Nineteen hundred years ago some unembodied evil spirits who were followers of Lucifer indicated to Jesus that they preferred the bodies of swine rather than to have no bodies at all. (Matt. 8:28-32) Now if mortal life is worth so much, how much is eternal life worth, and how far should one be willing to go to help bring it about? Of course, life does not get its value only from its dimension of length. Life comes in four dimensions. First, there is the length of life, or how *long we live.* Then there is the breadth of life or how *interestingly* we live. Third there is the depth of life or how *much* we live, represented by those great human qualities of love, worship, devotion, and service. Then there is the fourth dimension which might correspond to that more or less mysterious fourth dimension in space which is the purpose of life or *why* we live.

In ordinary situations we multiply the dimensions to get the total volume. What would *our* life's volume be if we were to multiply its greatest possible dimensions? First as regards the length of life: It is interesting to know that had we lived 2,000 years ago in Jerusalem our life expectancy at birth would have been approximately 19 years. Had we lived in George Washington's day in America it would have been 35 years. In the year 1900 the life expectation in America was 48 years. But the baby that was born in an American hospital this morning has an expectation of life of 70 years. We are making some progress in increasing the length of mortal life, yet not one person is satisfied. The only length of life that would ever be satisfactory to anyone is everlasting life.

A great love of life activated us in the spirit world. It continues with us here, and like all of our endowments from God, this love of life has a special purpose and significance. Victor Hugo once said, "A thirst for the infinite proves infinity." Surely this thirst for eternal life contains God's promise of its fulfillment. God did not plant this desire in our hearts to mock us. As someone has said, "God did not build a stairway leading nowhere." Joseph Addison stimulates us with the following interesting bit of philosophy. He said:

> It must be so—Plato thou
> Reasonest well!
> Else whence this pleasing hope,
> This fond desire,
> Things longing after Immortality?

Or whence this secret dread!
    This inward horror
Of falling into naught?
    Why shrinks the soul
Back on itself, and
    Startles at destruction?

'Tis the divinity that stirs
    Within us.
'Tis heaven itself that points
    Out a hereafter
And intimates eternity to man.
    Eternity! thou pleasing
Dreadful thought.

Certainly all would agree that the most valuable thing in life is life itself. The greatest of all the gifts of God is eternal life which God holds firmly in his hands.

Then suppose that we could multiply the length of life by its breadth. Life as its best, even in mortality, is filled with endless interest and wonder. After the creation, God looked out upon the earth and called it good. It is an earth of boundless beauty and continual fascination. When in our premortal existence we beheld the foundations of this earth being laid and knew that we were going to have the privilege of living upon it, we are told that " . . . all the sons shouted for joy." (Job 38:7) Then we walked by sight. We knew God. He is our Father. We lived with him. We knew that we were going to have to walk a little way by faith. But we were so delighted with the promised blessings of mortality that if we fully remembered now, what we surely understood then, then certainly no price would be too great to pay for life.

A good place to start work on this project of increasing the breadth of life is the place suggested by Mr. Thoreau, to live our appreciation every day. Life must not be allowed to go sour or become corroded by sin. When we think negative thoughts, we get a negative mind which limits life's breadth. When we think morose thoughts, we get a morose mind. When we think depraved thoughts, our minds become depraved. The scriptures tell us the awful results of thinking damned thoughts. On the other hand, we also know what can be accomplished in life by thinking inspiring happy thoughts. Edward Everett Hale once said that the best education comes from being perpetually thrilled by life. We may borrow some of this helpful philosophy from Irwin Cassel who sang:

I love life, and I want to live,
To drink of life's fullness, take all it can give.
I love life every moment must count,
To glory in its sunshine and revel in its fount.

Some of the greatest of life's joys are the joys of understanding. The most profitable understanding is to know the possibilities of our lives and what we can make out of them. One of the first questions that Adam and Eve were asked to decide when they were placed in the Garden of Eden was whether or not they would eat the fruit from the Tree of Knowledge of good and evil. And after they had eaten, God said, " . . . the man is become as one of us, to know good and evil." (Genesis 3:22) And I would like to point out in passing that the right kind of knowledge still tends to have that effect upon people. A flaming sword was placed in the Garden of Eden to guard the Tree of Life, but fortunately for us there is no flaming sword guarding the Tree of Knowledge of good and evil, and each of us may eat to his heart's content. Thereby we may greatly increase the breadth of our lives.

Then suppose we multiply the total of life's length and breadth by its depth. The objective of life is not just to live long, but to live well. It is not enough to live interestingly but to live beneficially. Life at its best is not measured only by its quantity but also by its quality. The goal of life is not merely what we can get out of it, but rather what we can become by it. Probably the eight most important words ever spoken are these, "So God created man in his own image. . . ." (Genesis 1:27) But each of us has also been en-

dowed with a set of the attributes of divinity, the development
of which provides one of our most thrilling opportunities.

The plan of eternal progression is the most wonderful
program for human growth, betterment, and happiness ever
known. What a stimulating thought, that according to God's
plan the offspring of God may during the long reaches of
eternity, aspire to become like the parent. The greatest of all
the joys of life, are not the joys of having, or even the joys of
doing, they are the joys of being—of being like God. Jesus
said, " . . . a man's life consisteth not in the abundance of the
things which he possesseth." (Luke 12:15)

Then there is the purpose of life—that is what gives life
its significance. The prophet said, "Men are that they might
have joy."

The author of a great hymn says:

> For a wise and glorious purpose,
> God has placed us here on earth;
> And withheld the recollection
> Of our former friends and birth.

Some day that recollection and those friendships will
be given back to us to our great delight and inspiration. But
in the meantime what a wonderful feeling to know that life
is not an accident or an afterthought, that above the dictators and above chance and above circumstance there is
God our Heavenly Father to whom every human being must
finally render an account of his life and receive his blessings
according to his works.

The main objectives of this life is to increase life in all
of its dimensions and thereby greatly multiply its total worth.
Our eternal salvation is earned by so many individual
thoughts, acts, and hours of work. These must be increased
in number and made better in quality, so that none of our
blessings will ever be lost.

Someone has said that we never lose eternal life by a

blowout. That always comes about by a series of slow leaks. A little ignorance, a little procrastination, a little thoughtlessness, a little indifference, a little sin and even before we know it, we may have lost eternal life. Certainly it would be the height of foolishness to so much dread to lose mortal life all at once and then deliberately to throw away eternal life a little bit at a time. Therefore, everything must be avoided that would reduce the dimensions of our lives. That is, we should shun the disobedience that may cut down life's length, the lethargy that may reduce its breadth and intensity, the sins that may destroy its depth, its Godliness, its joy, and the ignorance that may thwart its purpose.

The gospel of Jesus Christ is the perfect plan by which we may increase life's dimensions. The Savior said, "I am come that they might have life, and that they might have it more abundantly." (John 10:10) Then he gave the simple formula, "Come follow me." Every life must finally be judged by how well it complies with that one instruction. When our lives have reached their maximum in abundance, then eternity will be the measure of life's length. The celestial kingdom will be the measure of life's breadth. To be like God will be the measure of life's depth, and eternal joy will be the measure of its purpose. Then when we multiply how long—by how interestingly—by how much—by how come —we will have the thrilling satisfaction of seeing and living life at its best and greatest volume on an everlasting basis. Then we might feel a new and eternal application for the philosophy of Irwin Cassel's song as we also sing:

> I love life, and I want to live
> To drink of life's fullness,
> Take all it can give.
> I love life every moment must count,
> To glory in its sunshine and revel in its fount.

"All that a man hath he will give for his life" is still the greatest bargain in the world. May God help us to effectively spend our mortality to attain eternal life.

Do It Yourself

Some years ago while filling an assignment in one of the stakes of the church, a friend of mine asked if he could talk to me about a problem. He told me that he had been considerably disturbed by the fact that over a number of years he had never been invited to speak in any ward or stake meeting. One purpose of the Church as he understood it was to help its members develop spiritually, and of course he knew that we grow most rapidly by our own activity. He felt that if he had been called upon to give expression to his thoughts and have a greater participation in the activities of the Church, he would have made more satisfactory progress in his faith. Because this privilege had been denied him, he was considerably upset.

There is probably more than one solution to this particular problem, but I told my friend that this was one place where I felt certain I could be of substantial assistance to him, and that I would like to make a suggestion based on my own experience. In 1936 I was asked to serve as the bishop of my ward. This appointment came just before our stake quarterly conference, and it seemed quite likely to me that I would be called upon to speak in one of the meetings. So with considerable concern I very carefully prepared an outline of what I expected to say when the call came. But the conference came and went, and I was not called upon.

But three months later another conference was to be held, and I thought that certainly I would then be asked to say something, and so in anticipation I very carefully prepared another talk which I intended to give. But the next conference passed, and I was not called upon.

Since that time I have attended 72 stake conferences in my own stake, and I have prepared the written outline for every one of the 72, not one of which I have given. On two or three occasions I have been asked to speak, but each time my subject has been assigned and as a result I have 72 undelivered stake conference addresses.

Then I said to my friend, "Here is the best plan I know of to help you in your particular situation. To begin with I am going to give you an assignment right now to speak 30 minutes in Sacrament meeting next Sunday, and here is what I would like to have you do about it. First, go over the whole field of gospel subject matter and pick out the one idea that holds the greatest interest for you. Then read yourself full of that particular subject. Then get it organized, illustrated, and rehearsed. If you would care to, you may discuss it with your family or friends, but you be prepared next Sunday to give the most interesting, uplifting, thrilling, best organized and most aptly illustrated set of ideas of which you are capable on this particular subject. But that is not the end of the assignment. I am going to assign you to repeat that same process on some different gospel subject every Sunday for the next 52 weeks. Now, of course, it may just be that the bishop will not get around to calling on you, but the only losers will be those that don't hear you. You will have had done all of the thinking and made all of the preparation on 52 of the most thrilling and important of all possible subjects."

The great psychologist-philosopher William James said, "The mind is made up by what it feeds upon." Someone else said, "The mind like the dyer's hand is colored by what it holds. That is, if you hold in your hand a sponge full of purple dye, your hand becomes purple. But if you hold in your mind great ideas having to do with God and eternal life, your whole personality will be made up accordingly."

Wouldn't it be wonderful if each of us could be the

speaker every Sunday? The teacher always learns more than the student. Someone was once asked what he thought about a certain matter and he said, "I don't know, I haven't spoken on it yet." Before we speak on a subject we must think it through and make some decisions about it, and thereby we help to solve one of our most important problems of how to get good ideas into actual operation in our lives. Woodrow Wilson once called attention to this difficulty when he said, "The greatest ability of the American people is their ability to resist instruction." Unfortunately most of us have more of that particular talent than is good for us. This is especially true in the important realm of our spiritual welfare, even though one's religion is the most important thing about him. *That* is what determines what he believes in and stands for and lives by, and is willing to devote his life to, and we don't resist our own instruction as vigorously as that which comes from someone else. What could help us more therefore than to put ourselves on the program to do a little religious thinking each week.

Thomas A. Edison touched on the difficulty involved when he said, "There is no limit to which a man will not go to avoid thinking." Thinking can be a very disagreeable, unpleasant task for one who doesn't do it much. And yet Solomon said "As a man thinketh, so is he." Now I don't know just where that leaves us, if we are what we think and if we don't think. But it indicates a very important problem which requires our constant attention.

Ralph Waldo Emerson said, "What every man needs most is something to get him to do what he can." And it would help if each one undertook some responsibility for being his own Doctor of Divinity and do some of his own preaching. To trust this responsibility always to someone else or for us to merely read out of a book may not be sufficient to create strong convictions and the determinations to live by them. Some have read the entire Bible from cover to cover and not been greatly changed by the experience.

But when we ourselves think through some great ideas and then get them organized and written up and decisions made about them, they will have greater influence in our lives. We should not handle our religion as lightly as we sometimes do our New Year's resolutions, by merely saying, "I'm going to do better." We can give our resolutions greater depth and more definiteness by thinking them through and writing them down and making decisions about them and then attaching a timetable for a definite accomplishment.

Someone once said that he was going to quit smoking but he added, "Don't tell anyone because I may not want to go through with it." This is a common procedure by which we bring about our own failure.

Psychologists have said that ordinarily we remember only a very small percentage of what we hear. We retain a much larger portion of what we see. But we remember almost everything that we actually do. The gospel covers the most important area of our lives, but in addition it is the greatest do-it-yourself project ever known in the world. It is pretty difficult for one person to be religious for someone else. There is a very popular idea where a group of people get together and hire a minister to do their church work for them. There are others who say, "Let George do it." Both of these practices have serious disadvantages. We wouldn't want anyone to do our eating for us. No one can do our sleeping for us. How can we imagine that someone can do our thinking for us?

Just suppose that we had someone to do all of our church work for us; we had someone to do our teaching for us and pay our tithing for us and attend our meetings for us, and do our worshipping for us. Suppose that we let him also take over the responsibility for our prayers, our welfare work and the other things involved in being an effective follower of the Master.

We have some interesting examples in the scriptures of

the way someone had been denied the privilege of doing church work. For example, when David was king of ancient Israel the people were in great need of a temple. For a period of 460 years, from the time that Joshua had established them in their promised land until after the death of David, the only temple they had was the little portable tabernacle that the Israelites had carried on their backs during their 40 years of wanderings in the wilderness. The Lord wanted the people to have a temple, and David wanted to build a temple. But the Lord would not accept a temple built by David because he was unworthy and the Lord told David that the construction of the temple must wait and would be built by Solomon after David's death.

Later an angel appeared to David and told him that the Lord desired him to build an altar on which to offer sacrifice to Jehovah. As the place where the altar should be built, the angel had pointed out an elevated area used as a threshing floor in a wheat field owned by one of David's wealthy subjects whose name was Ornan. David told Ornan what the angel had said and asked if Ornan would sell him the land. Ornan told David that only would the land be available, but that David could have it free of charge. Ornan also offered to furnish the materials out of which the altar was to be built, and he offered to supply the wheat, the oil and the oxen needed for the offering—all without any cost to the King. David's reply to Ornan is profound and should be remembered. He said, "I will not offer unto the Lord an offering that doth cost me nothing." The Lord had given Solomon the privilege of doing an important part of the church work that should have belonged to his father David. But now that the Lord had granted David this lesser opportunity he intended to make the most of it. Like David, we can only get the maximum out of our church work on a do-it-yourself basis.

During the recent political campaign a certain newspaper man referred to Mr. Eisenhower as being "ear-minded."

In military service much of the direction is given by verbal command and soldiers are especially trained to use their ears. This same man referred to Mr. Nixon as being "eye-minded." In getting his legal education Mr. Nixon had been trained to look up cases and depend upon his eyes for much of his success, and in the process he had became "eye-minded." The eyes and the ears certainly have a very important part in developing our spirituality. But mostly we are "do-minded." It is what we *do*, that largely molds our lives and determines our destiny. It is a very old truth that faith without works is dead. It is also true that ideas without decisions are dead and resolutions without actions are dead also. When we stand before God to be judged, it will be our *works* that will count most. What we have *believed* and what we have *planned* and what we have *intended to do* will all give way to a consideration of what we have actually done. And we must have an effective program for integrating our works with our faith.

Mohandas K. Gandhi once pointed out that there were 999 people who believed in honesty for every honest man. It would be very difficult to locate a single person who did not *believe* in honesty. And yet we remember poor old Diogenes who went around Athens with a lighted lantern in the middle of the daytime trying to find just one honest man. There are a great many people who believe in God who do serve him wholeheartedly. There are many people who believe in the celestial kingdom who are not headed in that direction. The greatest rewards in *this* life as well as in the *next* depend upon our ability as doers, and a very good place to *start* this program is in *doing* some of our own teaching and some of our own preaching.

Socrates became famous not so much because he taught people anything new, he merely got them to take action on the things that they were already certain about.

The Lord has said to the people in Moses' day as well

as in our own day, that we should be a chosen generation, a royal priesthood, a holy nation, a peculiar people. But how can anyone succeed in this important project without the cooperation of the one being helped.

To qualify for the greatest blessings we must feed our minds and train our souls, and put gospel ideals *in force* in our lives. A lifetime of listening and waiting for someone to give us an assignment may be insufficient for our spiritual needs. To realize our greatest opportunities we must take some of the initiative and certainly the most profitable way that we can spend our time is working in this great enterprise in which God himself spends his entire time which is to bring to pass the immortality and eternal life of man. If God works for us all of the time, certainly we should work for ourselves a part of the time. One of the important functions of this "royal priesthood" that he has given us is that we may be our own priests. We are called to be Saviors upon Mount Zion, and the first soul that one should bring to God is his own soul. May he so bless us that our do-it-yourself efforts will be crowned with a maximum of success.

Dr. Jekyll and Mr. Hyde

Iɴ 1855 Robert Louis Stevenson wrote his best-known literary success entitled *Dr. Jekyll and Mr. Hyde*. Mr. Stevenson first lived this experience in a dream where the plot presented itself. His dream was so real and so startling that he began uttering exclamations of horror in his sleep. Upon being awakened he immediately wrote down the experiences of his dream.

This interesting and instructive story centers around a kindly and very successful physician by the name of Dr. Henry Jekyll who at the height of his medical career conducted an exciting but disastrous experiment, in which he ventured into the evil possibilities of a split personality. Mr. Stevenson's story spotlights a problem that everyone is confronted with in some degree. The psychiatrists have written much about that duality that exists in human personality. Each of us has a kind of North Pole and South Pole in his character. One is negative, one is positive; one is inclined toward evil, one toward good. Faust said, "Two souls are lodged within my breast that struggle there for undivided reign." If not controlled this flow of power between opposites tends to cancel the effect of the will and causes frustrations, complexes, and a large number of psychosomatic diseases. Very frequently we see the unhappy victims of incessant, unresolved mental and emotional conflicts "living lives of continual desperation." Sometimes a personality goes to pieces in what we call a nervous breakdown.

One of H. G. Wells' characters might have been speaking for some of us when he said, "I am not a man but a mob." That is, we sometimes develop within ourselves a miscellaneous, heterogeneous personality population consisting of many antagonistic, uncoordinated impulses which waste our energy by fighting one another. Mark Twain made reference to this problem when he indicated that "Every person is like a moon which has a light side and a dark side." Then these opposing forces make war on each other, and the resulting internal conflict sometimes attains very serious proportions, depending upon the amount of our integration and control. When left uncontrolled the casualties of this damaging individual cold war fills the sickbeds, the reform schools, the penal institutions and the mental hospitals.

In Robert Sherwood's play *Abraham Lincoln,* Lincoln said of himself, "You talk about a Civil War. But there is one going on inside of me all the time." He said, "One of these days I may split asunder and part company with myself."

That was exactly what Dr. Jekyll decided to do on a scientific basis in his medical laboratory. Dr. Jekyll was endowed with unusual abilities. He was also inclined to vigorous industry with high standards of professional excellence. This combination of virtues and abilities had earned for him a fine reputation supported by a long list of scientific degrees and a large medical practice. Like most conscientious men Dr. Jekyll was very fond of the respect and sincere good will that he received from his fellow men. To say the least, his life was fully occupied, interesting, and successful.

Dr. Jekyll felt that his worst fault was a certain natural gaiety of disposition which seemed to be in conflict with his dignity, and a need he felt to wear a grave countenance before the public. But in trying to conceal his lightheartedness he felt that he was developing within himself a kind of duplicity which gave rise to an unpleasant feeling of guilt. This was more especially true because of the exacting nature of his high professional standards. As time passed it seemed that the split grew larger, further dividing his personality under the two general subdivisions of good and evil.

Both sides of Dr. Jekyll's nature were in dead earnest

and each was making a determined effort to win consideration for its own point of view. Dr. Jekyll recognized the claims of each faction, and because he adopted no stern policy of personality integration, the negative influences continually grew in power. To support his high ambition, and the religious dedication he gave to his work, Dr. Jekyll labored long and hard in relieving suffering, preventing disease and promoting the general public welfare. But then at other times he felt a strong desire to lay aside restraint and indulge the other elements in his nature. Then even to himself, he seemed to be another person. Later when he thought of some of the things that he had done, he had an uneasy feeling of regret and guilt. But inasmuch as he seemed not disposed to commit himself wholeheartedly to either side, this disturbing cold war within himself gradually increased in intensity.

He often reflected upon this annoying situation and wondered what should be done about it. It occurred to him how much more simple his situation would be if he were actually two people instead of one. That is, suppose that he could split off the undignified and unjust part of himself to go its separate way without enduring the straight jacket of his conscience and the continual accusations of his better self. On the other hand, this separation would leave the just part of himself free of any distraction or guilt to walk steadily and securely along his upward course. Then he would be able to advance his knowledge and enjoy the pure delights of service without embarrassment, or the danger of doing any injury to his professional standing.

Dr. Jekyll found this speculation so agreeable that he finally settled himself in his laboratory to try to separate these antagonistic elements and thereby relieve himself of what of late was becoming a rather unbearable conflict. Why should these incongruous elements be thus bound together and both forced to endure an inharmonious, unhappy struggle. He would separate these opposite Siamese twins of personality that had been so unfortunately, and he felt unjustly bound together. Finally a drug was compounded by means of which he could temporarily dethrone either of his personalities and give complete supremacy to the other. As he seemed to have two characters, why shouldn't he also have two physical identities? He could be the kindly, helpful, highly respected physician by day, living above any thought of wrong or shadow of suspicion. Then when he felt the need to indulge his less worthy self he could go into his laboratory, drink the potion and completely eliminate Dr. Jekyll so that his reputation would forever remain untarnished.

At first this transformation was brought about only with great difficulty. It was also a rather painful process, resembling a convulsion which shook his entire being. But after the medicine had done its work, something like a new birth occurred, and he stepped out on the other side of the curtain a new man. In his new role he felt much younger. He was lighter of body and happier in his disposition. He was considerably smaller in physical stature with a completely new physical appearance. He felt a freedom never known before. His double life could now be housed in separate tenements, and he felt that at last he could have peace. His two selves in no way resembled each other. No matter how much evil his unworthy self might be guilty of, he had only to take an opposite kind of drug and he would again be the kindly, faithful Dr. Jekyll beyond the reach of any criticism or punishment. Dr. Jekyll retained his own name for his better personality and gave his new identity the name of Edward Hyde.

The pleasures that he first sought in his new disguise were only undignified. But his strange immunity from punishment soon led him toward the monstrous. The evil within him now operated with a free rein, being no longer restrained by good. Evil braced and delighted Mr. Hyde like new wine. Each personality was soon clearly marked for what it was. As pure goodness shone upon the countenance of Dr. Jekyll, so undiluted evil was broadly and plainly written upon the person of Mr. Hyde. The body of Edward Hyde bore the signature of Satan on its face. Yet when he looked in the glass he was conscious of no repugnance. Rather, he felt a thrill of relief to be free from the continual censure of the disapproving conscience of Dr. Jekyll. Every other human being was a commingling of good and evil. But Edward Hyde alone in all the ranks of mankind was pure evil. He took pleasure only from that which was bad, but after his evil appetite had been fully satiated, he could return from his excursions of depravity, go into his laboratory, take another drug and again stand forth as the kindly, unblameable Dr. Henry Jekyll.

But appetite grows by what it feeds upon. As his double careers went their unrestrained ways, his hunger for evil increased. When the devil within him was chained up for too long a period, it began to growl for license. He suffered a thousand deaths when confined for long in the fires of abstinence. And each indulgence gave his unbridled evil a more furious propensity to ill. He had been stripped of all of the balancing instincts by which even the worst of mankind may walk with some degree of steadiness among the temptations. But with all restrictions removed, to be tempted however slightly, was to fall.

He soon noticed that the intervals when he was Dr. Jekyll were growing shorter in duration. This he recognized as the warning handwriting upon the wall, and so he tried to give up his role as Mr. Hyde. He hated and feared the brute that stirred so uneasily within him. But his evil self so long indulged now exercised a kind of control that could not easily be denied. At intervals more and more frequent, Dr. Jekyll would again find himself raging and lusting with the passions of Hyde. Hyde was always burning with anger and lusting to inflict pain, and in the intervals between, the animal within him sat licking the chops of his memory.

Finally his evil nature stung him into the frenzied pitch of murder. In an early morning return from one of his evil expeditions he clubbed to death a fellow human being. Once his passions were unloosed to commit this capital sin, the spirit of hell raged within him. With a transport of glee he mauled the unresisting body, tasting delight with every blow. A demoniac glee stimulated his trembling excesses. And it was not until weariness had begun to set in that his evil passions were satisfied, and he fled from the scene to conceal himself from pursuit in the person of Dr. Jekyll.

But it was not easy to forget the spilling of a brother's blood. Dr. Jekyll had done strange things with his body, but he was unable to put his mind beyond the reach of judgment. He felt a cold chill of terror run through his heart as he thought about the murder. In the most earnest prayer mixed with bitter tears he sought to smother the crowd of hideous sounds and images that were swarming in his memory against him.

Dr. Jekyll tried to compensate for the evil done by Mr. Hyde. But the ugly face of sin kept staring into his soul. He felt a nausea and distaste for life accompanied by a deep-seated terror. It was not the terror of death. His soul was hounded by a deeper and more awful dread. As evil had first destroyed the balance of his personality, so it was now destroying the very foundations of his soul. He had brought upon himself a punishment so dreadful that it could not be named. And as he was the chief of sinners, so he was the chief of sufferers also.

As the change from Dr. Jekyll to Mr. Hyde had become more frequent, it had also become more easy. Then one night he went to bed as Dr. Jekyll and awoke as Mr. Hyde. The change had taken place without the drug. He rushed into his laboratory and took a double dose of the restorative that recalled Dr. Jekyll. But six hours later he felt again the automatic pangs that would change him to Edward Hyde. Again the Dr. Jekyll drug had to be administered in increased amount.

In the following weeks it was only under the constant stimulation of the drug that he was able to wear the countenance of Dr. Jekyll. At any hour of the day or night he might be taken with a warning shudder foretelling the change to his dreaded self. If he slept or even dozed for a moment in his chair, it was always as Mr. Hyde that he awakened. Now almost without transition his fancy began swarming with images of terror and his soul would begin boiling with causeless hatreds. His body now seemed too weak to contain the raging energies of his evil self. The power of Hyde had grown with the sickliness of Jekyll. He now knew that his better self was being permanently overthrown, the power to change was being forfeited and the character of Edward Hyde was becoming irrevocably his.

Dr. Jekyll felt that only those consigned to the deepest hell could ever know the full dreadfulness and horror of the Bible statement saying, "The way of the transgressor is hard." After all, who can understand what it is like to be completely abandoned to evil. Dr. Jekyll's pitiful cry for help and forgiveness was the cry of a lost soul. He had been blasted by a prodigy sufficient to stagger the unbelief of Satan. His was an incurable malady that both tortured and deformed the sufferer. His life was shaken to its very roots; sleep had become impossible; and the most deadly terror sat by him at all hours of the day and night. He knew that all was lost and that he was approaching the last time that Henry Jekyll would ever be able to think his own thoughts. He had no horror of death. His only horror was that of being what he was. And thus the unhappy experiment of Dr. Jekyll and Mr. Hyde came to its mortal end.

And some day when we come to the end of our own lives, how fortunate we will be if we have so integrated our deeds under the direction of our better selves that our lives will have the happy ending that God intended.

Fathers

In 1872, Julia Ward Howe made the first known suggestion that we set apart a special day in honor of our mothers. Later on Anne Jarvis and others led important Mother's Day movements until in 1914 the second Sunday in May was set apart and nationally recognized as Mother's Day.

At about that time Mrs. John Bruce Dodd of Spokane, Washington began an observance of a day called Father's Day. The third Sunday in June was finally set apart for that purpose on a national basis in 1936, and a national Father's Day committee was formed in New York to select the father of the year annually.

Most human beings receive their highest rank in accomplishment through their parenthood. Next to God, parents are our greatest benefactors. They provide us with life. We inherit from them our abilities and our characteristics. They give us our most helpful training. They start us on our way in the world. What could be more fitting, therefore, than to set aside these two special days in which to show proper honor and reverence to those to whom we owe our existence and at the same time to think about the significance that parenthood has for every individual life.

There are some who believe that the universe operates as a result of blind chance and that human affairs have no divine significance. There are others who have great difficulty in believing in such miraculous doctrines as the literal resurrection of the body and the eternal continuation of life beyond mortality. So frequently we have difficulty believing in something that we cannot understand. But if we believed in only those things that we understood, then our list of beliefs would be extremely short. For who can understand sunlight or electricity or how the grass grows? And probably the most unbelievable of all the miracles is the process of procreation involved in parenthood. It has always seemed to me that anyone who can believe in his own birth should have no trouble in believing in any of the other miracles of God.

That is, if you can believe in creation, if you can believe that two microscopic cells can be brought together, and then by a series of subdivisions form other cells so completely unlike themselves, to create this great masterpiece of bone and sinew, flesh and blood, vision, energy, intelligence, character, and enthusiasm which makes up a great human being—if you can believe in that, which *no one* understands, then it should not be difficult to believe in any of the other miracles of God.

The greatest blessing of life is life itself. And so on these two special days we put on our best clothes and with flowers and smiles, kind deeds and pleasant words, we try to show our appreciation for life and all of the other benefits received from our parents.

The wonder of this parent-child relationship impresses itself upon us especially because God himself is a father. The spirits of all men and women were begotten in heaven before the earth was created, and one of the greatest events in the history of our world was the birth of God's only Begotten Son in the flesh. About that event the holy scripture says that the Angel Gabriel was sent from God to a city of Galilee named Nazareth, to a virgin . . . whose name was Mary . . . and the angel said unto her, "The Holy Ghost shall come upon thee, and the power of the Highest shall overshadow thee: therefore also that holy thing which shall be born of thee shall be called the Son of God." (Luke 1:35) The Savior came into the world as all of us have come, through the wonder of physical birth.

Think of the thrilling benefits that we would have missed

if, like those who followed Lucifer, we had never been permitted a mortal birth. Certainly we should show by our actions that we are grateful for this blessing. Isn't it interesting that the most effective way to please our earthly father or our Heavenly Father is to make the most of our own lives? Nothing could be truer than the Bible proverb that says, "A wise son maketh a glad father."

Of course Father's Day and fatherhood are not only honors; they also require that we carry responsibility. Parents at their best have many times indicated their willingness to give their lives if their children could have a greater opportunity. All parents like to see qualities of nobility develop in their children, even though they fail to develop those same qualities in themselves. We want our children to go to church even though we stay at home. Many parents do things themselves that would break their hearts to see their children do. It is a wonderful Father's Day thought to remind ourselves of the love which God manifested for his only Begotten Son, and yet he permitted his only Begotten Son to sacrifice his life for us who are also his children. Probably the finest way for any father to keep Father's Day is to set a good example for his own children, for while our children may not follow our instruction, they will follow us.

There is an interesting sentence that appears in various forms many times in the Bible. The book of First Kings says about one son, "And he walked in all the *sins* of his father, which he had done before him: ... " (I Kings 15:3) Second Chronicles describes the different activities of another son by saying, "And he walked in the ways of Asa, his father, and departed not from it, doing that which was right in the sight of the Lord." (II Chronicles 20:32) Every man is interested in Father's Day either from a present or a prospective point of view, and every man should give some thought to improving the quality of the parental office which he holds.

When Napoleon was asked what was the greatest need

of France, he replied, "Mothers." He said, "If France has good mothers, she will have good sons." But as we approach what well may be the hour of our country's greatest need, what could be more appropriately patriotic than for each of us to supply our country and our children with better fathers?

The dictionary gives the term "father" many interesting meanings. The first and most common is "one who has begotten a child." But the dictionary says that a father is also one who is an inventor or the founder of a trade or a profession. We say Hippocrates was the father of medicine. Someone else was the father of the atomic bomb. The Bible speaks of the fathers of righteousness and the fathers of faith. *Ideas* and *ideals* also have to have fathers.

Philip, the ancient king of Macedonia, was the father of Alexander the Great. When Alexander was twelve years old, Phillip arranged for Aristotle, the great Macedonian orator and philosopher, to become the companion and teacher of young Alexander. Later Alexander said that Aristotle was his father. What he meant was that while he had received his body from Philip, Aristotle was the father of his mind.

On this Father's Day if you would like to have the challenge of a great idea, here is one of the best that I know. Physical paternity is a miraculous office. But fathers are supposed to be far more than the fathers of physical bodies. Suppose then that in our efforts to improve our worthwhileness as parents, we also think about our *mental* paternity and our *spiritual* paternity. Sometimes those who share the physical relationship of father and son may be no relation spiritually. A child may bear a closer spiritual resemblance to his teacher than to his father. And Alexander even went so far as to say that he was more indebted to Aristotle for knowledge than he was to Philip for life. I once heard a man making a personal claim by a hereditary process to the spiritual virtues of his parents. He said, "Like Nephi of old I was born of goodly parents." Someone called his attention to the fact that Laman and Lemuel also had goodly parents, yet from the point of view of their righteousness they possessed none of the family characteristics. Sometimes we think about heredity like the contemporaries of Jesus who kept reminding the Master that they had Abraham as their father. But Jesus said to them that "God is able of these stones to raise up children unto Abraham." (Matt. 3:9) Then Jesus traced their spiritual paternity for them by saying, "Ye are of your father the devil, and the lusts of your father ye will do." (John 8:44) Abraham was their physical ancestor, but their thoughts, attitudes, and behavior patterns were from Satan. While the office of physical fatherhood is tremendously important, we must not forget our office as the father of ambitions and ideals and faith, and in these fields characteristics are not passed on by the usual laws of physical heredity.

Physical fatherhood is given freely to all of the animal creation from the top to the bottom. But we must give our children spiritual qualities by other processes. We must also accept full responsibility for any failure. It has been said that the first question that God will ask every parent is, "Where are your children?" What a dismal experience it might someday be to commemorate Father's Day in eternity with the consciousness that our own children had been forever lost. On several occasions Jesus asked this interesting question: "What doth it profit?" He said, "What doth it profit a man though he gain the whole world and lose his own soul?" And someone has made a Father's Day adaptation of that question to read, "What doth it profit a man though he gain the whole world and lose his own son or his own daughter?"

We have two interesting parallel Father's Day stories about David and Jephthah. Before King David had seated himself securely upon the throne of ancient Israel, he had many antagonists to overcome, and one of these was his own son, Absalom. Absalom had rebelled against his father and had drawn away a part of the army of Israel. On the day that the decisive battle was to be fought between them, David did not personally go to the battlefield. But he instructed his generals that under no circumstances should any harm befall Absalom. All day long David waited and watched for the news from the battle. As the battle progressed, it became clear to Absalom that he could not win, and so he tried to save himself in flight. His mount ran under some lowhanging boughs, and Absalom became entangled in the branches. His pursuers, not knowing the instructions of the king, took advantage of the situation, and Absalom was slain. Then a runner was dispatched to tell the king the good news. David ran out to meet the messenger, and his first question was not who had won the battle, but he said, "Is the young man, Absalom, safe?" The messenger bowed low before the king and told him that Absalom was dead. David had gained the whole world, so to speak; his last opposition had been crushed; he was now securely seated upon the throne of Israel. But he had lost his son, and he went mourning up to his house saying, "O my son Absalom, my son, my son Absalom! would God I had died for thee, O Absalom, my son, my son!" (II Sam. 18:33)

Jephthah, one of the great warriors of Israel, made a vow to the Lord that if the Lord would give him victory over his enemies, when he returned from the battle, he would sacrifice to the Lord the first thing that he met. He probably believed that God would provide a suitable sacrifice of his own choosing. Jephthah won a great victory, but when he returned from the battle, the first thing that his eyes rested upon was his own daughter. Jephthah loved his beautiful daughter more than anything in the world, but he was bound by his vow, and he offered her as a sacrifice for his military success. Like David, Jephthah, had gained the whole world but he had lost his daughter.

On this Father's Day we might well inquire what any success doth profit us by which we may suffer the eternal loss of a son or a daughter. Everyone reaches his highest achievement in rearing Godly children. Therefore on this day we might remind ourselves to give to the world good mothers and good fathers and then it will have achieved the maximum good of having good children.

Father's Day

WE HAVE A very interesting custom among us of setting aside special days to think about special things. For example, we set aside the second Sunday in May as Mother's Day. This is a day for honoring our mothers. It is traditionally a day of family unity and happiness. On this day we put on our best clothes and perform our most thoughtful acts to honor and please our mothers. Closely associated with Mother's Day we set aside another special day for the same purpose. We designate the third Sunday in June as Father's Day.

The importance of both of these great days was given *divine* emphasis and approval some 3400 years ago when God descended in fire upon Mt. Sinai and to the accompaniment of lightnings and thunders said, "Honour thy father and thy mother." (Exodus 20:12) Of course, the *observance* of this commandment brings more benefit to the children than to the parents, for when we honor an ideal the honor gets into our lives and lifts them up.

> When the high heart we magnify
> And the sure vision celebrate;
> And worship greatness passing by,
> Ourselves are great.
> John Drinkwater

But in addition to the second Sunday in May and the third Sunday in June, God himself has set aside for our special observance not one day, but 52 days, not as holidays but as holy days. These special days might also be called "Father's Days," not the Father's Day that comes on the third Sunday in June, but the Father's Day that comes on the first day of each week which is set aside for us to honor and please God, our Heavenly Father. It is plainly stated in the scriptures that God is the Father of our spirits. Jesus taught us to pray, saying, "Our Father which art in heaven." Jesus said to Mary, " . . . go to my brethren, and say unto them, I ascend unto my Father, and your Father; and to my God, and your God." (John 20:17)

The Apostle Paul has reminded us that "We have had fathers of our flesh which corrected us, and we gave them reverence." Then he asks, "Shall we not much rather be in subjection unto the Father of spirits, and live?" (Heb. 12:9) And one way that we can best honor the Father of our spirits and put our lives in subjection to his will is by the proper use of these special "Father's Days" set apart for that purpose.

The relative importance of this great day that we call the Sabbath might be indicated to us by the frequency of its reoccurrence. That is, we have one day to honor Washington, one day to honor Lincoln, one day for Thanksgiving, one day for our nation's birthday, and then our Father in heaven in his wisdom has set aside one-seventh of all the days to honor God. But *this* day is also set aside *particularly* for *our* benefit, for when we honor God we tend to become like him.

The importance of *this* day was *also* emphasized to the world 34 centuries ago when out of the fires of Sinai God said, "Remember the sabbath day, to keep it holy." (Ex. 20: 8) In fact, it has been said that our civilization could never have survived for a half century if it had not been for this one day in seven that we call Sunday. This is the day when we try to reach a pinnacle in our lives by living at our best. This is the day when we put on our best clothes and think our best thoughts and read our best books. This is the day when we associate with the people we love the most. This is the day for which we usually reserve the best meal of the week. This is the day when we lay aside the cares that usually concern us during the other six days, and we go to the house of prayer and let our minds reach up and try and understand the things of God and eternity.

This special day when we worship God and honor him in our lives has great significance to us, for the human mind has some of the qualities of the tendrils of a climbing vine. It tends to attach itself and draw itself upward by what it is put in contact with. What a thrilling idea that one day of each week is especially set apart for us to put our minds in contact, and our lives in harmony with him in whose image we were created.

We have heard of the wonders that have been accomplished when men and women have, over a long period, regularly set aside even fifteen minutes a day for special study and self-improvement. By this means many people have raised themselves to great heights of accomplishment. This same principle diligently applied to the Lord's day would almost immediately transform our lives.

Alexander Hamilton has often been referred to as a genius, and he himself has given us his formula. He said, "Men give me some credit for genius but all the genius I have lies in this; when I have a subject in mind I study it profoundly, day and night it is before me. I explore it in all its bearings. My mind becomes pervaded with it. The result is what some people call the fruits of genius whereas it is in reality the fruits of study and labor." How would you like to become a genius in the things of God? How would you like to become a genius in those great principles that determine the eternal destiny of our own souls. All too frequently even on the Sabbath day we lose sight of the purpose of life and we concentrate our efforts on those things that have no lasting value. We sometimes desecrate the Sabbath by putting our minds in contact with the things that lead us away from God and eternal life. We make this special day a holiday instead of a holy day.

Some people confuse this "Father's Day" with "Labor

Day" and our less worthy appetites are allowed to crowd out the great interests for which the day was set apart. As William James, the great Harvard psychologist has pointed out, "That which holds our attention determines our action." What a tragedy then when we attend to the wrong things.

Someone has written:

NO TIME FOR GOD

No time for God,
What fools we are;
To clutter up our lives,
With common things,
And leave without the Lord of life,
And life itself.

No time for God, as well to say
No time to eat, to sleep, to live, to die
Take time for God.
Or a poor misshapen thing you'll be,
To step into eternity
And say to him,
I had no time for thee.

Only when we make God and his will central in our lives can we develop that constructive religious talent that will mold us into what we were intended to be, and give us direction back into the presence of the Creator.

One of the fundamental laws of our existence which also emphasizes the importance of the Sabbath day is to the effect that "As a man thinketh in his heart, so is he."

Mind is the master power that builds and molds
And mind is man
And ever more he takes the tools of thought
And fashions what he wills
Bringing forth a thousand joys,
A thousand ills.
He thinks in secret and it comes to pass,
Environment is but his looking glass.

In what we do on the Sabbath we may usually see our own eternal future reflected. In 1935 Clarence Day, Jr., wrote a play entitled, *Life with Father*. Suppose we borrow that idea to apply to our eternal lives and imagine ourselves as worthy to live forever with God. What would such a life be like? We speak of Americans as enjoying the highest standard of living. Try and imagine what the standard of living will be for those who live with God in the celestial kingdom.

Then by way of contrast suppose we consider the prospect of eternal life *without* our Heavenly Father. Suppose that we should become a part of that innumerable company of whom it is said, " . . . where God and Christ dwell they cannot come, world without end." (D & C 76:112) This situation will be accomplished by some simply because they put their minds in contact with the wrong things. A physician often judges the health by the appetite. We can also determine spirituality in about that same way. It is easy to ruin our appetite for the things of God by putting our minds in contact with the opposite kind of things.

Suppose that we sometime find out that by our sins of omission or commission we have apostatized from God, and thereby forever excluded ourselves from his presence.

Then we may find that one of the most devastating of all human emotions is this sense of being alone, of not being wanted, of being unworthy. What would it be like to feel unfit for the presence of God, and to have forever lost our eternal exaltation because we had mistrained our appetites. The greatest of all the gifts of God is eternal life—that means "life *with* Father." And these 52 wonderful days have been set apart especially to help us prepare, not only for this life but also for that magnificent experience which lies beyond our mortality. Our time of preparation is very short even if it is filled to its maximum with good works.

One of our inspiring hymns says, "We feel it a *pleasure* to serve thee, and we love to obey thy commands." What a wonderful attitude to develop toward the Sabbath day. One of the most important of God's commands and one that should give us the greatest pleasure has to do with our observance of that *best* day of the week, the Sabbath. That is our Heavenly Father's Day. That is the special day when we try a little more enthusiastically to please God as at the same time we mold our eternal lives. What a thrilling idea to put our minds regularly in contact with God and his will on each of these fifty-two *special Father's Days* which have been spaced one every seventh day throughout the year.

This divine command has not only come down to us from the fires of Sinai but it has also been the law of all ages and specially renewed by direct command of God in our own day when again God has said to us in substance, "Remember the sabbath day to keep it holy."

A Famine in the Land

I WOULD LIKE to retell briefly one of the most interesting stories of the Old Testament. It has to do with what is probably the most famous family in history—the family of Abraham, Isaac and Jacob. It is from this one family that most of our great scriptures have come. This was the family through whose lineage the Savior himself was born.

Early in his life Abraham was selected by the Lord to establish a new nation and was given the name of Father of the Faithful. Abraham had a son whose name was Isaac; Isaac in turn had a son whose name was Jacob; and Jacob had twelve sons who became the leaders of the twelve tribes of Israel.

The eleventh of Jacob's sons was named Joseph and was the favorite of his father. Jacob loved Joseph more than any of his other sons, and thus brought the hatred of his brothers upon him. But not only was Joseph favored by his father, he was also favored by the Lord who gave him inspired dreams. Joseph dreamed that the family were binding sheaves in the field and Joseph's sheaf stood upright, and all the other sheaves bowed down before it. When he told his dream to his brothers, they hated him the more.

Then Joseph had another dream in which the sun, the moon, and eleven stars also bowed down before him. In these dreams it seemed that Joseph was setting himself above his brothers and even above his father and mother, and so Jacob rebuked Joseph, but the scripture says that Jacob remembered the things that Joseph had said.

It was the responsibility of the older sons to tend the

sheep, whereas Joseph was kept at home with his father. But when Joseph was 17 years of age, his father sent him to visit his brothers and determine how they were getting along. When they saw him approaching, they said, "Behold the dreamer cometh," and they conspired among themselves to take his life. However, Reuben persuaded them not to slay Joseph; instead they sold him to a company of Ishmaelites from Gilead who were going down into Egypt. The price they received from Joseph was twenty pieces of silver or approximately eleven dollars in American money.

But even in Egypt God did not forget Joseph, but continued to manifest his will to him in dreams. And some years later when the Pharaoh himself had a dream, Joseph was sent for and made known to the Pharaoh that there would come seven years of plenty throughout all the land. This would be followed by seven years of famine bringing with it a great food scarcity and the accompanying hardship. Pharaoh was impressed that Joseph was a man of ability and integrity and so he placed him in charge of this great Egyptian welfare project. Accordingly Joseph faithfully stored up the surplus grain in Egypt's bounteous years, and when the famine began, the granaries were opened that the people might be fed.

But this famine was not confined to Egypt, and when Jacob up in Canaan learned that there was corn in Egypt, he sent his sons there to buy food. When they arrived they were immediately recognized by their brother Joseph who was now second in authority to the Pharaoh himself. When finally Joseph made himself known to them they were naturally very frightened. But Joseph quieted their fears by saying to them, ". . . be not grieved, nor angry with yourselves, that ye sold me hither: for God did send me before you to preserve life." (Gen. 45:5) Unwittingly, even though with evil intent, his brothers had carried out the Lord's purposes, and Joseph loaded their sacks with corn, and sent them back to

Canaan. And thus for eleven dollars two nations were saved from starvation.

But there is another very interesting and closely related account of an even more serious famine foretold in the Old Testament. In the eighth chapter and eleventh verse of Amos we read these words, "Behold, the days come, saith the Lord, that I will send a famine in the land, not a famine of bread, nor a thirst for water, but of hearing the words of the Lord: and they shall wander from sea to sea. and from the north even to the east, they shall run to and fro to seek the word of the Lord, and shall not find it. (Amos 8:11-12)

This projected famine for hearing the word of the Lord was foretold and written about by many of the ancient prophets. Isaiah gives us the reason for this famine when he said, "The earth also is defiled under the inhabitants thereof; because they have transgressed the laws, changed the ordinance, broken the everlasting covenant. Therefore hath the curse devoured the earth, and they that dwell therein are desolate: . . . " (Isaiah 24:5-6)

History gives us the details concerning the breaking of this everlasting covenant after it had been established by Jesus. It was not many years after the crucifixion that the people began to abandon the great doctrines and change the simple Christian ordinances. The everlasting covenant was broken and the authority established by Jesus was eventually lost from the earth.

One by one the apostles were put to death. Peter, Andrew, Simon, and Philip were crucified. James and Paul were beheaded. Bartholomew was flayed alive. Matthew was slain with a battle axe. Thomas was run through with a lance. James was beaten to death. Thaddeus was shot through with arrows. Barnabas was stoned, and Mark was dragged to death in the streets of Alexandria. And John, the last living apostle, was banished to a rocky little island called Patmos located in the Aegean Sea. Without divine leadership, the church soon sank to the level of a purely human institution. The authority was taken over by unauthorized leaders, and what had been the church of Jesus Christ became the church of the Roman Empire.

Isaiah had clearly pointed out the consequences of this apostasy from God when he said, "For, behold, the darkness shall cover the earth, and gross darkness the people: . . . " (Isaiah 60:2) And as had been foretold, the world slipped deeper and deeper into the long, spiritual night that we refer to as the Dark Ages.

But it has been pointed out that "God always provides the remedy before the plague." Some 600 years B.C. an Israelitish prophet by the name of Lehi was directed by the Lord to leave Jerusalem just prior to its destruction, and lead a little colony of people to this Western continent. One of the interesting things about this was that Lehi was a direct descendant of Joseph who was sold into Egypt, and this colony bound for what is now America brought with them a number of sacred records including some of the writings of their famous ancestor Joseph. Joseph had always been favored of the Lord; the Lord had not only shown Joseph the future history of Egypt, but he also showed him what would befall some of his posterity in our day. Lehi quoting from the writings of Joseph says as follows:

"Yea, Joseph truly said: Thus saith the Lord unto me: A choice seer will I raise up out of the fruit of thy loins; and he shall be esteemed highly among the fruit of thy loins. And unto him will I give commandment that he shall do a work for the fruit of thy loins, his brethren, which shall be of great worth unto them, even to the bringing of them to the knowledge of the covenants which I have made with thy fathers. . . . (II Nephi 3:7)

"And his name shall be called after me; and it shall be after the name of his father. And he shall be like unto me; for the thing, which the Lord shall bring forth by his hand, by the power of the Lord shall bring my people unto salvation. (II Nephi 3:7, 15)

Joseph Smith fulfills all of these predictions, Joseph who was sent into Egypt in describing this great prophet of the latter days said, "And his name shall be called after me." That is, Joseph. He said, "It shall be after the name of his father." Joseph Smith's father's name was Joseph. Then he said, "And he shall be like unto me for the thing that the Lord shall bring forth by his hand by the power of the Lord shall bring my people unto salvation."

The mission of Joseph, the son of Jacob, was to go before the face of the Egyptian famine to preserve life. The mission of Joseph Smith was to go before the face of the spiritual famine foretold by Amos for exactly the same purpose. Joseph, the son of Jacob, opened the Egyptian granaries that people might not perish in the famine for bread. Joseph Smith, in response to the direct commandments of the Lord opened the granaries of spiritual truth to abate the famine mentioned by Amos which was not a famine for bread nor a thirst for water, but for hearing the word of the Lord.

After several centuries of spiritual darkness, great relirous leaders began a reformation. Many churches were organized in protest against the famine that was devouring the earth and making desolate its inhabitants. The many Protestant churches were trying to get back what had been lost although none of them claimed a direct command from God for so doing. Certainly if the authority given to Peter to "bind on earth and in heaven" was lost, the Lord himself must restore it.

It is the testimony of the Church of Jesus Christ of Latter-day Saints that this restoration has been made by divinely authorized messengers through the Prophet Joseph Smith. Also through Joseph Smith the Lord has given to the world in our day three great volumes of new scripture, making crystal clear every principle of the gospel as taught by

Jesus of Nazareth. And once again there is heard upon the earth the authoritative statement, "Thus saith the Lord."

Some time ago I attended the dedication of a meeting-house in Colorado. After the service, luncheon was served during which I sat by a man who told me that until recently he had been a minister of one of the great Christian churches, but a date had just been made for him to be baptized into the Church of Jesus Christ of Latter-day Saints.

He told me that during his twenty-five years in the pulpit he had been frequently disturbed by the fact that each minister taught a different doctrine in the same church from the same Bible, whereas even Jesus said, "My doctrine is not mine, but his that sent me." (John 7:16)

A few weeks prior to our meeting this man had attended a ministerial convention of his church in Chicago. One morning he had had breakfast with the moderator of the meeting and they had discussed these doctrinal differences existing within their organization. They decided to conduct a survey among those present to learn the exact extent of these differences. And so they asked each minister present to fill out a questionnaire giving his personal beliefs about the great doctrines taught in the Bible. The result showed an even wider difference than either had expected. And so this minister handed in his resignation. He was no longer willing to take upon himself the tremendous responsibility of assuming to speak in the name of the church. He knew of Paul's warning to the Galatians saying, "Though we, or an angel from heaven, preach any other gospel unto you than that which we have preached unto you, let him be accursed." (Gal. 1:8) Certainly such a warning could not be less important in our days of confusion than it was in the days of Paul.

Paul had spoken to the Ephesians and said, "One Lord, one faith, one baptism, one God and Father of all." What a long way the famine has taken us from that concept spoken by Paul in the name of Jesus Christ. Because of this confusion men have been running to and fro seeking the word of the Lord, and have not been able to find it. There are now some 250 contending Christian sects all claiming to accept the Bible as the inspired word of God, and the only authoritative guide in faith and doctrine. According to a survey made a few years ago 78 of these sects practiced baptism by immersion, many sprinkled, 68 had optional forms, 67 practiced infant baptism, many had no baptism, 37 required no adherence to any doctrine of any kind. Ninety-five per cent of all of the people said they believed in God, but most of them had very little conception of the *kind* of God they believed in.

The Protestant churches came into being because of a protest or an argument with the mother church. The Civil War gave the occasion for many additional churches to be organized. The Church of England came into being because the Pope would not grant a divorce to Henry the VIII. There are many state churches. It was Emperor Constantine, not the servants of the Lord, that made Christianity the church of the Roman Empire. Queen Elizabeth II of England became the titular head of two separate churches the moment her father died. She is the head of the Church of England which is Episcopalian, and also head of the church of Scotland which is Presbyterian in organization. Elizabeth is an Episcopalian while in England and a Presbyterian while in Scotland. As Queen, Elizabeth personally appoints the archbishops who are nominated by whatever government may be in power at the moment.

A few weeks after the minister mentioned above had handed in his resignation, two humble missionaries of the Church of Jesus Christ knocked on his door and told him they had a message. He invited them in, and they gave him a series of lessons, not teaching their own doctrine, but quoting the word of God from these great new scriptures; every doctrine being supported by "Thus saith the Lord."

When they told him about the personality of God, he said, "Who said so?" And they read to him word for word what the Lord had said. He wanted to know about infant baptism, and they read to him the revelation of the Lord to the Prophet Mormon saying. "Thus saith the Lord." They did similarly with each of the other great doctrines in turn. It is my opinion that no one would want or dare to disbelieve these sacred writings if he only understood the facts. This sacred information is available to anyone who desires to investigate, and only he who fails to seek fails to find. We need not be scholars to understand the simple gospel truths. The original disciples of Jesus were humble untrained men, yet they knew the truth and had a testimony in their hearts.

The granaries of truth are now open. The bread of life is now available and Jesus has said, ". . . seek, and ye shall find; knock, and it shall be opened unto you." (Matt. 7:7)

Five Grains of Corn

WE HAVE A very helpful custom among us of setting aside special days to think about special things. We set aside the second Sunday in May as Mother's Day, and on that day we let our minds reach up and try to understand those considerations for which the day was set apart. We set apart the third Sunday in June as Father's Day for similar reasons. And someone has pointed out that the human mind has some of the qualities of the tendrils of a climbing vine. It tends to attach itself and draw itself upward by what it is put in contact with.

We have many other wonderful days. There are Memorial Day and Easter and Pioneer Day. We set aside the fourth day of July as our nation's birthday. On this day we put our minds in contact with freedom and what it means, and what it has cost, and what it would be like if it were lost.

Then we have another special day called Thanksgiving. We set aside the fourth Thursday of November as a day to count our blessings and build gratitude and appreciation into our lives. And as Cicero, the old Roman statesman, reminds us, "gratitude is the mother of virtues." And as we recount our blessings, we increase them.

Thanksgiving is distinctly an American holiday. There is nothing like it any other place in the world. Thanksgiving is also unusual in several other respects. It does not commemorate a battle won nor the fall of a city. It does not mark the anniversary of a great conqueror nor the birthday of a famous statesman. It does not commemorate the writing of a historic public document nor the launching of a new constitution. Rather, Thanksgiving is a time set apart by Americans to give expression to the deep gratitude felt for the rich productivity of American soil. It also serves us as a memorial of the dangers and hardships through which our ancestors have passed, and it gives us the opportunity to make a fitting expression to God for all of his goodness to us.

Thanksgiving comes to us once a year by presidential proclamation. But to every grateful man and woman it comes as frequently as hearts filled with appreciation may direct.

Some early New Englanders had an interesting Thanksgiving Day custom by which they kept their minds in contact with gratitude. At their Thanksgiving dinners they placed five grains of corn by every plate as a voluntary reminder of those stern, harsh days of winter when the food supply of the Pilgrims had become so depleted that only five grains of corn were rationed at one time to any individual.

The early Pilgrims wanted their children to remember the sacrifice and hardship necessary to make possible the settlement of a free people in a free land. They wanted to keep alive the memory of that long sixty-three day trip taken in the tiny *Mayflower*. They desired to keep in their hearts the picture of that "stern, rockbound, New England coast" and the inhospitable greeting it extended to its first post-Columbus settlers. The Pilgrims wanted to remember that first terrible winter which took such a toll of lives. They did not want their descendants to forget that on the day in which their ration was reduced to five grains of corn, only seven healthy colonists remained to nurse the sick. And nearly half their total number lay in a wind-swept graveyard on the hill. They also wanted to remember that when the Mayflower sailed back to England in the spring, only sailors were aboard.

The display of five grains of corn at each Thanksgiving Day plate was a fitting reminder to keep their heroic past fresh in their memories. The corn served as an appropriate symbol to help the Pilgrim forefathers keep their gratitude to God alive and vital. Suppose that at this particular time we should borrow the Pilgrim's Thanksgiving Day symbols, what would five grains of corn at our plates signify to our minds?

The first might represent our gratitude for life itself. Henry Thoreau, the early-day American philosopher, once said that we should thank God every day of our lives for the privilege of having been born. And then he went on to speculate on the rather unique supposition of what it might have been like if we had not been born, and he pointed out the great many blessings that we would have missed as a consequence. In the days of Job it was said, "All that a man hath he will give for his life." The greatest blessing in life is life itself. There is no hardship that we would not endure, there is no expense in which we would not involve ourselves to prolong life even for a week or a month. This natural love of life has been implanted in us by God our Father to help us appreciate this tremendous gift, the full importance of which we do not yet understand. As we feel and express our gratitude for our own lives as well as for those of our family and friends, all are increased in importance.

The second grain of symbolic corn by our Thanksgiving plate may well serve to remind us of the great abundance with which we have been blessed in this land handed down to us by the Pilgrims and the Pioneers. When we think of the bounty of our land, we may well be reminded of what the Lord said to the ancient Israelites about the land flowing with milk and honey which he had promised to give to them.

As they were about to cross the River Jordan to take possession of their Land of Promise, the Lord said to them, "And thou shalt inhabit cities which thou didst not build, and thou shalt eat from vines which thou hast not planted, and thou shalt drink from wells which thou didst not dig." Every American finds himself in exactly that same situation. That is, there is not one of us who does not eat from vines which he hasn't planted, and drink from wells which he didn't dig. Then the Lord said to the Israelites, "And when thou hast eaten and are full, beware lest thou forget the Lord thy God." (See Deut. 6:11-12) There is always a great benefit comes when we remember our blessings and their source.

There has never been a time in history that any people has had such a lavish abundance as we ourselves have. One of the biggest problems in the United States on this Thanksgiving Day is that presented by our huge surplus. Someone said that, "One of our most difficult problems in America is how to stay awake on a full stomach." At this harvest season we are grateful for our bounties of food and clothing, our good health, our homes and our lands, and the millions of miracles and marvels that characterize America in this great age of wonders and enlightenment that we call the dispensation of the fulness of times. Our granaries and storehouses are overflowing. The Lord has poured out his blessings upon this land that there is not room enough to receive it. Yet forgetfulness and ingratitude continue to be among our chief weaknesses.

The third grain of corn by our Thanksgiving plate may help to put our minds in contact with the blessings we receive from our country. One does not need to know very much about early American history to be impressed that a peculiar providential favor has always attended this land from its very beginning. The founding fathers frequently discussed it, Abraham Lincoln mentioned it in his Thanksgiving Day Proclamation of 1863. But latter-day revelation has given us the sure word of the Lord that the Constitution of the United States was established by wise men that God had raised up for this very purpose. (D. & C. 101:77-80) God himself has set this land apart as a sanctuary of freedom. (Ether 2:8-12; II Nephi 10:10-11; I Nephi 22:7; I Nephi 13:12)

It has been said that ours is a nation in which every man

is royal, but no man cares to wear a crown. Yet in the deepest chambers of our souls each is conscious that we do have a king. We sing—

> Our Father's God to thee,
> Author of liberty, To thee we sing.
> Long may our land be bright,
> With freedom's holy light;
> Protect us by thy might
> Great God our king.

The great communist nations claim that we are behind them in the rocket race for the moon. But the third grain of corn by our Thanksgiving Day plate reminds us to be grateful that we are not behind them in freedom or in worship or in our desire for justice and fairness among all men. We are grateful that we are not subject to the oppression of tyrants and murderers who are lacking in a sense of right or wrong.

In the United States we have just gone through a great political election to decide who would represent us in the governing councils of our country for the next four years. We have been sharply divided on issues and people. We have settled the matter by an appeal to the ballot box. No blood was shed, no life was in danger, no one had any thought of trying to liquidate his opponent. No one even pounded with his shoe or threatened to throw it at anyone. Now all Americans will settle down and give full support to the government that they, under God, have created. Now we will all unite in building a greater America and help to carry out our divine mission to promote freedom, justice, and happiness in the world.

The consciousness of America's inadequacies that show themselves at election time is not an antonym of love. It is like the doctor's alertness to his patient's disease: it is merely a token of his concern, just as the nurse's sensitivity is a sign of her usefulness.

J. B. Priestley once said, "We should behave toward our country as women behave toward the men they love. A loving wife will do anything for her husband except to stop critizing and trying to improve him."

How appropriate at this Thanksgiving time are the words of America's Lincoln who said, "With malice toward none; with charity for all; with firmness in the right, as God gives us to see the right, let us strive on to finish the work we are in; . . . to do all which may achieve and cherish a just and lasting peace among ourselves and with all nations." We will do as Washington suggested and "set up a standard to which the wise and the good may repair."

Now suppose that we let the fourth symbolic kernel remind us to be grateful for our part of the work of the world. Certainly our work is one of our greatest blessings. In one of the most important of all the religious commandments God said, "By the sweat of thy face shalt eat thy bread." That is not a command of punishment but a command of opportunity.

Our work is not merely the way we get our bread, it is also the way we develop our industry, build our characters, strengthen our abilities, and bring about most of the other benefits of our lives. The land of the Pilgrims now produces for us in abundance. The desert of the Pioneers has blossomed as the rose. And through our work we may make about any contribution that we desire for ourselves, our fellow men, and to God. At this Thanksgiving season we may well join Charles Kingsley who said,

"Thank God every morning when you get up that you have something to do that day which must be done. Whether you like it or not, being forced to work and forced to do your best will breed in you temperance and self-control, diligence and strength of will, cheerfulness and contentment, and a hundred virtues which the idle never know."

Only one symbolic grain of corn remains. Can we do better than to direct it to put our minds in contact with God, our Eternal Father who is our greatest benefactor? By the light of a smoking lamp on the Mayflower, our Pilgrim Fathers before landing at Plymouth, inserted these words into the Mayflower Compact, "We whose names are underwritten have undertaken for the glory of God to establish in Virginia the first colony for the advancement of the Christian faith." Ten years later in 1630 other Pilgrims in the New England Federation Compact Agreement said, "We all have come into these parts of America with one and the same end, namely to advance the kingdom of the Lord Jesus Christ." We must not forget our purpose.

America was established as a kind of laboratory or experiment station to show what would happen to any people who cared and dared to follow Jesus Christ.

As we have grown from our national babyhood there have been other manifestations of God's goodness to us. The gospel has been restored in a fulness never before known in the world, so that the pathway to eternal life is now perfectly marked and brilliantly lighted. God has not gone out of business, but has indicated that most of our important history yet lies ahead of us. Certainly, our most important opportunity is to be true to the God of this land who is Jesus Christ. (Ether 2:12)

Shakespeare said, "Oh, Lord who lends me life, lend me a heart replete with thankfulness," and may that thankfulness be great enough to become the mother of an inquiry into the truths of the gospel and obedience to God its author, is my humble prayer.

Freedom

O NE OF THE great days of our year is Independence Day. *This* year we celebrate the 184th anniversary of the signing of the Declaration of Independence. On July 4, 1776 the greatest nation ever known in history was born, and to commemorate this great event we set aside this one day in each year to think about our freedom and what it means and what it has cost and what would happen if it were lost and what we can do to increase our country's success and enhance its greatness and blessing.

To appreciate this great day properly we should be familiar with some of the important factors that have made our nation what it is. We know that centuries before Columbus, a great civilization flourished upon this land. At some periods in their history divinely inspired prophets lived among them. Their writings were gathered together in what might be thought of as "An American Volume of Scripture," called The Book of Mormon. This book contains prophecies foretelling the destruction of their ancient civilization because of the wickedness of their people. But it also tells many things about the great nation that God should raise up in our day upon this land. This inspired book tells us many of the secrets accounting for our historic success and that God has a special mission for this nation to perform. Centuries ago God decreed that this land should be choice above all other lands, that it should be preserved as a sanctuary of freedom, that it should be free from captivity and from the domination of foreign nations and dictators. (Ether 2:8-12; II Nephi 10:10-11; I Nephi 22:7)

Then on December 16, 1833 the Lord gave a revelation

to Joseph Smith the prophet saying that the laws and the Constitution of this nation were established by him, and he said that it " . . . should be maintained for the rights and protection of all flesh, according to just and holy principles; that every man may act in doctrine and principle pertaining to futurity, according to the moral agency which I have given unto him, that every man may be accountable for his own sins in the day of judgment. Therefore, it is not right," said the Lord, "that any man should be in bondage one to another and for this purpose have I established the Constitution of this land, by the hands of wise men whom I raised up unto this very purpose, and redeemed the land by the shedding of blood." (D. & C. 101:78-80)

What a thrilling thought to know from the Lord himself that it was by his hand that our freedom was established. That he has been interested in, and has fostered our success as a nation. He has made this land the land of opportunity and prosperity that it is. God led Columbus to these shores, to make this land available to those who desired to be free. (I Nephi 13:12)

Recently a discussion has been carried on in *Life* magazine as to whether or not we have now lost the sense of the divine purpose that actuated the founding fathers. It is pointed out that this is particularly important now, since "America is the world's chief home and hope of freedom. If we refuse, or if we are unable to defend it, the cause of freedom may be lost to the world for a thousand years to come." "The world has an acute need of a convincing working model of a free society." But freedom is not only a civil right it is also a religious principle. God himself dedicated this land as the citadel of freedom, and we who live here have been given the special responsibility not only of preserving freedom but also keeping democracy, individual enterprise, and morality alive in the world.

As President Lincoln inferred, our blessings are not produced by any superior wisdom or virtue of our own except as we prove ourselves worthy of those blessings. And how pleased the Provider of our benefits would be if on this our national birthday we should enthusiastically acknowledge him and make a determined resolution to pay him honor with righteous lives.

This particular anniversary has a special significance because it comes when our freedom is probably in greater jeopardy than ever before in our history. We are presently opposed by a powerful combination of nations that is dedicated to the task of destroying freedom, not only among us, but in every other part of the world. For us who have grown up in a land dedicated to liberty and democracy, it is a little difficult to imagine that in our highly civilized world there are powerful human beings who if they thought they could, would without a moment's hesitation seek to deprive every person in the world of this God-given gift of freedom.

Especially is this startling in view of the fact that the idea that men should be free did not originate with us nor in our time. Freedom and free agency were ordained by God in heaven before this world was created. (Moses 4:1-3; Abraham 3:22-28) But even then there were those who attempted to subjugate and enslave the minds and wills of men. The war in heaven which expelled Satan and his followers was a battle for freedom. Lucifer and a third of the hosts of heaven had proposed, and then supported with force a plan to introduce compulsion into God's program of human salvation. It is very interesting that Satan has never given up this doctrine of force and compulsion, and he has imposed it upon everyone who has come sufficiently under his influence. More than once in our generation we have seen this influence attempt to enslave the minds and bodies of men by means of a world war. But our nation has always lived in defiance of despotism no matter from what source it may have arisen. "This world would be a far different and more unhappy place if there had never been a United States of America."

As we have seen giant Russia force her will upon the freedom-loving people of little Hungary and other subjugated nations, how could we fail to recognize the characteristics of the master mind of Satan behind the scenes? Surely we have been reimpressed with the importance of our God-given mission to promote freedom against the tyranny and force of godlessness. We know that freedom and free agency come from God and that force, compulsion, and deceit come from Satan. God banished Lucifer from heaven. Now Lucifer through his tools is trying to banish God from Russia. Who could have seen the communist leader sabotaging the chances for peace offered by the Paris Summit Conference, without recognizing a continuation in our world of that satanic philosophy which caused the war in heaven? And so far as I know, has caused every other war since that time.

Unlike those who believe in God, the chief representative of the great atheistic Russian state recognizes no power in the world superior to his own. While he was recently our guest in this country, he went about among us talking of burying us and our way of life. He talked about competing with us in the manufacture of guided missiles, intercontinental rockets and other instruments of enslavement and destruction. How clearly he represented himself then, and in Paris, as the tool of him who from the beginning has been the father of trouble, bloodshed, deceit, and enslavement. As someone has said, "Man was not born to have someone else's foot on his neck, or someone else's hand over his mouth." Our foreign guest said nothing about competing with us in human dignity or in freedom and opportunity for his fellow human beings.

On this Independence Day we should turn our thoughts to God and righteousness and center our minds on those things pleasing to him, who is the author of freedom and peace. Some 1900 years before Khrushchev, the Prince of Peace was born into the world. An angelic chorus announced his birth by singing of "Peace on earth, and good will among men." Though Jesus could command legions of angels to enforce his will, yet he spent his life trying to establish righteousness by the most peaceful means, and righteousness is the only sound basis for peace or progress or good will or freedom. Jesus said, " . . . ye shall know the truth, and the shall make you free." (John 8:33) Jesus representing God his Father, is the greatest advocate of peace, liberty and human dignity ever known. And all of these things were ordained in heaven, and our nation has been given the divine mission of fostering them in our day.

It has been said that "if the Soviet bloc wins world domination then our other problems will cease to matter very much one way or the other." For as Emerson has said:

> Of what avail is plow and sail,
> Or land or life, if freedom fail.

Peace and freedom are identified with the very destiny of humanity itself. Without them, many of the greatest benefits of our lives become meaningless. It is said that our task as Americans in view of our divine mission is not only to help the world to find enough to live on, but also help it find enough to live for.

And while on this particular birthday we are on the very brink of war and catastrophe, think of the encouragement we have in knowing that we are fighting for those principles of which God himself is the author. In *Paradise Lost* John Milton puts these words into the mouth of the Creator:

> I formed men free, and free they must remain
> Till they enthrall themselves.
> I will not change their nature
> Nor revoke the high decree
> That hath ordained their freedom,
> They themselves ordained their fall.

We may also ordain our own fall as a nation by departing from the righteous principles on which this nation was founded. On the other hand, we may entitle ourselves to prosperity, success, happiness, and all of the other blessings of heaven, if we are obedient to the God of this land who is Jesus Christ. (Ether 2:12) Montesquieu once said that "Countries are well cultivated, not as they are fertile but as they are free." And it might be added that we are free, not as we conquer others but as we carry out our own divine mission. Emerson who was one of our greatest American spokesmen said, "I wish to see America a benefactor such as no country has ever been. The office of America is to liberate, to abolish kingcraft, priestcraft, and ignorance." This newest brand of tyranny called communism is like all of the old brands in that it is founded upon ignorance, force, poverty, and a widespread belief that freedom and morality are not meant for all people. If we are to fulfill our destiny we need to recapture the spirit of '76. We need to capture the spirit of the Prince of Peace who said, "Man shall not live by bread alone." Our main problem is that we have paid too little heed to that instruction, "but have gone on stuffing ourselves with every kind of bread except the kind that Christ offered."

One noted religious leader said that "Unless we are willing to accept the diagnosis of the book on which our culture is founded, we will continue along the road to disaster and ruin."

When President Dwight D. Eisenhower took his second oath of presidential office on January 21, 1957, he raised his right hand in the air and rested his left hand upon the Bible opened to the 33rd Psalm which says, "Blessed is the nation whose God is the Lord." We must understand that great truth, that above the dictators and above chance and above circumstance there is God our Heavenly Father to whom all men must finally render an account of their lives.

I would like to close with the testimony of the great American prophet, Joseph Smith, who said, "The constitution of the United States is a glorious standard. It is founded in the wisdom of God. It is a heavenly banner. It is to all those who are privileged with the sweets of its liberties, like the cool-shades and refreshing waters of a great rock in a thirsty and a weary land. It is like a great tree under whose branches men from every clime can be shielded from the burning rays of the sun." (D.H.C. Vol. 3, Page 289-305)

Gird Up Your Loins

IT IS ALWAYS a very helpful experience to think about the outstanding qualities of a great man. One of my favorite great men is the Prophet Job. As the Old Testament book about him opens we see him as a man of great wealth and power. Later he is reduced to poverty and misery, with an almost unbearable load of calamity and suffering. Then in the third period Job's former wealth and power are multiplied and restored to him. But through good times and bad, Job is constant and unchanged, not only in his devotion to God but also in his attitude toward life generally.

There are some men who can't stand up under even a little adversity; others go down in a heap before prosperity. The slightest change one way or the other makes or breaks certain kinds of men. But Job was as faithful and true in one condition as in the other. His righteousness was in himself, not in the circumstances by which he was surrounded. I always get a great thrill when I read of Job, out of the very depths of his tribulation saying, " . . . while my breath is in me, and the spirit of God is in my nostrils: My lips shall not speak wickedness, nor my tongue utter deceit. . . . till I die I will not remove mine integrity from me." (Job 27:3-5)

Feel the power of this great prophet's spirit as he says, "Oh that my words were now written! oh that they were printed in a book! That they were graven with an iron pen and lead in the rock for ever! For I know that my redeemer liveth, and that he shall stand at the latter day upon the earth: And though after my skin worms destroy this body, yet in the flesh shall I see God: Whom I shall see for myself, and my eyes shall behold, and not another; though my reins be consumed within me." (Job 19:23-27)

Even God was proud of Job, and God said to Satan, "Hast thou considered my servant Job, that there is none like him in the earth, a perfect and an upright man, one that feareth God, and escheweth evil? and still he holdeth fast his integrity, although thou movedst me against him to destroy him without cause." (Job 2:3) What a satisfaction it would be to merit that kind of an expression from the Creator.

But one day the Lord put Job on the spot and out of the whirlwind asked him to answer some questions. And to get him prepared the Lord said to him, "Gird up now thy loins like a man; for I will demand of thee, and answer thou me." (Job 38:3)

All of my life I have heard this interesting expression "gird up thy loins" and I was never quite sure just what it meant. It seems that in Job's time the girdle was an important part of a soldier's uniform. It not only held the uniform together, but it gave the soldier's body firmness and power in battle. I suppose that we could say that both figuratively and literally it stiffened his spine. Therefore when a soldier was preparing for some strenuous action he would put on his girdle, or in other words, he would gird up his loins.

Before the era of modern medicine various internal organs were supposed to be the seat of certain qualities and powers. Courage was thought to reside in the heart; irritability came from the spleen; the gall bladder was thought to be the source of bitterness; but *stamina* and *power* were based in the intestines. We infer something like that even nowadays when we talk about intestinal fortitude and stick-to-it-iveness as coming from the area behind the belt buckle. Someone once misinterpreted the phrase, "indomitable courage" and called it "abdominable courage."

But no matter what it is called, this quality is almost all-important to our success in life. It might be said about courage what James M. Barrie once said about charm. He said, "If you have it, then nothing else matters much, and if you don't have it—well—then nothing else matters much either."

But certainly we need to develop in our own lives more of this rugged, righteous, tough-minded, tenacious abdominal strength which is so necessary in solving the difficult problems of our day. And probably no expression puts the punch into real accomplishment quite as well as the Lord's phrase to Job, "Gird up now thy loins like a man." That sounds like the Lord meant business and intended that Job should not only put on his girdle but his thinking cap as well. Like Job we all want to be good soldiers, and it seems to me that it would be a good idea, if at least in our thinking we would reinstate the girdle as a part of our soldier's uniform, particularly for those who are engaged in the work of the church and other kinds of human betterment.

In the picturesque language of the Bible, the girdle has also been used as an expressive figure of speech. King David, the celebrated warrior of ancient Israel in praising the Lord said, "Thou hast girded me with strength to battle." (II Sam. 22:40) He added, "Thou hast . . . girded me with gladness (Psalm 30:11) Isaiah refers to the coming of the Savior by saying, "Righteousness shall be the girdle of his loins. . . ." (Isaiah 11:5) In Peter's first general Epistle to members of the church he said, "Gird up the loins of your mind." (I Peter 1:13) In fact, if anyone plans on doing anything worthwhile, he had better be properly girded for the occasion.

It is interesting that so many scriptural texts also refer to success and our eternal salvation by using the figure of speech of a battle. David said, "The Lord mighty in battle." (Psalm 24:18) The children of Israel under Moses sang, "This Lord is a man of war." (Exodus 15:3) But this is more than a mere figure of speech. Before the Lord was the Prince of Peace he was Jehovah the warrior under whose leadership

Lucifer was expelled from heaven. In that unusual contest Jehovah must have represented great leadership qualities and skillful action at their best. We were a part of those pre-mortal battalions and must have learned much from Jehovah's courage and leadership ability.

We are still under obligation to be "good soldiers," and should some day be able to say as did the Apostle Paul, "I have fought a good fight. I have finished my course, I have kept the faith." But in any success it is helpful to think about the characteristics required of a good soldier. For we must also learn to be effective fighters, not to fight against anyone, but to fight for everyone.

The church, the community and every individual should be constantly waging war—a war for peace and happiness and righteousness—a war for God and Godliness, a war for our own eternal exaltation and the welfare and happiness of our children. We should be waging a constant war against ignorance, sin, and sloth.

We must be effective fighters against discouragement, inertia, and lethargy. At the same time we must never allow ourselves to be discouraged or negative. The largest single group of casualties in the recent world war were psychiatric. They were the men who broke down under the mental stresses and the personality pressures of military life.

Victory usually goes to those who gird up their minds with the right kind of thinking and then never stop fighting until the victory is won.

Paul tried to teach the Ephesians how to be good Christian soldiers. The lesson is also a good one for us. He said, "Finally, my brethren, be strong in the Lord, and in the power of his might. Put on the whole armour of God, that ye may be able to stand against the wiles of the devil. . . . Stand therefore, having your loins gird about with truth, and having on the breastplate of righteousness; And your feet shod with the preparation of the gospel of peace; Above all, taking the shield of faith, wherewith ye shall be able to quench all the fiery darts of the wicked. And take the helmet of salvation, and the sword of the Spirit, which is the word of God." (Eph. 6:10-11, 14-17)

What a great formula for our success! Suppose that we examine this direction a phrase at a time.

First, "Be strong in the Lord." There is so much to be done, and we need great strength for doing it. We must not lose any more ground. Weakness is not Godliness.

Second, "Put on the whole armour of God . . . having your loins girt about with truth." What a wonderful girdle is truth. That would permit no falsehood to get into our lives. Certainly we must know the will of the Lord. We must be true to our best capabilities and our greatest potentialities.

Third, "Having on the breastplate of righteousness." The breastplate is supposed to protect the heart. The breastplate of righteousness would particularly guard against all evil influences, as well as against all defeatism and negative thinking; all attitudes of weakness, failure and sin must be kept out of the heart. If we are righteous, our conduct will stand up under the scrutiny of the most just and competent judge.

Fourth, "And your feet shod with the preparation of the gospel of peace." A good heart is important to a soldier's success, but so are good feet. No one will ever go far as a warrior who is a tenderfoot or who doesn't get good service out of his feet. One of the greatest assets in spreading the gospel or in winning a war is to have willing, tireless, highly maneuverable feet. Success is never lost as long as the fighter stays on his feet.

Fifth, Then Paul said, "Above all, taking the shield of faith wherewith ye may be able to quench all the fiery darts of the wicked." Anciently burning arrows were used in warfare. It was necessary to extinguish these fiery darts before too many fires destroyed the chances for victory. If we lower the guard of our shield of faith, we are exposed to the damage of these poisonous burning arrows. The poison of too many of these fiery darts of the wicked soon starts us to thinking about surrender. Among the things most necessary to our success is the strong protection of a good solid shield of faith.

Sixth, "And take the helmet of salvation." The helmet protects the head. The head is the headquarters. It houses the soldiers' administration and control. The head is the source of thinking power. The most effective army is usually the one that has the best plans and the most useful ideas. No war is over until someone quits fighting. And victories are won when someone is first overcome in his thinking. If the psychological war can be won, then the rest is easy.

Every week the church and every other worthwhile organization suffer a long list of psychological casualties. Some lose their self-confidence; some become discouraged and afraid. Many are offended and when we lose the psychological war, about the only thing that can be done is to put us among the casualties and release us from service.

Seventh, "The sword of the spirit which is the word of God." Most good soldiers are judged by the way they use their swords. The sword of the spirit which is the word of God can have great power in people's lives. Effectively used it conquers all before it. No matter how the battle goes we should maintain a firm grip on the word of God.

God intends us to carry forward his word. Few battles are ever won by always being on the defensive. We must be aggressive fighters. "The advance" is the most effective of all military maneuvers. "To attack" is the shortest road to victory. Those who understand the importance of how to use the word of God, become the real successes in the battle of life. The finest armor is useless if we ourselves are unarmed.

The sword is closely related to the girdle. That is, the sword is the instrument by which we advance, and the girdle holds the uniform together and best represents the whole.

When the Lord says to Job and to us, "Gird up now thy loins like a man," he not only means that we should be completely dressed and ready for battle, but that we should be capable, industrious, responsible fighters.

When the Utah pioneers were coming across the plains some of them began to get weary and discouraged. Then at the request of Brigham Young, William Clayton wrote the great hymn, "Come, Come, Ye Saints." Then when they wanted to stiffen their own spines a little they sang:

> Gird up your loins
> Fresh courage take,
> Our God will never us forsake.
> And soon we'll have
> This truth to tell,
> All is well, all as well.

That is not only a great hymn, it is also a great success formula. It is a great philosophy of life which everyone needs if he is to become superior to the problems to be solved in our day. As Peter suggests, we need to "gird up the loins of our minds." We need to gird up the loins of our spirits. We need to put on the whole armor of God and get ready for the greatest accomplishment we have ever known. This is a day of high speed and great power, and we need great character qualities to overcome our problems and make the most of our opportunities.

God is now saying to us. "Gird up now thy loins like a man." And why shouldn't we? We are not incompetents or weaklings or failures—but children of God with important responsibilities, and we should gird up our loins and acquit ourselves like men in every situation.

May God bless us that we may be great warriors and like Job may prove worthy of the confidence of our Commander-in-Chief.

The Glory of the Sun

Some friends of ours have recently returned from a trip abroad. Most of their time away was spent in the Holy Land. When they began planning this trip two years ago, they wrote to the steamship companies, airlines, travel bureaus and libraries for information about the places and peoples they expected to visit. Inasmuch as their special interests centered in Palestine they had a large map especially prepared on which the places, events and dates of their particular interest were noted. Then for nearly two years, with the help of some good reference books, they restudied every chapter in the Bible. Upon their return they indicated that this had been one of the most wonderful experiences of their lives. The benefit they had received had been in proportion to the preparation that they had made.

With this in mind I would like to mention another important journey. In this country we pride ourselves on being extensive travelers. We like to go to new places and see new things and have wonderful experiences. Isn't it interesting then to remember that everyone of us already has a reservation, for the most important and the most exciting trip that anyone will ever make? That is when we will take that final trip beyond the boundaries of mortality.

There is a very important similarity between this postmortal journey and some others that we are familiar with, in that in each case the benefit received will be in proportion to the preparation made. In fact most all of life is preparation. We prepare for school, we prepare for marriage, we prepare for our life's work, we prepare for death. In the pre-existence we prepared for mortality. In mortality we are preparing for eternal life.

Because of the overwhelming importance of this scheduled journey and the new life that it will inaugurate, God himself has provided us with the sacred scriptures to serve us as an authentic guide, a kind of travel literature by which we may prepare for a magnificent experience beyond this life. The gateway to immortality is death, and because we usually think of death as unpleasant, we sometimes fail to make adequate preparation for it. But lack of preparation does not cancel the trip, it just changes the destination.

The school of mortality is like any other school in that only those who have made satisfactory preparation will receive the highest awards. The scriptures tell us that there is one place above all others that we should plan to attain. The Apostle Paul mentioned this in an interesting letter sent to the members of the Church at Corinth. He indicated to them that they had a choice between three possible destinations, each greatly differing in desirability from the others.

He pointed out that after the resurrection those who had not "sinned unto death" would be classified into three main groups according to their preparation. He said, "There are also celestial bodies, and bodies terrestrial: but the glory of the celestial is one, and the glory of the terrestrial is another. There is one glory of the sun, and another glory of the moon, and another glory of the stars: for one star differeth from another star in glory. So also is the resurrection of the dead." (I Cor. 15:40-42)

Other scriptures also point out the fact that the most desirable of these kingdoms is the one that Paul refers to as "the glory of the sun." It excels the other kingdoms in glory as the blazing noonday sun excels the soft light of the moon or the twinkle of a tiny star. This is the glory that God himself has instructed us to prepare for. Every single commandment that he has given has to do with the celestial kingdom.

The Lord has given no direction about getting into either of the lesser kingdoms. We get into these only by the degree of our default from the celestial.

In this same letter to the Corinthians Paul said, "Eye hath not seen, nor ear heard, neither have entered into the heart of man, the things which God hath prepared for them that love him." (I Cor. 2:9)

We can imagine luxury, elegance and beauty costing billions of dollars. In America we speak of our rising standard of living. But who can even conceive of the standard of living in this place where God himself dwells in the "glory of the sun."

In our own day some wonderful things have happened having a direct bearing on our eternal success. Direct revelations from God have vastly enriched our travel literature and given us far greater knowledge about our own future possibilities. On February 6, 1832, at Hyrum, Ohio, the Lord gave to Joseph Smith and Sidney Rigdon a vision regarding these three kingdoms of glory spoken of by Paul. He also told them about another kingdom not mentioned by Paul which is not a kingdom of glory. This vision is recorded word for word in the 76th Section of the Doctrine and Covenants. From any standpoint it is one of the greatest documents in all human literature.

In the 51st to the 53rd verse the Lord tells us exactly how to qualify for the celestial kingdom. He tells us a great deal about what it will be like. There will be no sin there. Celestial glory is the order in which God himself dwells. The glory of God is so great that no mortal in his natural state can live in God's presence. (D & C 67:11-13)

The Lord has also told us where this glory will be located. After the earth has filled the measure of its creation it will go through a series of changes and find its final destiny as the celestial kingdom. When God created this earth he looked upon it and pronounced it very good. Then the earth was defiled by the sins of its inhabitants. But that curse will be removed and after the millennium and the final judgment, the earth shall be purified, resurrected, glorified and celestial-ized to become the permanent abode of those who have lived here and have qualified for celestial glory. But God has made it very clear that if we desire to live here eternally we *must* be prepared. His exact words are, "If you will that I should grant you a place in the celestial world, you must prepare yourself by doing the things that I have commanded you." This is not just some man's idea, this is the word of the Lord. He says:

" . . . he that endureth in faith and doeth my will, the same shall overcome, and shall receive an inheritance upon the earth when the day of transfiguration shall come; When the earth shall be transfigured, even according to the pattern which was shown unto mine apostles upon the mount; of which account the fulness ye have not yet received."   (D & C 63:20-21)

On December 27, 1832 the Lord added another impor-tant chapter to our great literature on this subject known as the 88th Section of the Doctrine and Covenants. Speaking of the earth he said:

"For after it hath filled the measure of its creation, it shall be crowned with glory, even with the presence of God the Father;

That bodies who are of the celestial kingdom may pos-sess it forever and ever; for, for this intent was it made and created, and for this intent are they sanctified."

The Lord has also told us that those who are not quali-fied must be cast out. He says,

"And they who are not sanctified through the law which I have given unto you, even the law of Christ, must inherit another kingdom, even that of a terrestrial kingdom, or that of a telestial kingdom.

"For he who is not able to abide the law of a celestial kingdom cannot abide a celestial glory.

"And he who cannot abide the law of a terrestrial kingdom cannot abide a terrestrial glory.

"And he who cannot abide the law of a telestial kingdom cannot abide a telestial glory. Therefore he is not meet for a kingdom of glory. Therefore he must abide a kingdom which is not a kingdom of glory.

"And again, verily I say unto you, the earth abideth the law of a celestial kingdom, for it filleth the measure of its creation and transgresseth not the law—

"Wherefore, it shall be sanctified; yea, notwithstanding it shall die, it shall be quickened again, and shall abide the power by which it is quickened, and the righteous shall inherit it." (D & C 88:19-26)

Not only will the earth be celestialized and beautiful, but all who live upon it will be resurrected celestial personages capable of receiving a *fulness* of celestial glory. Try to understand what you, as a celestial personage, will be like, with quickened senses, amplified powers of perception, and vastly increased capacity for understanding and happiness, made suitable to live in the presence of God.

The Lord says of all such, "These are they whose bodies are celestial, whose glory is that of the sun, even the glory of God, the highest of all, whose glory the sun of the firmament is written of as being typical." (D & C 76:70) But a celestial person is not just a celestial body. The Lord says that the celestial excels in *all* things. (D & C 76:92) That means a celestial mind, a celestial personality, a celestial family and celestial friends. Beginning in the 55th verse of Section 76 the Lord says,

"They are they into whose hands the father hath given all things.

"They are they who are priests and kings, who have received of his fulness, and of his glory;

"And are priests of the Most High, after the order of Melchizedek, which was after the order of Enoch, which was after the order of the Only Begotten Son.

"Wherefore, as it is written, they are gods, even the sons of God." (D & C 76:55-58)

What an inspiring portrayal of your possible dignity and destiny!

Now just suppose that we don't qualify. Suppose that we have paid insufficient attention to our inspired literature in which the Lord is trying to give us direction. Suppose that we must then content ourselves with one of the lower kingdoms with something less fine and far less satisfying. Suppose that we are among those that must be cast out, that we must live elsewhere forever, not only away from our family and friends but also excluded from the presence of God. The scripture speaks of outer darkness. It tells of weeping and wailing and gnashing of teeth. Who can understand the depth to which our grief may go when we realize that we have missed the celestial kingdom? The Prophet Joseph Smith said that the greatest misery of departed spirits is to know that they come short of the glory that others enjoy that they could have had." (*H. of C.*, Vol. 5:425)

Some of us even in this life have known the intense regret that can come because of a wasted opportunity or some defiling sin. "Of all sad words of tongue or pen the saddest are these, It might have been." The most devastating of all human emotions is the sense of being alone, of being unwanted, of being unworthy. We were born on this earth; we were placed here to get ready; we inherited the right to live here forever, unless through our own disobedience and sin we disqualify ourselves.

In conclusion I would like to read a statement made

many years ago by President Charles W. Penrose about the earth when it becomes celestialized. He said, "The earth will die like its products but it will be quickened again and resurrected to celestial glory. It has been born of the water and will be born of the spirit, purified by fire, from the corruption that once defiled it, developed into its perfections as one of the family of worlds fit for the Creator's presence. All its latent light awakened into scintillating action, it will move up into its place among the orbs governed by celestial time, shining like a sea of glass mingled with fire. Every tint and color of the heavenly bow radiates from its surface.

"The ransomed of the Lord will dwell upon it. The highest beings of the ancient orbs will visit it. The garden of God will again adorn it. The heavenly government will prevail in every part. Jesus will reign as its king. The river of life will flow from the regal throne. The tree of life whose leaves were for the healing of the nations will flourish upon the banks of the heavenly stream and its golden fruit will be free for the white-robed throngs that they may eat and live forever. This perfected earth with its saved inhabitants will then be presented to the Eternal Father as the finished work of Christ."

What a thrilling experience lies ahead if we are only able to translate the word of the Lord into appropriate preparation and thereby qualify, with our families and friends to live forever in that wonderful place which has been so aptly described as "the glory of the sun!"

He Is Risen

(Matt. 28:6)

T ODAY WE commemorate one of the most important events that has ever taken place upon the earth. It greatly affects the individual life of every human being who ever has, or ever will live here. Many years ago in the Garden Tomb of Joseph of Arimathea on the outskirts of Jerusalem, the universal resurrection was initiated upon this earth. As a consequence, every person, whether his life has been good or evil, shall sometime have a literal bodily resurrection. This tremendous benefit comes to us with no effort on our part, for as in Adam all die, even so in Christ shall all be made alive. (I Cor. 15: 22) However, the *kind* of resurrection that each receives will be determined by the kind of life that he has lived.

It is difficult to conceive of anything more important to us individually or collectively than the things that we memorialize at Easter time. And one of our greatest opportunities is to understand and believe in the Easter message.

One of our most serious problems is the difficulty we sometimes have in actually getting great ideas into operation in our lives. Because some religious truths cannot be demonstrated by the usual methods, we sometimes believe them on a fractional or marginal basis, which usually results in our action being indecisive.

But nothing in the scriptures could be more clearly or authoritatively stated than the literalness and actuality of the resurrection of Jesus. If we can fully believe this with no reservations, then it is an easy step to believe in our own resurrection. And as our power to act comes from our ability to believe, a strong belief in our resurrection will help us to make it a glorious one. We ourselves are hurt if we just half-believe or if we try to spiritualize or explain away this great doctrine which is the very foundation of the Christian religion.

What greater accomplishment could be ours than to have an unshakeable testimony of the glorious message of Easter as given by the word of the Lord and recorded in the Holy Bible.

Here are some of the facts about the death and resurrection of Jesus. He was hung upon the cross at about nine o'clock in the morning. (Mark 15:25) He remained there for six hours or until three in the afternoon. (Mark 15:34) From 12 till 3 Luke says there was a darkness that covered all of the earth. At the end of this period of darkness and disturbance in nature, Jesus cried out with a loud voice, "Father, unto thy hands I commend my spirit." And then he died.

Joseph of Arimathea obtained permission from Pilate to lay the body of Jesus in the nearby tomb that he had prepared for himself. Then Matthew says:

"Now the next day, that followed the day of the preparation, the chief priests and Pharisees came together unto Pilate, Saying, Sir, we remember that the deceiver said, while he was yet alive, After three days I will rise again. Command therefore that the sepulchre be made sure until the third day, lest his disciples come by night, and steal him away, and say unto the people, He is risen from the dead: so the last error shall be worse than the first. Pilate said unto them, Ye have a watch: go your way, make it as sure as ye can. So they went, and made the sepulchre sure, sealing the stone, and setting a watch." (Matt. 27:62-66)

Now suppose that in imagination we go and stand before the tomb very early in the morning of that first Easter Sunday while I read to you what the Apostle Matthew has recorded in the 28th chapter of his gospel. We remember that the entrance to the sepulchre had been closed with a great stone to which the Roman seal had been affixed and over which a guard of Roman soldiers were standing watch. Then Matthew says:

"In the end of the sabbath, as it began to dawn toward the first day of the week, came Mary Magdalene and the other Mary to see the sepulchre.

"And, behold, there was a great earthquake: for the angel of the Lord descended from heaven, and came and rolled back the stone from the door, and sat upon it.

"His countenance was like lightning, and raiment white as snow:

"And for fear of him the keepers did shake, and become as dead men.

"And the angel answered and said unto the women, Fear not ye: for I know that ye seek Jesus, which was crucified.

"He is not here: for he is risen, as he said. Come, see the place where the Lord lay.

"And go quickly, and tell his disciples that he is risen from the dead; and, behold, he goeth before you into Galilee; there shall ye see him: lo, I have told you." (Matt. 28:1-7)

Matthew also says: "And behold, the veil of the temple was rent in twain from the top to the bottom; and the earth did quake, and the rocks rent; And the graves were opened; and many bodies of the saints which slept arose, And came out of the graves after his resurrection, and went into the holy city, and appeared unto many." (Matt. 27:51-53)

That is, Jesus was the first fruits of the resurrection, but others were also resurrected, and just as surely as we now live, everyone of us will some day be resurrected. Our problem comes from the fact that it is difficult to understand and believe something that we have not actually experienced.

We are like Thomas. We must first put our fingers into the prints of the nails, and thrust our hands into his side before we can believe.

When the women entered into the tomb, the body was gone. (Luke 24:3) Jesus had risen. He had conquered death not only for himself but also for everyone of us.

While we are thinking about this great event may I read to you some lines entitled "The Guardsman" written by one who in imagination represented the Roman officer in charge of the soldiers detailed by Pilate to watch the tomb. The author uses his imagination to fill in between the lines of the scripture, and they may help us to make this great event memorable to our minds. In telling his sweetheart of his experiences before the tomb, Maximus, the Roman officer said:

"My Sylvia, 'tis long since we have met, so kissed, so held each other to heart! I thought to greet thee as the conqueror comes, bearing the trophies of his prowess home, but Jove hath willed it should be otherwise. Jove, say I? Nay, some mightier, strong God, who thus hath laid his heavy hand upon me; No victor, Silvia, but a conquered man—who seeks to hide his weakness in thy love.

"How beautiful thou art! The years have brought an added splendor to thy loveliness. With passion of dark eye and lip rose red, struggling between its dimple and its pride. Yet there is something that looms *between* thy love and mine; come, girdle me about with thy true arms, and pillow on thy breast this aching and bewildered head of mine; Here, where the fountain glitters in the sun among the saffron lilies—and I will tell, if so that words will answer my desire, The dreadful fate that has befallen me.

"Down in Jerusalem they slew a man, or God—it may be that he was a God—those mad, wild Jews whom Pontius rules. Thou knowest Pilate, Silvia, a vain man, too weak to govern such a howling horde as those same Jews. This man they crucified. I knew naught of him, never heard his name, until the day they dragged him to his death; then all tongues wagged about him and his deeds; Some said he claimed to be their king, some that he had blasphemed their deity. 'Twas certain he was poor and meanly born. No warrior he, nor hero; and he taught doctrines that surely would upset the world; so they killed him to be rid of him. Wise, very wise, if he were only man, not quite so wise, if he were half a God!

"I know that strange things happened when he died. There was a darkness, and an agony, and some were vastly frightened—not so I. What cared I if that mob of reeking Jews had brought a nameless curse upon their heads: I had no part in that blood guiltiness.

"At last, he died, and some few friends of his took him and laid him in a garden tomb. A watch was set about the sepulchre, lest these, his friends, should hide him and proclaim that he had risen as he had foretold.

"Laugh not, my Silvia, I laughed when I heard the prophecy; I would I had not laughed:

"I, Maximus, was chosen for the guard with all my trusty fellows. Pilate knew I was a man who had no foolish heart of softness—all unworthy of a man. I was a soldier who had slain my foes; my eyes had looked upon a tortured slave as on a beetle crushed beneath my tread;

"I gloried in the splendid strife of war, lusting for conquest; I had won the praise of our stern general on the scarlet field; red in my veins the warrior passion ran—for I had sprung from heroes, Roman born!

"That second night we watched before the tomb, my men were merry; on the velvet turf, bestarred with early blossoms of the spring; they diced with jest and laughter.

"All around the moonlight washed us like a silver lake, save where that silent sealed sepulchre was hung with shadow as a purple pall.

"A faint wind stirred among the olive boughs; methinks I hear the sighing of that wind in all sounds since; it was so dumbly sad; but as the night wore on it died away, and all was deadly stillness; Silvia, that stillness was most awful, as if some great heart had broken and so ceased to beat.

"I thought of many things, but found no joy in any thought, even the thought of thee. The moon waned in the west and sickly grew her light sucked from her in the breaking dawn.

"Never was dawn so welcome as that pale, faint glimmering in the cloudless, brooding sky.

"Oh, Silvia, how may I tell thee that which next came to pass? I have been mocked at, when I told the tale, for a crazed dreamer, punished by the gods, because he slept on guard; but mock not thou! Silvia, I could not bear it, if thy lips should mock the vision dread, of that Judean morn.

"Suddenly the pallid east was all aflame with radiance, that bent upon our eyes as from the noonday sun, and then we saw two shapes, that were as the immortal gods, standing before the tomb; around me fell my men as dead; but I, though through my veins ran a cold tremor never known before, withstood the shock, and saw one shining shape roll back the stone.

"The whole world seemed ablaze, and through the garden came a rushing wind, thundering a paean, as of victory.

"Then that dead man came forth! O Silvia, if thou could'st but the face of Him have seen.

"Never was such a conqueror. Yet no pride was in it—naught but love and tenderness, such as we Romans scoff at, and his eyes bespake him royal. O my Silvia, surely he was no Jew—but very God!

"Then he looked full upon me. I had borne much staunchly but that look I could not bear! For what man may front a God and live? I fell prone as if stricken by a thunder-bolt; and though I died not; somewhat of me died that made me man.

"When my long stupor passed, I was no longer Maximus, I was a weakling with a piteous woman soul; all strength and pride, joy, and ambition gone. My Silvia, dare I tell thee what foul curse is mine because I looked upon a God?

"I care no more for glory, all desire for honor and for strife is gone from me, all eagerness for war. I only care to help and save bruised beings, and to give some comfort to the weak and suffering. I cannot even hate those Jews; my lips speak harshly of them, but within my heart, I only feel compassion; and I love all creatures, to the vilest of the slaves, who seem to me as brothers.

"Silvia, scorn me not for this weakness; it will pass, sure-ly 'twill pass in time, and I shall be Maximus, strong and valiant once again, forgetting that slain God. And yet, and yet, He seemed like one who could not be forgot."

The greatest hope of every person in the world is em-bodied in the Easter message of the resurrection. Christian peoples generally say to the world that they believe that Christ rose from the dead, but the Church of Jesus Christ of Latter-day Saints says to Christians and to all others that we *know* that Christ rose from the dead, because this same Jesus who walked upon the waters, healed the sick, suffered in Geth-semane, died upon the cross, came forth from the tomb and said to Thomas, "Reach hither thy hand and behold my side," has appeared again to men in our own day and has revealed again the greatest truth in the world—that God lives, that Jesus Christ is his Son, that the Savior of the world lives, and be-cause he lives everyone of us shall live also.

May God help us to make the Easter message a controll-ing part of our lives, that in the resurrection we may find our peace in the Glory of the Sun.

J Day

Branch Rickey, the great baseball manager, was once asked what was his greatest day in baseball. Mr. Rickey said, "I don't know. I haven't had it yet." Life is made up of a lot of wonderful days that are interesting to think about. But if you were asked to pick out the one single day that in your opinion would be the greatest of all of your days which one would it be? You may select the day of your birth. That was certainly a great day. That was the day you came into the world. That was the day when your life, with all of its opportunities, began. That was when many wonderful things were determined for you. You may think that the greatest day will be the day of your death. Death is the gateway to immortality. We live to die, then we die to live.

There are many other wonderful days. There is your graduation day. There is the day you began your life's work. There is your wedding day. There are some important "days of decision," when vital issues are determined upon. These are like hinges upon which an entire future may turn. There is another very interesting day called resurrection day. What an exciting day that will be. A reunion with old friends is always a thrilling experience, but what a stimulating thing it will be to be reunited with yourself. On your resurrection day your body and spirit will be joined together in a glorious union which will never again be subject to dissolution.

Now of all of these and other great days, which is the stand-out day of your entire existence? The correct answer is probably the same that Mr. Rickey gave—"You haven't had it yet."

There is an interesting day best known to the soldiers

of World War II called "D Day." That was a term used to indicate an unspecified day on which some crucial military operation was to take place. In World War II this date was June 6, 1944. That was the day when the Allied invasion forces swarmed onto the beaches of Normandy to re-establish their foothold in Western Europe. This was the beginning of the end of the European War. August 15, 1945 was VJ Day, or Victory in Japan Day.

But there is an unspecified day mentioned in the scripture on which another crucial operation is to take place. This is another "J Day" or "judgment day." Judgment Day is a term used throughout the scriptures indicating a settling-up day. This is a day for balancing the books. Through the ages the prophets have looked forward to this important day and have called it by various names such as "the day of reckoning," "the day of the Lord," "the great and terrible day." To some it might be thought of as "doomsday." But to some scriptural writers, this day stands apart from all other days and needs no qualifying phrase. They refer to this day by merely saying "*the* great day."

If we were going to participate in some very important social or business function, we would want to know as much as possible about it in advance. We would want to know who was going to be there, what the purpose of the occasion was, and what would be expected of those present. There is a great deal of this information available about judgment day. We know who is going to be there. We know that *we* will be there, *God* will be there, all of the children of God will be there. Even Satan and his angels will be there. The Prophet Jude said, "The angels which kept not their first estate but left their own habitation, he hath reserved . . . unto the judgment of the great day." (Jude 1:6) We know the purpose of the judgment; we know who the judge will be. We know the points on which the judgment will be made. We know the source of the evidence. But how would you like to see an actual, authentic preview of judgment day itself, with you in it? John the Revelator makes such a preview available to us as recorded in the Book of Revelation. Suppose then that we turn the picturing power of our minds to their clearest focus, while we project the account of the judgment as we will someday experience it. You remember that after all of the other apostles had been killed, the Apostle John was banished to a rocky little island in the Aegean Sea called Patmos. There the Lord gave him a very important revelation. It was so important that thereafter this apostle has been called John the Revelator. It was not given just for his benefit, but for the benefit of all of us who should live after that date.

The Lord specifically asked John to write down what he saw so that we might see it also. John says that while he was in the spirit on the Lord's Day, he heard a voice behind him. It was a great voice as of a trumpet, saying, "I am Alpha and Omega, the first and the last, and what thou seest write in a book." It has always been the program of the Lord to give revelations to the one appointed for that purpose. Then we get the message from him. John says that he turned to see who spoke and he saw one like unto the son of man, clothed with a garment down to the foot. Then John tried to describe this glorious personage. He said, "His head and his hairs were white like wool, as white as snow. His eyes were as a flame of fire. And his feet like unto fine brass, as if they were burned in a furnace. And his voice as the sound of many waters." So glorious was this personage that John says, "When I saw him I fell at his feet as dead. And he laid his right hand upon me saying unto me, Fear not; I am the first and the last: I am he that liveth, and was dead; and behold, I am alive forever more . . . and have the keys of hell and of death." (Revelation 1:17-18)

Think how important that message is to everyone who has or will live upon the earth. Think what it would mean to hold the keys of death and hell. And then John transmits to us this stimulating preview of what we are some day going actually to experience. Anciently men communicated with each other by means of pictures. We still think in pictures, but we transmit those pictures to others by means of words. When someone is relating an experience to you, he is translating into words a picture that he has in mind. You receive the words and then you translate the words back into pictures. In your mind you actually visualize the particular thing he is describing. This picturing power of the mind can be one of our most important abilities. That is, we see with our minds. When one says, "I just can't see myself doing that," he doesn't mean that he lacks eyes—he lacks picturing power. We must see before we can understand.

I would now like to read to you some of this revelation, and while you are getting parts of the picture focused in your mind, I would like to make a few comments about it. John says:

"And I saw the dead, small and great, stand before God; and the books were opened: and another book was opened, which is the book of life: and the dead were judged out of those things which were written in the books, according to their works." (Rev. 20:12)

The fundamental law of the universe is this immutable, inexorable, irrevocable law of the harvest which says, "Whatsoever a man soweth, that must he also reap." That is a tremendously important idea to always keep in mind. Then John continues.

"And the sea gave up the dead which were in it; and death and hell delivered up the dead which were in them: and they were judged every man according to their works.

"And death and hell were cast into a lake of fire. This is the second death.

"And whosoever was not found written in the book of life was cast into the lake of fire." (Ibid. 20:13-15)

It is a very stimulating experience to try to imagine

yourself waiting before the judgment bar to find out what the book says about what your final status will be. Some are going to be very unhappy when they get the information. The Bible speaks of outer darkness where there will be weeping and wailing and gnashing of teeth. Try and *preview* that situation, or just suppose that your name can't be found in the Book of Life. What a lot of excitement *that* is going to cause. How will we feel about loved ones who don't qualify? On the other hand, how grateful and relieved we will be if we finally locate our names and those of our families and friends written high up the list of the Book of Life.

John continues this tremendous vision by saying to this group:

"And I heard a great voice out of heaven saying, Behold, the tabernacle of God is with men, and he will dwell with them, and they shall be his people, and God himself shall be with them, and be their God.

"And God shall wipe away all tears from their eyes; and there shall be no more death, neither sorrow, nor crying, neither shall there be any more pain: for the former things are passed away.

"And he that sat upon the throne said, Behold, I make all things new, and he said unto me: Write: for these words are true and faithful. . . .

"He that overcometh shall inherit all things, and I will be his God and he shall be my son." (Ibid. 21:3-5,7)

What greater day could there be than such a VJ Day or victory on judgment day? If we have only qualified for the blessings shown in the vision!

But suppose that we *don't* qualify. John describes the unhappy situation of one such group as follows:

"But the fearful, and unbelieving, and the abominable and murderers, and whoremongers, and sorcerers, and idolators and all liars, shall have their part in the lake which burn-eth with fire and brimstone: which is the second death." (Ibid. 8)

I don't know what the arrangement will be when we stand before the great judgment bar of God. We may not have to wait in line, though my memory always brings back pictures of people waiting in a long line to get their auto licenses or their movie tickets or pay their taxes. And I try to understand how I will feel while I am in this judgment day lineup waiting for the book to be opened to that very important page marked with my name. What will the verdict be and how will I take it?

We have seen people stand before earthly judges to receive sentence. We know a little bit about how some of *them* have felt. After the sentence some have fainted; some have wept bitterly; some have completely gone to pieces emotionally.

One of our biggest problems is that we are such incurable optimists. No matter what our conduct may be, we always picture the result as "a happy ending." But we can learn wisdom by also thinking about the alternatives.

Of course there will be many degrees of rewards and punishments. As Paul said to the Corinthians, "There are also celestial bodies, and bodies terrestrial: but the glory of the celestial is one, and the glory of the terrestrial is another. There is one glory of the sun, and another glory of the moon, and another glory of the stars. For as one star differeth from another star in glory, so also is the resurrection of the dead." (I Corinthians 40-42)

Only those will inherit a lower kingdom, who have not made definite arrangements to inherit a higher kingdom.

Someone has pointed out that "If you don't think about the future you can't have one." The Prophet Joseph Smith once said that the greatest misery of departed spirits is to know that they come short of the glory that others enjoy, that they could have had. (*History of the Church*, Volume 5, page 425) We come short mostly because we haven't made preparation for something better.

Someone has said that "hell is truth seen too late." That is, the judgment is not a place where you go to say I am sorry and I will do better next time. On judgment day the evidence will all be in, the decisions will have been made, and the judgments handed down. Whatever our present attitude may be, when we stand before God, every one of us will *then* want to be a faithful, devoted, effective follower of Jesus Christ. But if we have not taken note of the requirements and lived thereby, we may find that our opportunities have forever passed us by.

To prevent this suppose that at regular intervals we impress upon our own minds the great truths of this vision by turning our picturing power to its clearest focus while we project again the account of the judgment, as we will someday actually experience it.

John said, "And I saw the dead, small and great, stand before God; and the books were opened: and another book was opened which is the book of life: and the dead were judged out of the things which were written in the books, according to their works."

And God has given us this great promise:

"And he that overcometh shall inherit all things, and I will be his God and he shall be my son."

We all like to think about inheriting from a wealthy parent. What is more to be desired than to inherit from God. For Jesus has promised, "Then all that my father hath shall be given unto them." If you could only project your vision into the future and find yourself a member of this group, then if someone should ask you again, what is the greatest moment of your life, you would certainly say, as did Mr. Rickey, "I haven't had it yet." May we look forward to this great day with an ambition strong enough to bring about the greatest blessings seen by the great Revelator.

Joseph Smith

IT HAS been said that a nation's greatness is usually written in the biographies of its great men. Some of the reasons that America is great is because of the people who settled here, the motives they possessed, the standards they have lived by, and the ambitions they have developed. America is great because of the ideals that have been handed down by her people. The world has no greater resource than that of a great man.

Thomas Carlyle once said, "You cannot look upon a great man without gaining something from him." The ancient Romans used to capitalize this idea by making statues of their greatest Romans and setting them up in their homes. Then as they looked at the statue, they thought about the qualities of the man it represented, and as they thought about him, they borrowed his virtues for their own lives.

We have done something very similar in America when we have set aside the birthdays of our great men and held their lives up before our minds for consideration and review.

Sometime ago I re-read one of Abraham Lincoln's anti-slavery debates. Lincoln's opponent had argued that they could not afford to free the Southern slaves because there were some four million of them, each had an average value to his owner of approximately $1,000. He reasoned that if they freed the slaves, they would upset the economy of this little group of people by some four billion dollars which they could not afford. But in addition, he said, who would take care of the corn, the cotton and the tobacco crops?

When Lincoln came to the platform he brushed all of these considerations aside as immaterial. He said, "There is only one question you need to answer in order to decide the question of slavery and that is this: Is slavery right or is it wrong? Is it right for some men to hold other men in bondage?" Suppose that in the future whenever we have a difficult problem come up that we apply Lincoln's formula for solving it. All we need to do is to ask ourselves, is it right or is it wrong? We are all made richer when we think of the great virtues of Abraham Lincoln.

There is another great American whose life and work has had, and in increasing measure will have, a very important influence upon our thinking. He was a contemporary of Abraham Lincoln, being a little over three years old when Lincoln was born. His name was Joseph Smith, the great American prophet, and I would like to hold up for your consideration some thoughts about him.

Any man's greatness is judged by the work that he does. If he isn't great in what he does then he isn't great. It has been suggested that a man's worth to the world should be judged by the answers to four basic questions. Those questions are:

1. Who gave him his assignment?
2. What was the size and importance of the job that he did?
3. How well did he do his work?
4. What did he leave to posterity?

First. Who gave Joseph Smith his assignment? That is, who is it that says that he is great? Sometimes Republicans believe a man great whereas the Democrats may disagree. Or a son may make an appraisal of his father's virtues that may not harmonize with the general opinion. It is, of course, a little bit difficult to appraise the calling of one of the prophets who have received their assignments from God. It is very interesting that many of the prophets have received their divine calling at a very early age. Noah was ordained at age 10. (D. & C. 107) Samuel had a personal visit from the Lord in the Temple at Shiloh when he was just a child, probably age 12. (I Sam. 3:10, 21) David was anointed king of ancient Israel when he was just a shepherd boy, and waited many years before ascending the throne. (I Sam. 6:12) Joseph was sent into Egypt on an errand for the Lord when he was 17. (Gen. 37:2) Jesus taught the wise men in the temple at 12. (Luke 2:42) Jeremiah was called when a mere child, probably age 13. (Jer. 1:6) Mormon, one of the great prophets of pre-Columbus America was called at age 10. (Mor. 1: 10) Joseph Smith received a visit from the Father and the Son at age 14½. (Joseph Smith 2:7)

The Lord has an interesting advantage in the selection of a great man because he knew each one in the spirit world before this life began. In the first chapter of the book of Jeremiah we find out when God selected Jeremiah. Jeremiah said, "Then the word of the Lord came unto me, saying, Before I formed thee in the belly I knew thee; and before thou camest forth out of the womb I sanctified thee, and I ordained thee a prophet unto the nations. Then said I, Ah, Lord God; behold, I cannot speak: for I am a child." (Jer. 1:4-6)

In one of the greatest visions ever given in the world, we find out something about how the Lord works. The Prophet Abraham was shown his own premortal existence and he records that experience saying: "Now the Lord had shown unto me, Abraham, the intelligences that were organized before the world was; and among all these there were many of the noble and great ones; And God saw these souls that they were good, and he stood in the midst of them, and he said: These I will make my rulers; for he stood among those that were spirits, and he saw that they were good; and he said unto me: Abraham, thou art one of them; thou wast chosen before thou wast born." (Abr. 3:22-23)

We believe that our standing in eternity will be influenced by our faithfulness in this life. It is also logical that our lives here were influenced by our antemortal existence. We know that Jesus was ordained before he was born. (John 1:1-12) But the Prophet Joseph Smith says that "Every man who has a calling to minister to the inhabitants of this earth was ordained to that very purpose in the grand council in heaven before the world was. (DHC 6:364)

Question number two—What was the size and importance of the job done by Joseph Smith? Of course, it is not always possible to judge fully a situation when we are so close to it. But what kind of man would one expect to be selected by the Lord to open and lead the greatest and last of all the gospel dispensations, the dispensation of the fulness of times.

The great prophets of old looked enviously down to our age of wonders and enlightenment. This is the greatest of all ages. This is the day that is to prepare for the glorious second coming of Christ to the earth. It is interesting to remember that almost every other dispensation was wiped out by apostasy. That even applies to the dispensation of Jesus. But our dispensation has been given the promise that the gospel shall never again be taken from the earth until the Lord shall come again. One could scarcely conceive a more important assignment than to stand at the head of the last dispensation.

The third question is, "How well did he succeed?" The following appraisal of the work of the Prophet Joseph Smith was given by Josiah Quincy, noted writer and distinguished citizen of Boston. Mr. Quincy interviewed Joseph Smith at Nauvoo, Ill., just before his martyrdom. Later he wrote a book entitled, *Figures from the Past,* and on page 376 he asks this question:

"What historical American of the 19th century has exerted the most powerful influence upon the destinies of his countrymen?" Mr. Quincy then proceeds to answer his own question by saying, "It is by no means impossible that the

answer to that interrogatory may be thus written: Joseph
Smith, the Mormon prophet. And that reply, absurd as it
doubtless seems to most men now living, may be an obvious
commonplace to their descendants. History deals in surprises
and paradoxes quite as startling as this. The man who estab-
lishes a great religion in this age of free debate, and who was
and is today accepted by hundreds of thousands as a direct
emissary from the most high, is not to be disposed of merely
by pelting his memory with unsavory epitaphs."

In section 135 of the Doctrine and Covenants, the Prophet's contemporaries made this appraisal of his life after his
death. And I quote—

"Joseph Smith, the Prophet and Seer of the Lord, has
done more, save Jesus only, for the salvation of men in this
world, than any other man who ever lived in it.

"In the short space of twenty years, he has brought forth
the Book of Mormon, which he translated by the gift and
power of God, and has been the means of publishing it on
two continents; has sent the fulness of the everlasting gospel,
which it contained, to the four quarters of the earth; has
brought forth the revelations and commandments which com-
pose this book of Doctrine and Covenants, and many other
wise documents and instructions for the benefit of the children of men; gathered many thousands of the Latter-day
Saints, founded a great city, (Nauvoo) and left a fame and
name that cannot be slain.

"He lived great, and he died great in the eyes of God
and his people; and like most of the Lord's anointed in ancient times, has sealed his mission and his works with his own
blood; . . ." (D & C 135:3)

Fourth. The fourth question is, "What did he leave to
posterity? Moses left us a great heritage including the Ten
Commandments." Isaiah, Ezekiel, Jeremiah and the other
Old Testament prophets left the Old Testament chapters that

bear their names. Matthew, Mark, Luke, Peter, James, John, Paul, and others left a series of wonderful letters and other writings that have been of great service and inspiration to the world.

But Joseph Smith has given to the world three great *volumes* of new scripture outlining in every detail the simple principles of the gospel. He has restored to the world the sure knowledge of a personal God. The Christian world says we believe in God. Joseph Smith says in substance, "I know there is a God, for I have seen him." Joseph Smith has written down that everyone may read an account of this greatest vision of which the world has a record.

He received several visits from Moroni, the American prophet of pre-Columbus times who delivered the Book of Mormon to us.

Through Joseph Smith, the Aaronic and Melchizedek Priesthoods have been restored to earth by John the Baptist and Peter, James and John who held the keys of these priesthoods in their own dispensations. Joseph Smith reestablished under direct command from God the ancient custom of building temples where special ordinances can be performed that are not acceptable to God in any other place.

On March 27, 1836 the first temple of this dispensation was dedicated at Kirtland, Ohio. A few days later on April 3, 1836, Joseph Smith and Oliver Cowdery retired to the temple pulpit around which veils were dropped, and after silent and solemn prayer they received the following vision and personal manifestation of the Lord. The Prophet said:

"The veil was taken from our minds, and the eyes of our understanding were opened. We saw the Lord standing upon the breastwork of the pulpit, before us; and under his feet was a paved work of pure gold, in color like amber. His eyes were as a flame of fire; the hair of his head was white like the pure snow; his countenance shone above the brightness of the sun; and his voice was as of the sound of the rushing of great waters, . . . "   (D & C 110:1-3)

"After this vision closed, the heavens were again opened unto us; and Moses appeared before us, and committed unto us the keys of the gathering of Israel from the four parts of the earth, and the leading of the ten tribes from the land of the north.

"After this, Elias appeared, and committed the dispensation of the gospel of Abraham, saying that in us and our seed all generations after us should be blessed.

"After this vision had closed, another great and glorious vision burst upon us; for Elijah the prophet, who was taken to heaven without tasting death, stood before us, and said:

"Behold, the time has fully come, which was spoken of by the mouth of Malachi—testifying that he (Elijah) should be sent, before the great and dreadful day of the Lord come—

"To turn the hearts of the fathers to the children, and the children to the fathers, lest the whole earth be smitten with a curse—

"Therefore, the keys of this dispensation are committed into your hands; and by this ye may know that the great and dreadful day of the Lord is near, even at the doors." (D & C 110:11-16)

Joseph Smith died a martyr at age 38 "and greater love hath no man than this, that he lay down his life for his friends."

The fact that many people do not believe this message is only following the pattern of the past which applies even to the days of Jesus himself. Not only is it so, that many do not believe, many will not even listen, and yet thousands of members of the Church bear testimony that this message is true. And all men are invited to investigate and gain a witness for themselves.

A Journey through Hell

IN THE EARLY part of the fourteenth century, the Italian poet, Dante, wrote his great literary masterpiece entitled *The Divine Comedy*. In those days a comedy was not something that was funny. A comedy was something with a happy ending. A more understandable title for our day would have been "The Divine Experience" or "The Divine Story." Thomas Carlyle said that in his opinion *The Divine Comedy* was the most remarkable of all books. It was based on the scriptures, to which Dante added generously out of his own imagination.

The book is divided into three parts. Part one is "The Inferno." It tells of an imaginary trip which Dante made through hell. In Dante's story hell was the place where departed spirits were consigned who were forever lost. These were the ones whose lives were so warped, twisted, and perverted, that there was no hope. Then Dante traveled through a second kingdom which he called "Purgatory." This was a place of purification where certain spirits who had not sinned unto death were cleansed through suffering, then educated, and made worthy to ascend unto heaven. The Bible refers us to this place as the place where Jesus went and preached to the spirits in prison who had been disobedient in the days of Noah some twenty-five centuries earlier. (I Peter 3:19-20)

Then the happy ending came when Dante concluded his journey in what he refers to as "Paradise" which was that place where the righteous lived forever with God. Dante believed that it was his mission in life to show men hell, and that seems to me to be a necessary and a very important

mission. However, it is a pretty *difficult* assignment because
generally we don't like to think about things that are unpleasant, even to avoid them. Think how reluctant we are
to think or talk about death or the consequences of sin, and
so we bury our heads in the sand so to speak, to hide from
those truths that we do not like. But unpleasant things do
not cease to exist just because they are ignored. And a far
better way to avoid an unpleasant prospective situation is to
do a lot of the right kind of thinking about it in advance.

One of our biggest problems so far as our eternal exaltation is concerned is that we are such *incurable* optimists.
We usually have an overwhelming, unshakeable belief in our
own "happy ending," regardless of what we do leading up
to it. But Jesus talked about many unpleasant things such as
repentance, and the possibility that even some of the elect
may be lost. He *probably* talked as much about hell as he
did about heaven. He said, ". . . wide is the gate, and broad is
the way, that leadeth to destruction, and many there be that
go in thereat." (Matt. 7:13) Yet comparatively very *few*
people ever think of themselves as being in that particular
group.

Shakespeare was probably trying to get us to think a
little more realistically about our own situation as over one-
half of all of his plays were tragedies. Shakespeare understood what is very important for us to understand, that unless we do something specific about it, every life does *not*
have a happy ending.

We are reminded of our natural optimism when we say
that in our business affairs we work under "the profit system."
That is just not true. We work under the profit and *loss* system, and that is the *same* system that regulates our eternal
welfare.

With the thought in mind of helping ourselves to avoid
this useless loss, suppose that *we* take a mental journey simi-

lar to the one that Dante took. And a good place to begin is where Dante began—in hell.

It was reported that a certain minister once announced that his next Sunday's sermon would be about hell. A newspaper man went to hear him and then commented that the minister was certainly full of his subject. But it is thought to be a very good idea at least to get enough of the ideas about hell into our *minds* that we may avoid actually going there in person. Hell must be a very exciting place, but there are a great many advantages to first making this trip in the imagination. One advantage is that it is a little easier to get out if we don't want to stay. Another advantage is that we may not want to go there in the first place.

I would like to point out in passing that hell is a divine institution. It was not established by Satan as some of our present-day institutions seem to have been. Hell was established by God for a very important purpose. You remember that in the council of heaven Lucifer rebelled and drew away one-third of all of the hosts of heaven after him. The Lord said, "And they were thrust down and thus came the devil and his angels: And, behold, there is a place prepared for them from the beginning, which place is hell." (D & C 29:37-38) There are some people who don't believe in hell. Many others have just never thought about it either one way or the other.

Of course, we have the direct word of God on *many* occasions that there is a hell. Reason also tells us that there must be a hell. We know that the basic law of the universe is this unchangeable, irrevocable law of the harvest that says "Whatsoever a man soweth, that must he also reap." If everyone is going to be judged according to his works, then if there is a heaven there must be a hell. In the great enterprise of human salvation there must be different places for instruction and reformation, rewards and punishments. Unfortunately Satan and his angels are not going to occupy hell alone. In discussing the outcome of the judgment the Lord said, "And the righteous shall be gathered on my right hand unto eternal life; and the wicked on my left hand will I be ashamed to own before the Father. Wherefore, I will say unto them—Depart from me, ye cursed, into everlasting fire, prepared for the devil and his angels." (D & C 29:27-28)

In spite of its unpleasantness hell was established for a good purpose, just as penitentiaries are established for a good purpose, and mental hospitals are established for a good purpose, and reform schools and the organizations of Alcoholic Anonymous are established for a good purpose. There is a certain purification that sometimes can best be brought about only through suffering. The members of some religious organizations do what they call "whipping the flesh." They deliberately torture themselves, to help themselves understand the meaning of pain. They believe that a little suffering now may help them to avoid a lot of suffering later on.

But one of the most important success factors in life is to settle definitely our minds about the existence of hell. Dr. William E. Orchard, a noted religious leader, was once asked whether or not he thought the concept of hell might now be safely abandoned in this day of education and enlightenment. With a strange quietness in his manner Dr. Orchard replied, "I would not bank on it if I were you."

A student once asked his Sunday School teacher, "Is there a hell?" The teacher replied, "There is a hell all right, but we won't go into that now." But Dante thought it was important that we should go in occasionally.

The Prophet Joseph Smith once said, "If you could gaze into heaven for five minutes, you would learn more than by reading all of the books that have ever been written on the subject." But we might also learn a great deal by gazing into hell for five minutes. That is, human nature is often more effectively motivated by the prospect of pain or loss, than by a comparable promise of reward. But if we go about it right, we can get good from both the promise of rewards, and a foreknowledge of punishments. Of course, no one is ever sent to hell by compulsion. Everyone who goes there goes there voluntarily by his own choices. And everyone who goes to hell goes there only because he just hasn't made definite plans *not* to go there. No one needs to go to hell who definitely makes up his mind to go some other place. And if the "picturing power" of our minds is sufficiently effective, we will be able to make some firm decisions about where we want to go, if as Dante did we visit all three places in advance. Suppose then that we first go in imagination and stand before the great gate of Dante's hell and consider its challenging inscription which reads as follows:

Through me you pass into a world of woe
Through me you enter into eternal pain;
Through me you join with souls forever lost,
All hope abandon ye who enter here.

Suppose that we become familiar with the real hell by reading the inspired words of the great scriptures and think about the importance of such messages as those contained in the 40th chapter of Alma, the 76th section of the Doctrine and Covenants, the sixteenth chapter of Luke, and many others.

It is thought that a thorough understanding of these passages pertaining to hell would forever free us from our difficult problems in obtaining eternal life. That is, it would not be very difficult to forsake our sins and get rid of our weaknesses if occasionally we could clearly see in advance the tragic consequences of our evil.

In trying to show us these kingdoms of hell and purgatory Dante pictures a series of circles or elevations. The top levels are inhabited by the spirits who have sinned least. And then as we descend from one layer to another into the depths of hell, the corruption and consequent suffering increases. Dante tries to picture the worst conceivable suffering of which his mind was capable. But the human imagination even at best is very limited in its power, and is not capable of giving more than a faint suggestion of the real experience. For example, note the difference between a toothache in your imagination and one in your tooth. For the same reason it is probable that no matter how vivid a description of hell might be, it must of necessity fall far short in its ability to convey to our minds the full impression of those who will actually suffer there. But to see it as clearly as possible in our minds can be a wonderfully helpful experience.

Suppose that we could go as Jesus did and talk with these spirits who had been confined to their prison house for many centuries. Just suppose that we could feel their regret and understand their suffering. Or suppose that we could learn first hand from them what brought them to this unhappy place. We would probably recognize a great many of our own personal sins. It has been pointed out that there are no new sins, there are only new sinners. As as example, one of hell's prisoners said to Dante, "Not what I did but what I failed to do lost me the right to live with God on high." And then from the point of view of his own hindsight he said, "This desire for God and goodness I knew too late."

One of hell's groups said, "Our lukewarm eagerness for doing good brought us to this place of misery." Another said, "We could not endure the toil unto the end and thereby forever lost the glory of our lives."

As Dante went into the lower regions he visited with some of those unfortunates who had sinned unto death. These had lived such lives that they could never be redeemed. For them there was no forgiveness. We do not know how intense either mental or physical suffering can be. We know that it can be severe enough to send one insane. And Dante pictures some of hell's inmates as afflicted with madness because some incurable grief had unhinged their minds.

One of hell's spirits said to Dante, "We beg that if ever

you escape from these dark places to look again upon the stars of heaven, see that ye speak of us to other men." And then attempting to discharge that obligation in our interests, Dante said, "Reader, as God may grant you reason, gather wisdom from reading this and then take council with yourself." We should also take council with God and his word, which tells us that there are at least two ways to cleanse ourselves from sin. One is by suffering. A great line in latter-day scripture says, "For behold, I, God, have suffered these things for all, that they might not suffer if they would repent; But if they would not repent they must suffer even as I; Which suffering caused myself, even God, the greatest of all, to tremble because of pain, and to bleed at every pore, and to suffer both body and spirit—and would that I might not drink of the bitter cup, and shrink—" (D & C 19:16-18)

The other way is repentance, as indicated by Walter Malone's poem entitled "Opportunity." He said:

Art thou an idler, then rouse thee from thy spell
Art thou a sinner, sin may be forgiven.

Each morning gives thee wings to flee from hell.
Each night a star to guide thy soul to heaven.

God has promised us that we may have any blessing that we are willing to live and we must pay the awful penalty of every sin. This helpful experience, of an occasional mental journey beyond the borders of mortality may help us to avoid the suffering of hell and find a happy ending in the celestial kingdom of God.

Kobojolism

IT IS VERY interesting what ideas and feelings occupy our minds when some particular word is brought into the focus of our attention. There are some great words like faith, courage, freedom, love and honor that can fill us with pleasant emotions and vitalize our ambitions. There are other words that bring with them a different kind of influence and feeling.

There is one word that has a rather dishonorable reputation that we call plagiarism. It is used to describe one who is guilty of a kind of literary or artistic theft. To plagiarize someone is to steal his ideas, expressions or artistic productions, and take the credit for ourselves. A plagiarist is a kind of counterfeiter. He tries to pass off the mental creations of others as his own. He is a kidnapper of ideas, and kidnapping is always a very serious offense. But in addition, these words themselves sometimes bring unpleasant emotions to our minds.

But it is the exact opposite of plagiarism that I would like to say something about. This also indicates a serious offense, but what is a little unusual about it is that so far as I can find, there is no word in the dictionary to describe it. That is, suppose that you try to think of a word that means the opposite of plagiarism. If plagiarism is where you put your name on the ideas and work of someone else, what would the word be to describe putting someone else's name on your ideas and work?

Many years ago Elbert Hubbard coined a word to fill this blank space in our language which he called "kobojolism." This word seems to me to fill an important need though it has never yet found its way into the dictionary. But even so there is probably far more kobojolism in the world than there is plagiarism. Kobojolism, like most other acts, comes in varying degrees of good and bad. For example, Mr. Hubbard points out that Plato was a kobojolist. Plato had been a student and was a great admirer of Socrates. The fame of Socrates went on increasing after his death and Plato capitalized on the reputation of Socrates to build up a large following for his own philosophy by putting Socrates' name on his ideas. Plato would say, "The great teacher said thus and so." Or, "This is what Socrates thought." By giving Socrates the credit for his own thoughts Plato gained prestige for himself and greater influence for his ideas. Because of the great name Socrates' ideas so labelled had immediate acceptance with a large number of people.

Benjamin Franklin was also a kobojolist. Franklin was a printer with many good ideas. But to avoid offending his readers with a continual display of his own wisdom, he created a fictitious character specifically for the purpose of kobojolization. The name of his non-existent helper was Richard Saunders. For many years Franklin published what he called "Poor Richard's Almanac." Franklin could praise Richard Saunders to the skies. He built up for Richard Saunders the reputation of being a poor but very wise and likeable person. Then Franklin merchandized his own literary effort by labeling it with the name of Richard Saunders. By this process he got the benefit of an effective third party influence and at the same time did away with the danger of any possible accusations of egotism against himself. It also made any need for restraint unnecessary and over and over again Franklin introduced his choicest literary gems by saying, "Poor Richard says—."

Nietzsche, the great German philosopher, did about the same thing with another specially made personal dispenser for his wisdom by the name of Zarathustra who was created by Nietzsche only for Nietzsche to quote.

Many people aim at the same end achieved by Plato, Franklin and Nietzsche by merely saying, "Someone said thus and so," without bothering to give any specific credit. But by this process they are able to push their wares to their heart's content, as it is easier to promote one's own ideas by kobojolizing someone else. This particular deception might be labeled as petty kobojolism. But there is also a kobojolism in the second degree. That is when someone passes off inferior mental merchandise for which he himself is unwilling to stand as sponsor. For example, someone may tell a profane or an immoral story, or he passes on some harmful scandal. He tries to get rid of any stigma that may attach to himself by saying, "Let me tell you one of John Doe's stories." By this device we attempt to take any satisfaction or credit to ourselves, while we debit the bad to the account of someone else. Then beyond all of these is what might be called grand kobojolism where we boldly write someone else's name on our sins and crimes.

We are all aware of our natural human tendency to shift blame away from ourselves. One man explained his lack of success in his business by saying, "My Father wasn't a pusher. Some of my friends had fathers who were pushers, but my father was too easy going, therefore, I haven't done very well." He held himself to be perfectly innocent of any blame while debiting his father with his lack of success. In other words, he kobojolized his father.

The story is told of a little girl who was a kobojolist. She once hit her brother over the head with her doll. When her brother's head broke the doll, she began to cry and said, "Now, look what you've done."

Mr. Khrushchev is a grand kobojolist in the worst sense of the term. In his self-righteous tirade at the Paris Conference he called God as his witness to prove that his heart was pure and his hands were clean. He gave everyone else credit for breaking up the Summit conference, for keeping the cold war going and for enslaving helpless peoples. He put the names of others on sins that were cut out for him and by him. He always gives someone else the credit for his own vile and premeditated evil.

All criminals are kobojolists. There is an old saying to the effect that "there is not one guilty man in prison." If you accepted the testimony of criminals, you would be forced to conclude that most inmates of the penitentiary are there because of circumstance, or the malice of the judge, or the dishonesty of the lawyer, or the injustice of the law. But as all criminals are kobojolists, so all failures are kobojolists and all sinners are kobojolists. Do you remember the reasons for the fall of man as given by Adam and Eve? When the Lord asked Adam why he had eaten of the forbidden fruit, he said, "The woman whom thou gavest to be with me, she gave me of the tree, and I did eat." Eve said, "The serpent beguiled me, and I did eat." (Gen. 3:12-13)

Most people would be horrified to be accused of plagiarizing someone else, and yet we kobojolize to our heart's content without even a word to describe what we are doing. In plagiarizing someone we are really paying him a compliment. But in kobojolizing we both discredit him and deceive ourselves.

I suppose that more than anyone else we kobojolize Satan. Mother Eve said, "The serpent beguiled me." That is still our most common excuse for ourselves. God never forces us to do right, and Satan has no power to force us to do wrong. Yet instead of squaring our shoulder and taking the blame we insist on putting Satan's name on our misdeeds and say, "The serpent beguiled me." I suppose that it will be just as difficult to find a guilty man in hell as to find a guilty man in the penitentiary.

Henry Ward Beecher was trying to get us to put the blame on the right account when he said, "We ought not to say how much the devil tempts but how strongly we are inclined."

Aristotle gave a very helpful philosophy that we should adopt for ourselves when he said to Alexander that the greatest enemy that ever confronts an army is never in the ranks of the foe, but always in your own camp. That is, who is the greatest enemy of America? Someone might say Russia or China, but that is ridiculous. Who sold our atomic secrets to the Russians? Who causes our strikes, wastes our natural resources, commits our crimes, gets us drunk and induces us to be dishonest and immoral? Or who is it that keeps me poor and ignorant and unsuccessful? It is always the enemy in my own camp. We talk about a wolf in sheep's clothing. We blame our parents for our failures, our teachers for our ignorance, and Satan for our sins, and yet when we catch the enemy and take off his disguise, whom do we find but ourselves? We plagiarize the virtues of others and kobojolize our own faults. We put our names on virtues that we don't possess and put the devil's name on the faults that we do.

An ancient Chinese prince worked out an interesting kobojolizing technique. He not only put the blame on someone else, but he also meted out the punishment that went with it. The prince always kept a whipping boy handy, and whenever anything went wrong in his affairs, instead of accepting the blame he would relieve himself by whaling the daylights out of his whipping boy. But this is only one physical manifestation of what most of us do to our mental and spiritual whipping boys.

It has been said that if you can't afford a whipping boy, don't be discouraged—your wife and children can make splendid substitutes. When you have a bad day at work, or if things don't go right in your personal affairs, or if you are just plain not making the grade, don't let it upset you, just take it out on the wife and kids when you get home.

The ancient Hebrews had a little different way of handling this problem of placing blame. Instead of a whipping boy they used what they called a scapegoat. They had a regular religious ritual by which they transferred their sins onto the head of a goat. Then they would chase the goat out into the wilderness, sending their sins along. (Lev. 16:21-22) If the scapegoat died, their sins died with him.

You have heard about some innocent person being made "the goat" for the misdeeds of someone else. Apparently this is where the custom came from. In our day we still maintain the custom except we don't bother to use the goat any more. Now we use our families or the church or the company we work for. A large national magazine recently made a survey which indicated that 75% of all the people in the United States hate their jobs. We pick the work we like the best, and then we turn our hate upon it. The reason is that most people use their jobs as a scapegoat. That is usually the most convenient place to pile our poison and frustration.

In getting married we select the one and only person in the world, and then turn her into a whipping boy, saying as Adam did, "The woman did it."

The opposite political party also serves us as a whipping boy or a scapegoat. The Republicans whip the Democrats, and the Democrats pile their sins on the heads of the Republicans. The country itself does not escape our kobojolism. We try to evade our taxes, shirk our duty and break the laws made for our protection. Then we say, "America is not what it used to be."

Our capital kobojolistic sin is committed against God. Something happens in our lives that is not to our liking and we frequently become bitter about life itself. We start a cold war against God even though he is trying to help us. We say life is unfair, that God doesn't like us. The world has almost always followed the pattern of killing the prophets. We close our minds to the holy scriptures, and pile our sins on the church. The more we kobojolize someone, the more we dislike him. It is hard to forgive a man to whom you have done an injury. He may forgive you, but you can't easily forgive him. Upon the cross Jesus forgave his crucifiers, but they never forgave him. They had put his name on too many things that he was not guilty of. Profanity is a kind of kobojolism. When something goes wrong for some people, with a curse and an oath they put the name of Deity upon it.

Isn't it strange that the people who serve God most earnestly love him best, while the people who commit the greatest sins against God like him the least? Jesus took upon himself our sins. In a way he serves as our scapegoat. Yet we pile our sins upon him. We should be very careful that we don't punish the wrong man too much.

One of the greatest virtues that we could ever develop is that of placing the blame for our personal sins exactly where they belong. Charles Dickens once said, "Everyone ought to think well of his own business." Certainly everyone ought to think well of his own family, and his own God, and one of the best ways to bring this feeling about us is to refrain from the sins of kobojolism.

If we desire to love God, we should keep his commandments. The more we serve him, the greater our love becomes. I pray that God will help us to properly take this name upon ourselves and be worthy of it that it will not be necessary for us to put our sins upon others. Then we will also be able to think well of ourselves.

Licked by the Fog

IN 1950 Florence Chadwick, the great American woman swimming champion swam the English Channel. Then on July 4, 1952 she undertook to swim the 21 miles of water lying between Catalina Island and the Southern California coast. The water was very cold, and a heavy fog lay over the sea.

When Miss Chadwick was just about a half mile from her destination she became discouraged and told her father in the boat nearby that she wanted to be taken out of the water. Her father knew that she had swum greater distances on previous occasions, and he tried to encourage her to go on. He pointed up through the fog and said in substance, "Florence, it can't be much farther, why don't you just swim a little longer? I am sure that you can reach the shore, and there will be victory and satisfaction and success. But she couldn't see the shore because of the fog, and it is sometimes pretty difficult to believe in something that you can't see; and she did not have enough of that faith that Paul describes as the substance of things hoped for and the evidence of things not seen, and so she went through with her determination to quit and was taken out of the water.

The next day she was interviewed by some newspaper men who wanted to know the reason for her failure. They also knew that she had previously swum greater distances, and if there was some special reason for her present failure they wanted to know what it was. And so in answer to their questions Miss Chadwick said, "No, it wasn't the cold water, and it wasn't the distance," she said, "I was licked by the fog." She then told the newspaper men that when she had been swimming the English Channel she had had a similar experience. As she neared her objective her fatigue and discouragement had made the success she sought now seem much less important than when she began. On that occasion also she had wanted to quit when on the very brink of accomplishment. But again her father had pointed up toward the shore, and this time there wasn't any fog, and she had raised herself out of the water just long enough to re-fix in her mind the image of her objective. This gave her a great new surge of strength, and she never stopped again until she felt under her feet the solid earth of the other shore.

Among the most common causes for failure in our religious activities or in life generally is that we, also, allow ourselves to be licked by the fog. We are continually being enveloped in the fog of weariness, the fog of discouragement, the fog of misunderstanding, the fog of fear, and the fog of sin. Jesus talked of people who for these and other reasons, even though they had eyes yet they could not see. That still remains one of our biggest problems. We don't see things clearly enough, and we don't see them soon enough, and we don't see far enough. Poor visibility is more than ordinarily treacherous because it conceals our objectives or produces a distortion that makes them seem of small consequence. It is so easy to start things, but it is more difficult to finish because the weariness and discouragement increases as we get closer to the shore. But we should remember that the darkest hour comes just before the dawn. It is when the sea reaches its lowest ebb that we can look for a change in the tide. That is the time we should get our second wind and make sure that the fog does not blight our ambition nor destroy our success when we are on the very shore of accomplishment.

So frequently we allow ourselves to be licked by the fog of ignorance. Upon the cross, Jesus said, "Father, forgive them, for they know not what they do." Unfortunate men crucified Jesus without really understanding what they were doing. Pilate did not know that Jesus was the Savior of the world, but why didn't he know? There is only one possible answer and that is that he had not invested the time nor made the investigation necessary to find the truth. Pilate could have found out who Jesus was just as any of us can find out who Jesus is if we work at it hard enough over a long enough period. In our investigations many of us follow the technique used by Pilate when he said to Jesus, "What is truth?" And then without waiting for a reply he turned and walked out of the room. Because of this procedure the fog of ignorance sometimes makes us its permanent victims, for only he who fails to seek fails to find. But almost all of the sins in the world are the sins of ignorance. When young people absent themselves from their church meetings, they don't really understand what they are doing, or when one thinks wrong thoughts, or breaks the Word of Wisdom, or engages in dishonest or immoral practices, he doesn't understand that these things are changing his entire life and preparing to rob him of his rightful success and happiness. Everyone should be very particular that he prepares himself to handle the fog of ignorance.

After the resurrection, Jesus appeared upon the Western Hemisphere where a great upheaval of nature, including tempests and earthquakes, had been the signs of his crucifixion. A terrible destruction was followed by three days of total darkness.

Later on a great multitude was gathered around the temple in the land of Bountiful discussing their changed conditions, when a voice was heard, "as if it came out of heaven; and they cast their eyes round about, for they understood not the voice which they heard; and it was not a harsh voice, neither was it a loud voice; . . . notwithstanding it being a small voice it did pierce them to the center . . . and did cause their hearts to burn. And it came to pass that again they heard the voice, and they understood it not. And again

the third time they did hear the voice, and did open their
ears to hear it; and their eyes were towards the sound thereof; and they did look steadfastly towards heaven, from
whence the sound came. And behold, the third time they
did understand the voice which they heard; . . ." (III Nephi
11:3-6)

It was the voice of the Father, introducing his Beloved
Son who appeared above them, clothed in a white robe. He
descended and stood in their midst. After he had introduced
himself he showed them the nail holes in his hands and the
wound in his side. Then he tried to teach them the gospel
but they were not prepared to learn, and he said to them, "I
perceive that ye are weak, that ye cannot understand all my
words which I am commanded of the Father to speak unto
you at this time. Therefore, go ye unto your homes, and
ponder upon the things which I have said, and ask of the
Father, in my name, that ye may understand, and prepare
your minds for the morrow, and I come unto you again." (III
Nephi 17:2-3) This idea of mind preparation will help clear
away the destructive fog of ignorance.

Sometimes we are licked by allowing a foggy murkiness
to get into our attitudes. Walter Dill Scott once said that
mental attitude was more important than mental capacity.
As an example, we might ask ourselves why it was that the
accomplishment of Nephi so far outdistanced that of his older
brothers, Laman and Lemuel. Certainly the difference was
not in their heredity, and we should keep in mind that Laman
and Lemuel were also "born of goodly parents." The difference was not in their environment, nor their education, nor
their opportunity, nor their physical power, nor their mental
ability. The difference was in their attitudes. It was in how
they looked at things. Laman and Lemuel went around in
a kind of spiritual fog. They didn't see things in their true
light. They thought their father was a dreamer. They were
afraid. They didn't believe in the scriptures. They had eyes

but couldn't see. The fog also got into their ears and their understandings. These same problems of low, spiritual visibility still bothers many of us. Through most of our problems are really blessings in disguise, sent to strengthen us, yet frequently because we don't see it clearly we turn away, reject the problem and lose our blessing.

One fog that is very destructive to our best interests is the confusion that takes us over when we fail to integrate our deeds and our creeds. When we believe one thing and practice something else we get a kind of split personality which is at the root of innumerable wrongs in our lives and in society generally. Most of us have so much more faith than we have works. Most of us *believe* so much more than we practice.

Most people firmly believe in success at the very moment that their deeds are bringing failure upon them. A great group of people believe in the celestial kingdom who are no closer to being on schedule now than they were five years ago. Many people believe in morality who are not moral. This produces a conflict which sets us against ourselves causing confusion and frustration. It not only blinds our eyes but also drowns out the still small voice of the spirit. Our problem arises because we practice too much segregation, we keep our creeds in one compartment where they cannot adequately influence our deeds, therefore thwarting the purpose of our lives which is not knowledge but action. Brigham Young once pointed out that any one can preach, but it takes a good man to practice. Sir James M. Barrie made the wise observation that, "The life of every man is a diary in which he means to write one story but actually writes another. And his humblest hour comes when he compares the volume as it is, with what he had hoped to make it." Someone has said that we get into much of our trouble because the present generation does not read the minutes of the past generation.

To clear away much of our fog and confusion we have

only to integrate deed and creed properly, then make some once and for all decisions. For example, do we believe that drunkenness and alcoholism are good? Have we definitely settled that question in our own minds? Have we decided about honesty, spirituality, and what our personal relationship with God ought to be? Do we understand the real destructiveness of sin in our lives? It is not just the *big* sins that do us harm, sin is sin whether taken in large or small doses. We usually have little difficulty in deciding what is good and what is bad for someone else, but the fog seems to thicken when we center the attention upon ourselves.

A wonderful suggestion for our success was made some years ago by the great Illinois football player Red Grange. At a dinner in his honor where he was designated the greatest athlete of all time, he was asked to tell the source of his success. He said, "I can give it to you in five words—I practice like I play." What a tremendous idea! Because we will also play as we practice. Every thought, every act, and every emotion goes into the general fund determining our success. Whether we are on the practice field or playing for the championship makes little difference. If one *does* less than his best during practice, he will *be* less than his best during the game. What we accomplish in the church or in life generally is in the long run determined by how we have practiced. The following poem making some suggestions on integration is closely related to and shows the negative side of the philosophy of Red Grange. It is entitled:

I KNELT TO PRAY

I knelt to pray as day began
And prayed, "O God, bless every man!
Lift from each weary heart some pain
And let the sick be well again."

And then I rose to meet the day
And thoughtlessly went on my way;
I didn't try to dry a tear
Or take the time a grief to hear.

I took no steps to ease the load
Of hard-pressed travelers on the road.
I didn't even go to see
The sick friend who lived next door to me.

But then again when day was done
I prayed, "O God, bless everyone."
But as I prayed, a voice rang clear
Instructing me to think and hear.

Consult your own heart e're you pray
What good have you performed today
God's choicest blessings are bestowed
On those who help Him bear the load.

And then I hid my face and cried,
"Forgive me, Lord, for I have lied.
Let me but live another day,
And I will live it as I pray."

How a well-integrated program of praying and living can clear away the fog and help us to see more clearly the real objectives of our lives. Some of us are getting pretty close to the eternal shore, and we need to stamp the idea into our minds a little deeper that eternal glory may be just ahead. We should frequently refix in our minds the image of our eternal objectives and then allow nothing to distort our perspective, or stifle the voice of the spirit. We can clear away many of the fogs of ignorance, sin, wrong thinking, indifference, or indecision by our own thoughtfulness and effort.

But if sometimes we might feel the weariness and discouragement to which our human flesh is heir, then let our faith point our minds up through the fog to remind us that the celestial kingdom may be only a half a mile away.

May God help us to prepare our minds to see and our hearts to understand that the fogs may be cleared away and that the wonderful objective that he has provided for us may stand out large and clear in our faces.

Lives

ONE OF the most influential books of the world goes under the title of *Plutarch's Lives.* Plutarch was a great Greek moralist and biographer who lived for seventy-five years beginning in 45 A.D. He studied in Athens, visited Egypt, and spent some time in ancient Rome. He made his greatest contribution to the world by writing the biographies of famous Greeks and Romans. He said, "My method is to study their history, and by the familiarity thus acquired, to habituate my memory to receive and retain images of all that is best and worthiest in their characters." He said, "To write their lives is like actually living and associating with them." We may receive them into our minds as our guests. We may entertain and be entertained by each in turn. And as we view their statures and judge their good qualities, we may select that which is most noble from each.

Plutarch said that he first commenced writing biographies for the good of others, but he continued to write them for his own sake. He said, "The virtues of a great man serve as a sort of looking glass in which I may see how to adjust and adorn my own life. I am thus able to free myself from any ignoble, base, or vicious traits. And what greater pleasure can one have?" And we might echo his exclamation and ask, what indeed? There is nothing so important as life, and Plutarch devoted himself to the study of that mysterious human element out of which all of our lives are fashioned.

Of course, the very heart of success centers in the individual himself, and it is of primary importance to us that we know as much as possible about the basic elements from which our lives are made up. Plutarch had some ideas and procedures to which we might very profitably give the most serious consideration.

There is in modern medicine a very interesting practice known as vivisection. This is the act of cutting into the tissues of a living animal in order to study the workings of its vital organs. Vivisection is not for the purpose of killing the animal, it merely provides the education by which the doctor hopes to keep others alive. From the practice of vivisection the investigator is able to learn how life works, and where it may go wrong, or how it may be improved.

Plutarch was a kind of vivisectionist. He cut into the experiences, attitudes, and personality traits of men to find out what makes them great and good, wise and successful. And as a good doctor can learn medicine by comparing diseased and healthy bodies, so we can promote our success in life by a kind of laboratory comparison of the similarities and differences in human lives.

In a long series of studies Plutarch compared the lives of noble Greeks and Romans. He wrote up his findings in some interesting biographies that he called *Parallel Lives*. For example, he wrote up the life of Theseus who settled Athens, and then set him side by side with Romulus, the founder of Rome. He studied Lycurgus, Solon, Pericles, Cato, Pompey, Tiberius, Demosthenes, Cicero, Demetrius, Antony, and dozens of other great Greeks and Romans. Then he compared them with each other. He appraised their virtues, weighed their faults, and, fully labeled, he placed them all on public display. He did some interesting personality vivisections that others might also learn "how to adjust and adorn their own lives." Sometimes seeing a wrong in the life of someone else teaches us how to prevent it from occurring in us.

On the other hand, the greatest influence in the world is the power of a good example. We need better working

models for our lives to go by.   Byron hurried across Europe
searching for an ideal to adore.   When we see man at his
noblest, we are able to appropriate the very essence of his
courage and faith to produce a sublime effect in our lives.
As a usual thing, those who enshrine no ideals experience no
growth.   What a glorious gallery of stimulating pictures we
have in the biographies of great human beings.   Your library
can be a wonderful storehouse where hundreds of the great
of all time are looking down upon you awaiting your command.   We may lift up our eyes to the peaks of their accomplishment and get from them the ability to draw ourselves upward.   These great men have all undergone the test
of time.   We do not have to accept their acts without knowing
the consequences in advance.   It also helps us to understand
our own lives better when we see our human characteristics in
operation in others.   The fine distinctions in values that are
so difficult to make in ourselves are easily recognized when
we study them in other people.   Once the solution has been
worked out, we can more easily apply the principle to ourselves.

Biographies are the histories of individual lives, considered as a branch of literature.   The delights of which are
among the most pleasant and profitable of all human inter-
course.   No entertainment is as cheap as reading, nor is there
any pleasure as lasting.   Have you ever had the experience of
lingering in front of a house at night where the lights are lit
and the blinds undrawn? Each floor of the house shows us a
different section of human life and being, and we wonder who,
and what they are.   What are their names? their occupations?
their thoughts and abilities?   And then some enterprising
biographer searches out the answers to every question and
every ambition.   He lights up their lives as the electricity
lights up the houses in which they live.

Then we see them going about their daily affairs, toiling,
failing, succeeding, hating, and loving until they die. Our

own futures can be greatly enriched by the poetry, music, art, and history that show themselves in other lives. Through the stimulation that can come by the study of biography we can learn not only about the surface of life, but we can also study it in depth and breadth as well. We may get valuable knowledge and vicarious experiences from those who have soared the highest as well as from those who have dived furthest into life's depths. At the closest range we are able to scrutinize both failures and successes, both good and bad. We can learn as much from the villain as from the hero. One teaches us the quicksands to be shunned, the other holds up the goals to be attained.

Sometimes we can learn faster from the experiences of others than from our own. Because of troublesome blind spots where we ourselves are concerned, our progress may be extremely limited when we have no other model to go by but our own. Isn't it interesting that the thing that we know less about than anything else in the world is our own individual selves. We don't know very much about where we came from or what the purpose of our life is. We do not know very much about our eternal destiny. We did not even discover the circulation of our own blood until about 300 years ago. We are familiar with the prevailing winds and the currents of the ocean. We are not so familiar with those powerful influences moving in our own lives. Twenty-five hundred years ago Socrates said, "Know thyself." Confucius said, "To understand yourself is the key of wisdom." And we can usually understand ourselves best when we see ourselves reflected in others without the hindrance of our personal prejudice or the distorted vision of self-interest.

What wonders are available to us in books where the wisest men picked out of every land, look down from library shelves waiting patiently to answer our questions and enrich us with their wisdom. During their lifetimes these men were inaccessible, and impatient of interrogation. But the thoughts that they did not uncover to their bosom friends are here fully written out for us, the strangers of another age. It has been said that "Books are embalmed minds." In a good book we may have the very essence of a good man, where his virtues are spotlighted and his faults are forgotten. "Through the great literature we can feel the fascination of moving to and fro over the vast reaches of time, as imperially as the astronomer moves through space. Such flights are exhilerating, they involve us in no peril, they attach to us no responsibility. They begin and end by our own fireside at our own convenience." These hours should be greatly expanded in most of our lives. As we do this important research we become experts in the responses of the human heart, whether they are Greek or Hebrew, Babylonian or English. "Biography abounds in religion, pathos, sympathy, and loving kindness. It contains a portrait of man's innermost feelings. It shows the beauty and wisdom of God attempting to reappear in the lives of men." Here we have a gallery of spiritual ideas in which we may meet Socrates, Moses, Shakespeare, and Mahatma Gandhi. We may even meet Christ himself. We may go with them as on some sacred mountaintop of life to be transfigured as it were, and spend some wonderful hours dressed in the shining garments of the mind.

Because of the unique terms which exist between author and reader, we are able to associate with sinners no less than with saints, and receive a helpful contribution from each. We are all curious to learn how men subject to our passions, contradictions, and disabilities have succeeded or failed in this great experience called life. Having entered the realm inhabited by those who live to us through the magic of biography, we soon meet friends for whom we have sought in vain among our actual living associates. Access to these great leaders in the flesh would have been impossible, but through their biographies, the most humble among us may have an absolute freedom of selection from a limitless variety that no one could have enjoyed among the living.

We can research the life of Napoleon or Bismarck or Lincoln. We can relive the experience of Booker T. Washington in his biography entitled, *Up from Slavery*. Then we may transfer our mental residence to the palace of Queen Victoria and live again in *Leaves from a Journal*. We can know the pathos and paradox of human passion involved in the fearful agony of Faust's final doom, and share his despair as he waits for the midnight bell which is to be the signal of his eternal destruction.

In his *Hearts of Men*, H. Fielding said, "I would have you go and kneel beside the Mohammedan as he prays at the sunset hour and put your heart in tune with his and wait for the echo that will surely come. "Unenviable is he whose heart ne'er ran over with silent admiration for the great of old. Those dead but sceptered sovereigns who still rule our spirits from their urns. They pass to us across the sea of time, their most cherished ideals and ambitions, and no matter what the cares or torments of your day may have been, at evening you can enter this magic city, forget the present, and follow in imagination those careers that closed in time so long ago, yet still live on with undimmed lustre on the timeless domain of the imagination. And during all of this delightful exploration, you can be learning more and more about human nature, that mysterious, primal element in which you yourself have your being." We can learn what a precious privilege it is to live, to understand, to think, to feel, to be, to love, and to enjoy.

It has been amply demonstrated that everything we hear, everything we read, everything we feel, every sermon, and every ambition leaves an impression upon our lives so that we are never quite the same thereafter. In our own right, we can live only once, but through others we may live a thousand lives and become expert architects in building our own eternal existence. With Plutarch, we may borrow from others all that is noblest and most worthy. "He is a rich man who can avail himself of all men's faculties and draw benefits from the labors of men in distant countries and in times past." By this process we may become citizens of what has been called, the "celestial city of fine souls."

Think of the unlimited treasures available to us in the Holy Scriptures. Here we can live with the great prophets, memorize their philosophy, and even absorb the spirit made available to us through the words of God himself. There is a sacred song that says, "I walked today where Jesus walked." And wouldn't it be a thrilling experience to go and stand on the very spot of ground where Jesus stood, while we undertook to capture the spirit of his life. And while it may not be practical to walk today where Jesus walked, there is something much more important that we can do and, that is, we can think today what Jesus thought. We can fill our minds and actuate our lives with the very attitudes that made him the Master of men. We are all aware of the fact that Jesus died for us. We are not so conscious that he lived for us also, that he is our example, that by reliving his life we can transfer his thought and motivations for our own success.

"He who merely knows right principles is not equal to him who loves them." May we love the good and be effectively moved by the great powers placed in our hands by the magic of Biography.

Lord Is It I?

ONE OF THE last and most important of the mortal responsibilities of Jesus was to prepare the twelve for the burdens of the ministry that would soon rest upon them. As they were eating the Last Supper in the upper room, the disciples must have been startled to hear the Master say, ". . . one of you shall betray me." Matthew says, "And they were exceeding sorrowful and began every one of them to say unto him, Lord, is it I?" (Matt. 26:21-22)

Betrayal is a terrible thing, and one of the best ways to deal with it, or with any other fault, is to dig it out of the mind and heart and destroy it before it has been committed. By bringing this matter up before all members of the Twelve, the Lord might have been trying to get them to do a little real soul searching while he was still with them. The main problem centered in Judas, but the Master also had a lesson for the eleven; for after Judas had left the upper room and the others had finished their meal, sang a hymn, and gone out into the Mount of Olives, Jesus said to the Eleven, "All ye shall be offended because of me this night."

Peter himself who later became such a great power for good and willingly gave up his life for the Master, here gave evidence of his own need for self-examination. He said to Jesus, "Though *all* men shall be offended because of thee, yet I will never be offended." Then Jesus said to him directly, "This night before the cock crow thou shalt deny me thrice." Peter just couldn't believe that such a thing was possible. He said, "Though I should die with thee, yet will I not deny thee." And Matthew adds significantly, "Likewise also said all of the disciples." (Matt. 26:33-35)

When they came to Gethsemane Jesus said to them,

"Sit ye down here while I go and pray yonder." He took with him Peter, James, and John whom he especially asked to watch with him. Then he left them also and "went a little farther, and fell on his face, and prayed, . . ." It must have added much to his burden of sorrow to return and find his most trusted disciples asleep. It had been such a short time since they were all professing their loyalty and constancy, but they were unable to carry out the Master's simple request to watch with him for even an hour. Then he made a statement which we ourselves frequently have occasion to think about. He said, "The spirit indeed is willing, but the flesh is weak." (Matt. 26:39, 40)

We should prepare ourselves to combat this common tendency toward weakness as it so often manifests itself in so many of us. One minute we are so positive that we can handle any situation, and the next we may be falling down on our own most cherished expectations. Peter seemed so sure of himself at the supper, but before the crowing of the cock, even he, Peter the Rock, the stalwart, the chief disciple, had done exactly the thing that he had so stoutly declared he would never do. Without any intention of doing so, he had denied the Master. We do not know all that happened that night, but Jesus had foretold that all of the Eleven would be "offended" because of him, quoting the prophecy that when the shepherd was smitten, the sheep would be scattered.

These interesting reactions in the most faithful disciples of Jesus point out some of our own possible dangers. For we also carry around with us the seeds of many sins. We may *strengthen* our determination and ability to do good by exploring our own hearts occasionally with the disciples' searching question, "Lord, is it I?" For only by keeping in mind our own possibilities to err are we able to destroy our mistakes before they are committed. Thomas Carlyle once pointed out "that the greatest of all faults is to be conscious of none." That also indicates where many of us are most likely to go astray. We can sometimes get off the track almost without knowing it. Most sins are at first so small that they may be unidentifiable.

Judas allowed the evil in his own soul so much latitude that it destroyed him. We should be aware of our own possibilities in that direction. Sin is still the basic problem in the world, and none of us are free from the scourge that it may bring into our lives. Even the chosen Eleven had some serious problems in doing their duty. To begin with none of them could stay awake to sustain the Master, even for that period when under the burden of their sins he was sweating great drops of blood at every pore.

This liability to err is sometimes very strong even in the best people. And it may overcome them if they are not constantly on guard. Paul said to the Corinthians, "Wherefore let him that thinketh he standeth take heed lest he fall." (I Cor. 10:12) Listen to the confession that the former great Saul of Tarsus wrote to Timothy. He said, "who was before a blasphemer, and a persecutor, and injurious: but I obtained mercy because I did it ignorantly in unbelief." (I Timothy 1:13) But even though Paul lived a good life after his miraculous conversion, yet he could never undo the damage he had already done. No matter how sincere his repentance, it was impossible to bring Stephen back to life or wipe out the other injuries that he himself had done to the cause. How bitter a thing it is to have to look back on one's own past and say to one's self, "A blasphemer and a persecutor and injurious, such was I." Or how bitter a thing it is to look on our own lives after they have become pitted and scarred with evil!

The difference between success and failure in our lives may frequently be found in this ability to search our own souls and repent before the wrong thought has gone too far. Certainly many of our sins, great and small, might be avoided if we were a little more expert in the art of advance self-examination. Then we could dig out and destroy any harmful inclination before it had borne its evil fruit. We might with profit regularly turn the disciples' question upon ourselves and then insist on some frank, unbiased answers. Periodically everyone should require convincing proof of his own integrity and the ability to make good on his own hopes and the promises that he has made to himself.

Sometimes like the disciples, we may be thinking one thing at the very moment we are actually about to do something else. Peter hadn't the slightest intention of doing what he did. But his vigorous declaration didn't hold up even for one night. So frequently we cannot foretell what we ourselves will do under given circumstances.

We allow the wrong to be committed first and then question ourselves afterward. We sometimes say, "Why did I ever do such a thing?" Even then, we frequently do not wait for a satisfactory reply. Peter felt so badly after his denials that he "went out and wept bitterly." Judas also felt *intense* remorse, but he did not check himself soon enough. Then when the priests refused his offer to undo his evil deed, he threw down the betrayal money and went out and hanged himself. What a pity he could not have felt this sorrow sooner. Regret and tears have value only when they don't come too late, yet how frequently we do our most constructive thinking only after the sin has been committed. We lock the barn door only after the horse has gone, so to speak. If we could adjust the timing of our regret and feel our sorrow a few hours earlier, we could head off most of our damaging mistakes.

We may think of Judas in terms of the awful title "son of perdition." But his tragic experience reminds us that many of our own mistakes are caused by the same kind of ineffectiveness in introspection; our timer is frequently off so far as our regret for sin is concerned. When we are unable to detect an oncoming evil in ourselves, we leave ourselves completely unguarded because we have no protecting forethought. If we customarily spent half as much energy on prevention as we lavish on remorse, the whole complexion of our lives could be changed for good. Precaution is far more profitable as an instrument of success than even the most severe remorse.

Just suppose that someone were to suggest the possibility that Judas-like we might betray the Lord or his work, we would probably become indignant. We would be likely to feel absolutely certain that we could handle ourselves in every situation. But by this very attitude of non-suspect we frequently become a nurturing host to the very sin that is gathering strength to destroy us.

We should remember that Judas is not the only one who has been guilty of betrayal. Our wrong personal conduct may constitute a betrayal of our friends who look to us for an example. One who occupies a position of leadership in or out of the Church may mislead those who follow him. The Bible says, "We reap as we sow," but that is only part of the fact. Mostly we reap as others have sown for us. We reap as our parents have sown; we reap as our teachers have sown. And one of the most challenging ideas that I can think of is that those for whom we have leadership responsibility will reap as we sow.

Almost the last instruction that Jesus gave to Peter before ascending into heaven was the triple charge. "Feed my sheep." (John 21:16) A full and complete disobedience to which we can incur by merely doing nothing. To let the lambs die of starvation is not as spectacular as outright betrayal, but the result may be just as disastrous. It is interesting to remember that Jesus did not lose his eternal exaltation because of the treachery of Judas. But some of those under our direction may actually lose eternal life because of a simple default by a well-meaning leader. Leaders almost without realizing it, may *betray* their trust, or *deny* their calling, or *doubt* their responsibility or *sleep* on their opportunity. The *means* may be different but what about the final result?

President John Taylor once said, "If you do not magnify your calling, God will hold you responsible for those you might have saved had you done your duty." (*J. of D.* 20:23) That means that we are guilty of all of the good that we do not do. And when we accept our callings on that basis, we had better be well fortified with some effective means of preventing our own failure.

Some time ago a 64 year old man said, "If I had known 40 years ago what I know now, I would have lived different-ly." He said, "I wish I could live my life over again." But if even Judas had known and felt when he was planning the betrayal what he knew and felt just before committing sui-cide, *he* would also have done differently. "Foresight" has greater value in bring our success about than its belated cousin "hindsight."

To me one of the most inspiring traits in the life of the Master was that he did not have to commit a single sin in order to find out that it was wrong. There are some people who have to make every mistake personally. It will not help us much when we stand before the judgment bar of God to say, "I wish I could live my life over again." Even our "weeping, wailing, and gnashing of teeth," will then avail us little. We cannot relive our lives. Life permits us no re-hearsals. We cannot rehearse birth or death or success. But we *can* help ourselves by the simple processes of "preview-ing" and "pretesting" our acts for potential wrongs while the acts are still in the idea stage.

Betrayal in any degree is a terrible thing, but so is thoughtlessness, and so is incompetence, and so is sloth, and so is every other instrumentality by which eternal blessings are lost. It might, therefore, be very helpful to put ourselves on guard against possible errors by occasionally going down the check list of wrong with the disciple's searching inquiry, and say from our hearts "Lord, is it I?"

The Lost Bible

THERE IS an ancient legend that tells of a time when the world lost the Bible. Not only did the book itself disappear, but all traces of its influence were taken completely from the earth. Its doctrines had vanished, its philosophy, its commandments, its history, and its religion were all as completely erased from the records of the world as though they had never existed. The priceless Archives appeared as though vandals had pillaged them, slashing and despoiling the classical works of the world. The art galleries now displayed mostly a lot of empty frames. The valuable religious canvasses had been taken away leaving no trace of the thrilling artistry that had been inspired by the Bible.

Much of the finest music in the world was silenced; it had evaporated as though it had never existed. The mighty oratorios such as *The Messiah, The Creation,* and *The Elijah* were out of circulation forever. They had not only been removed from the libraries and galleries, but they had also been completely expunged from the minds and hearts of men. Beautiful hymns which for ages had expressed the hopes, the fears and devotions of millions were now silent. The beautiful Christmas carols, Easter anthems, and songs of Thanksgiving were now no more.

Libraries had been gutted and the writings of Shakespeare, Milton, Tennyson, Carlyle, Longfellow and countless others were dull and drab as they now lacked their former inspiration and beauty. The masterpieces of oratory were minus their most potent passages. Law books made little sense, for the fundamental principles of right and justice had been eliminated. The great documents of human rights such as the Magna Charta of Great Britain, the Constitution of the United States and the Declaration of Independence were now as sounding brass. Great values had become jumbled and confused. The precious gifts of the spirit were blurred and cancelled out, and in their places there was nothing but blankness.

When the Bible was lost, according to the legend, the Holy Spirit was also snuffed out and in its absence, man no longer grew tall of soul, gentle of spirit, courageous of heart, just and honest toward his fellow men, faithful in life and fearless in death. Life itself had become flat, empty and purposeless, for God, the author of the Bible, had also vanished, and man had no one left to worship but himself. The natural laws by which the universe had been governed now had no author and no master, but everything was left to chance, and confusion reigned.

Fortunately this is only a legend. Actually we still have the Bible. The book of books is still on the shelf where it has always been. The word of God is still available where we can turn to its greatest passages with a moment's notice. How fortunate we are to have this holy book in our immediate possession. It has given more inspiration to more people than any other book that was ever printed.

The fate of the nations themselves hang on the Holy Scriptures. Napoleon on St. Helena said, "The Bible is not merely a book—it is a living power . . . nowhere as in the Bible can be found such a series of beautiful ideas and admirable maxims which pass before us like the battalions of a celestial army. . . . The soul can never go astray while it has this book for its guide." The influence of this volume reaches into every corner of our lives. The Bible is the world's first book of religion; it is the world's first book of wisdom; it is the first book of history; it is the first book of literature. The writings of Shakespeare alone contain 550 Bible quotations and allusions. The poetry of Tennyson contains 330

Bible references. The works of Emerson are filled with Bible passages and philosophy. Jesus himself quoted 89 times from the Old Testament scriptures.

But although the Bible itself is safe and sound, yet there are many individuals to whom the Bible is still lost. What good does it do for one to have physical possession if he does not have mental and spiritual familiarity? A recent survey revealed that 92% of all American homes contain a Bible, but 72.5% of the people living in those homes said that they seldom, if ever read it. Thirty-four per cent of those questioned could not name a single book in the Bible. One man who could quote the batting averages of every important major league baseball player in the United States confessed that he could not quote one single verse from the word of the Lord. He had a Bible, but he knew nothing of its message.

This situation reminds us of the Forty-Niners who over a century ago started out for California, seeking gold. Many of them died of thirst while crossing the great American desert. Very frequently their bodies were found near the water holes. They could have saved their lives if they had only known that there was water within their easy reach.

Our spiritual situation is very similar. Jesus talked a great deal about the living waters that would save us from spiritual death. But many are dying of spiritual thirst with the water holes right under our noses. Many eternal deaths occur because those concerned have lost the Bible.

Some time ago the late Dr. Adam S. Bennion gave a series of Bible lectures. The first assignment made to the class members was for them to *find* their Bibles. They were not required to open them or dust them off or read anything out of them—just get them located. I suppose that in a little different sense that is about the number one need of our day —for every person in the world to find the Bible, not just to locate the book itself, but to discover its doctrine and love its inspiration. Suppose that we could just make the proper use of the Sermon on the Mount and the Ten Commandments. Suppose that we could really discover the message of the Golden Rule or find the lessons hidden in the Parables and the Beatitudes, and then put every instruction in force in our daily program.

Most of the sin, degradation and suffering in *this* world and in the world to come are and will be because of our misfortune in losing the Bible. We have lost its repentance, its righteousness and its wisdom. Sometimes we lose the Bible a little bit at a time by deliberately discarding those parts that don't suit our fancy.

This is one of the places where without question the Communists leaders of Russia excel us, as they have thrown away the Bible all at once. Even though the book itself may still be available, in Russia its great doctrines have been repudiated and its Christian ordinances have been intentionally discarded. Not only has the Bible been officially lost in Russia, but in harmony with the legend, the author himself has been banished from every part of his own earth presently occupied by the Russians.

The fact that the Russians now have no higher authority to go by than themselves certainly has much to do with the fact that they seem to have lost their sense of right and wrong. To bring about human slavery is one of their most cherished goals; they would deprive every human being of his God-given free agency without a moment's hesitation if they thought they could. In fact, they threaten that they are now poised and ready to destroy the world if their ultimatums are not followed. The problems that threatens Russia like that which destroyed Nazi Germany is that their leaders have lost the Bible. This has been the problem of the nations of the past, it is the problem of the nations in the present.

If we are to succeed as individuals or as a nation we must find the Bible, and we must find the Bible's author.

God promised to spare Sodom and Gomorrah if ten righteous men could be found. Maybe he would also spare us the devastation that has been foretold if we would turn our lives to him. One of our most important needs is for the great Christian churches to find the Bible. There are presently some 250 Christian denominations claiming to base their entire religion upon the great book. They say they accept the Bible as the inspired word of God, and the only authoritative rule of faith and practice. But many of the greatest doctrines taught by Christ and mentioned in the Bible are missing from their creeds. It is a very simple matter to accept the Bible when it is closed, but reject the fundamental Christian doctrines that are exposed to view when the Bible is open.

Almost everyone believes the Bible when it is closed. But when the Bible is opened, how much do we believe of the divinity of Christ, the atonement, the personality of God, the antemortal existence of spirits, the literal bodily resurrection, the degrees of glory, the eternity of the family unit, the authority of the priesthood, and the thrilling doctrine of eternal progression? It has been said that if Christ should come back to earth today he would certainly not be able to recognize in the contending sects led by unauthorized men, the one Lord, one faith, and one baptism that he established. He promised severe punishments to anyone who added to or subtracted from his doctrine. (Rev. 22:18-19)

A few years ago one of the greatest sectarian religious leaders of our day wrote a book in which he compared the doctrines taught in the Bible with what is presently being taught by popular religious leaders. This man pointed out from the scriptures that the God of the Bible was a personal God. There could be no question about that. Jesus taught that God was his Father (John 1:14), that Jesus was the first Begotten Son of God in the spirit, (Heb. 1:6, Romans 8:29) and the Only Begotten in the flesh. (John 3:6) But this minister making the survey said, "We don't believe that any more."

Then he explained what the survey indicated was presently believed about God by the ministers of popular Christianity. One of them said, "No one can possibly know about God. He is absolutely unknowable, indiscernible, and undiscoverable. He is not limited to boundaries and we can be sure that he has no body or shape." Another minister said that God was like a giant electronic brain. Many believed him to be some incomparable, mysterious essence that filled the universe that no one could understand. Another referred to him as a mobile, cosmic ether. The minister said, "Imagine Jesus praying to a mobile, cosmic ether." Jesus prayer, "My Father which art in heaven." Jesus said to Mary, "Go to my brethren and say unto them that I ascend unto my Father and to your Father and unto my God and to your God." (John 20:17)

Jesus was literally begotten by his Father; (Luke 1:35) he had a body like his Father; (D. & C. 130:22) he resembled his Father; (John 6:46, 14:9) he prayed to his Father. (John 17:5) He did the will of his Father. He taught the doctrine of his Father (John 7:16), and his Father's voice spoke approval of his work. (Matt. 3:17, 17:5)

The minister handling the survey said that those who wrote the Bible believed in a literal, bodily resurrection. There could be no question about that. The body of Jesus came out of the tomb and was seen by many during the forty days between his resurrection and ascension. He said to Thomas, "Reach hither thy finger, and behold my hands; and reach hither thy hand, and thrust it into my side: and be not faithless but believing." (John 20:27)

Summing up some of the other great doctrines of Christ this minister said, "The virgin birth is no longer an accepted historic fact. The second coming of Christ is an outmoded phrasing of hope. The inerrancy of the scriptures is incredible." Then this minister commented that "almost nothing is left of this great volume of scripture that if accepted could save the world." But through disbelief, disobedience, and false teaching, many churches and many individuals have in very large part lost the Holy Bible, and consequently they have lost themselves and their blessings.

The Church of Jesus Christ of Latter-day Saints declares that God the Father and his Son, Jesus Christ, have again visited the earth and declared again that the Holy Bible is the word of God, and that every single doctrine is important. May God help us in our individual investigation and search to really find the Bible, and make every one of its life-giving truths an important part of our lives, that we may thereby find ourselves.

Lucifer

ONE OF OUR most helpful self-improvement activities is the study of biography. We can best understand the traits of success and failure as they show themselves ready made in others. Disraeli, a former British Prime Minister, once said that "One could not know anything about mankind without learning something about himself." When we have before us actual working models of success and failure, then we can make effective adaptations to serve our own need. Of course, the greater our example, the more we can learn from him. That is one reason why the most profitable of all knowledge is the knowledge of God. Jesus said, "This is life eternal that they might know thee, the only true God and Jesus Christ whom thou hast sent." Joseph Smith said, "If men do not comprehend the character of God, they do not comprehend themselves." And someone said that the greatest discovery that anyone ever makes is to discover God. With a full understanding that the purpose of his mission was to be our pattern, Jesus said, "Take my yoke upon you and learn of me." That is one of the scriptures most thrilling lines and our eternal lives depend upon our successful compliance.

But learning can usually be brought about most effectively when we see accomplishment on both its negative and its positive sides. We can best understand white when we see it on a black background. We learn most quickly by contrast. Some events show us what to do; others show us what we should avoid. Both saints and sinners have something to teach us.

As the greatest good is God, so the greatest evil is Satan. God and Satan form the extremes of good and bad, and both may serve an important need in us. As the Apostle Paul said, ". . . all things work together for good to them that love God, . . ." (Rom. 8:28) That is, if we have the right attitude, if we think straight, if we do right, if we love God, then even Satan himself can make a substantial contribution to our welfare. If he so desired, God could destroy Satan at any instant—then why doesn't he? He himself has given us the answer. He has said, "And it must needs be that the devil should tempt the children of men, or they could not be agents unto themselves; for if they never should have bitter they could not know the sweet—" (D & C 29:39) Therefore, if Satan has something to teach us, we ought to find out what it is.

Some time ago I heard one of the great ministers of the world speak about Satan. He began by saying that he was sure that such a personage existed. Of course, that is a fact that everyone must accept, who accepts the Bible. On many occasions Jesus talked about Satan. In the fourth chapter of Matthew there is an account of the personal interchange that took place between Jesus and Satan following the baptism of Jesus and his long fast in the desert. Jesus triumphed over Satan's most severe temptations. His victory served him as a kind of final examination before beginning his official ministry.

Certainly no one who believes in Jesus or in the Bible can disbelieve in Satan. The fact that he exists is not only made perfectly clear in the scripture, but we see many evidences of his work in our present day society. But one of our problems comes from the fact that many of the details about him are lacking from the Bible, and some of the Bible references are so fragmentary as not to be clearly understood. Commenting on this fact the minister just referred to said, "We don't know where the devil came from, it is all very speculative. No one knows for sure." However, modern day revelation has given us a great deal of additional information about this important and very influential personage.

We learn about Satan for the first time when we first learn about ourselves. The first mention made of us in the scripture tells us that we were assembled in a grand council of heaven where our earth life was being discussed and a Savior was being selected.

The Prophet Isaiah gives a partial view of the proceeding when he said, "Also I heard the voice of the Lord, saying, Whom shall I send, and who shall go for us? . . ." (Isaiah 6:8) Modern revelation tells us that there were two who responded. One was the first Begotten Son of God in the spirit who was particularly qualified for this special mission. He answered and said, "Here am I, send me. Father, thy will be done and the glory be thine forever." But another also spoke, it was Lucifer, the brilliant son of the morning, and he said, "Behold, here am I, send me. I will be thy son and I will redeem all mankind, and not one soul shall be lost. And surely I will do it, therefore give me thine honor." And the Lord said, "I will send the first. And the second was angry and kept not his first estate; and, at that day, many followed after him." (Abraham 3:27-28; Moses 4:1-4)

Using the free agency that we all had in heaven, Lucifer rebelled against God, and he was required to bear the responsibility for his acts, in consequence of which John the Revelator says: "And there was war in heaven: Michael and his angels fought against the dragon; and the dragon fought and his angels, And prevailed not; neither was their place found any more in heaven. And the great dragon was cast out, that old serpent, called the Devil, and Satan, which deceiveth the whole world: he was cast out into the earth, and his angels were cast out with him. And I heard a loud voice saying in heaven, Now is come salvation, and strength, and the kingdom of our God, and the power of his Christ: for the accuser of our brethren is cast down, which accused them before our God day and night. And they overcame him by the blood of the Lamb, and by the word of their testimony; and they loved not their lives unto the death. Therefore rejoice, ye heavens, and ye that dwell in them. Woe to the inhabiters of the earth and of the sea! for the devil is come down unto you, having great wrath, because he knoweth that he hath but a short time." (Rev. 12:7-12)

About this same event Isaiah comments as follows: "How art thou fallen from heaven, O Lucifer, son of the morning! how art thou cut down to the ground, which didst weaken the nations! For thou hast said in thine heart, I will ascend into heaven, I will exalt my throne above the stars of God: I will sit also upon the mount of the congregation, in the sides of the north: I will ascend above the heights of the clouds; I will be like the most High. Yet thou shalt be brought down to hell, to the sides of the pit. They that see thee shall narrowly look upon thee, and consider thee, saying, Is this the man that made the earth to tremble, that did shake kingdoms;" (Isaiah 14:12-16) Satan drew away a third part of all of the hosts of heaven after him. (Rev. 12:4, D & C 29:36-38)

It is interesting to contemplate the kind of personage Lucifer must have been to have been able to contend so successfully even with God, and to have influenced such a vast number of the hosts of heaven to follow him, in preference to God the Father, and his pre-eminent first-born Son in the spirit. It has been estimated that 80 billion people have lived upon the earth since Father Adam. Even if that represented all of the two thirds who remained faithful to God, even then the number that followed Satan would have been 40 billion. What a tragedy to lead such a vast army to their eternal doom.

The New Testament prophet Jude says, "And the angels which kept not their first estate, but left their own habitation, he hath reserved in everlasting chains under darkness unto the judgment of the great day." (Jude 6) In speaking of this event in our own day, the Lord said, "And they were thrust down, and thus came the devil and his angels; And, behold, there is a place prepared for them from the beginning, which place is hell." (D & C 29:37-38)

We know what great misfortunes have sometimes befallen men in this life when they have let their unrighteous ambitions get out of control to bring failure and unhappiness to themselves and others. But here we have the greatest of all disasters in the form of eternal suffering brought upon billions. Lucifer's disobedience was greatly regretted in heaven as the Lord says, "And was called Perdition, for the heavens wept over him— . . ." (D & C 76:26)

Lucifer's proposal for using force to bring about accomplishment is particularly interesting right now when freedom and free agency is again by far the most critical issue in the world. Lucifer argued that he would save everyone even though it was by compulsion. He had said, "Not one soul shall be lost." (Moses 4:1) His appeal must have been based in part on what we all knew, that if we were given our free agency, then this world would be a place of sin and suffering, poverty and disease, ignorance and death. We knew that if everyone did as he pleased there would be war, bloodshed and heartbreak, that many would use their agency to bring misery and eternal destruction upon themselves and others. But what must have been most disturbing of all was that we knew that only "a few" would ever get back into the presence of God in the highest degree of glory. Yet the advantages of freedom were so tremendous in the minds of God and a majority of his children that a war was fought to preserve it, and Lucifer was expelled because he sought by force to deprive us of it. It is interesting that to this day Satan has not changed his opinion.

Modern revelation tells us that this nation has been set apart as the sanctuary of freedom, that dictators should not prosper here. And it is our mission to safeguard freedom in the world against the evil powers that would rob us of it. What a thrill it should give us to be a part of the most powerful, world stronghold of freedom and the leading representative in the world for that idea for which God and all of us fought in the war in heaven.

As we know much about Lucifer's past, we also know quite a lot about his present and his future. He is still carrying on his desperate rebellion against God. He is raging furiously to overthrow any and every part of the work of God and all of those who opposed him in the council of heaven. His influence will continue as long as he has the freedom of action of which he tried to deprive others by force. He will continue until the glorious second coming of Christ to judge the world, after which the millennium of peace will begin upon the earth. During the ensuing thousand years Satan will be bound and have no power.

John the Revelator says, "And I saw an angel come down from heaven, having the key of the bottomless pit and a great chain in his hand. And he laid hold on the dragon, that old serpent, which is the Devil, and Satan, and bound him a thousand years, And cast him into the bottomless pit, and shut him up, and set a seal upon him, that he should deceive the nations no more, till the thousand years should be fulfilled: and after that he must be loosed a little season." (Rev. 20:1-3) The scripture makes plain that after the thousand years he will be loosed for only a short time, but it will be long enough again to cause great bloodshed and trouble.

John the Revelator says, "And when the thousand years are expired, Satan shall be loosed out of his prison, And shall go out to deceive the nations which are in the four quarters of the earth, Gog and Magog, to gather them together to battle: the number of whom is as the sand of the sea." (Rev. 20:7-8)

We are greatly stimulated by thinking of the lives of some great men and contemplating the good that they have done in raising others to success and happiness. But what about the stimulation in thinking of the eternal misery and degradation of billions because of following the wrong influence. Or, think of those who have gone over to the side of Satan during their second estate, many of whom will share his fate in hell. In our own day the Lord has warned us of our own danger saying, "And the righteous shall be gathered on my right hand unto eternal life; and the wicked on my left hand will I be ashamed to own before the Father; Wherefore I will say unto them—Depart from me, ye cursed, into everlasting fire, prepared for the devil and his angels." (D & C 29:27-28) If he who was once designated as the light bearer has lost his exaltation and has led so many people to their destruction, then we should be warned of our own danger and leave evil strictly alone.

Suppose we could picture the suffering of Satan or understand our own situation if we allow ourselves to be led away by him. Then we will have eternity in which to think of the words of the poet who said, "Of all sad words of tongue or pen, the saddest are these, It might have been." Satan may bring a great benefit to us if we learn how to make effective use of both the good and bad in the influence of others.

Memorial Day

ONE OF THE most unusual of all of our special holidays is the one known as Memorial Day. This is a day set apart especially to help us to remember. On this day we look back into the past with an expression of gratitude for the love and benefactions of those who have gone before.

This interesting day had its beginning on May 5, 1868 when General John A. Logan, then Commander-in-Chief of the Grand Army of the Republic, issued an order appointing May 30th of that year as a day for the living to remember the dead. It was a special day to decorate the graves of those who died during the Civil War. Since then, May 30th has been our official day of memories. This is the day when we live again the great moments of yesterday, and put blossoms upon the graves of those we love and wish to honor.

This is *one* of those days that we make memorable with flowers. We select flowers for the expression of our finest sympathies. The beauty and fleetingness of flowers make them the most fitting symbols of sentiments too difficult for language. Mrs. L. M. Childs has said, "How the heart of man blesses flowers. They are wreathed around the cradle, the marriage altar and the tomb. They deck the breast of the youthful bride; they festoon the altar. They twine around the tomb as a perpetual symbol of the resurrection. Their fragrance and beauty ascend in perpetual worship before the Most High." Flowers serve as a kind of special symbol of Memorial Day and help us more adequately to feel its special meaning.

But Memorial Day has become far more than a day of

patriotic appreciation. It is also a day for a special kind of thought. It is a stimulating practice to lay fragrant, beautiful flowers upon the graves of our departed dead. But it is even *more* stimulating to relive ideas and feelings and thereby bring about a renewal of our love and appreciation. Remembering is one of the most significant things we ever do. We store up beautiful and useful memories for future need much as a squirrel stores up acorns. Then by the exercise of this miraculous power of memory we may reproduce at will what has already been thought or experienced.

For example, one great man tells us of his art in memorizing peacefulness. He once spent a week in beautiful Hawaii. There he watched the waves wash up upon the shore. Over his head long streamers of sunlight were bursting through the clouds. Graceful birds were gliding in the breeze. He said, "I laid back my head and shut my eyes. Suddenly, I became aware of the fact that I could see all of this peace and beauty with my eyes shut as plainly as I had seen it with my eyes open. Then I said to myself, 'If I can see it now with my eyes shut, why can't I also see it in ten years from now? Why can't I return to this beauty at will, and draw healing and satisfaction from the peaceful picture in my memory.'" God provided us with a memory to enable us to store up beautiful experiences of peace, beauty, love, faith, joy and accomplishment. Memories are among our most precious possessions; and God expects us to treasure them and always have them available in good supply so that we can return to them, or draw upon them when strength is needed.

And, after all, what is more important in life than to set up standards, and accumulate wonderful experiences, and ideals which when rerun by the memory can reinspire our lives? The quality of each life is largely determined by the number and kind of pictures that have been stored in our hearts.

A little girl was leaving her home in the mountains and moving away with her family to a new place of residence. Just before getting into the car, she stood aside, facing the beautiful mountains that she loved so much, and began a process of opening and closing her eyes. Her mother said to her, "Marjorie, what are you doing?" Marjorie said, "I am photographing the mountains so that I can take them with me to Kansas." One of our greatest possible ideas is that we can also photograph courage, faith, righteousness and love in such a way that they will also go with us and hold our lives at their best in all of our future years. The memory makes a record of every shining thing, then plays it back with music through the years.

It is important to train the eye to *see* beauty. It is just as important to train the memory to *hold* it. In fact, it has been said that education itself consists not so much in merely being taught as in being reminded. Life at its best is always to remain faithful to the greatest beauty we have ever seen, and the highest inspiration we have ever felt. A memory can be trained to always see virtue, beauty and faith as it was experienced at its highest point.

One of the main hazards threatening the quality of our lives is forgetfulness. Many of us are like Scrooge in Dickens' "Christmas Carol." Scrooge had forgotten the significance and beauty of Christmas. So the Spirit took him back into his own early life for a rerun of the Christmases of his youth. There Scrooge relived, reabsorbed and he recaptured the lost spirit of Christmas. When Scrooge came back into his own presence he said, "I am not the man I was." To change ourselves for good is one of the functions of memory. We ought to remember, however, that while we can rerun memory, we cannot rerun life. Therefore, we must make available to the memory only that kind of experience that we desire to determine our accomplishments.

I would like to share with you what to me is a very useful idea for this day when we think about remembering. It is said that Whistler once painted a tiny picture of a spray of roses. The artistry involved was magnificent. Never before it seemed had the art of man been able to execute quite so deftly a reproduction of the art of nature. The picture was the envy of the artists who saw it, the despair of the collectors who yearned to buy it for their collections. But Whistler steadfastly refused to sell it. "For," he said, "whenever I feel that my hand has lost its cunning, whenever I doubt my ability, I look at the little picture of the spray of roses and say to myself, 'Whistler, you painted that. Your hand drew it. Your imagination conceived the colors. Your skill put the roses on the canvas.' Then, said he, 'I know that what I have done I can do again.'

"Therefore, hang on the walls of your mind the memory of your successes. Take council of your strength, not your weakness. Think of the good jobs you have done. Think of the times when you rose above your average level of performance and carried out an idea, or a dream, or a desire for which you had deeply longed. Think of the great moments in your life—hang these pictures on the walls of your mind and look at them as you travel the roadway of life."

By a similar process we may also borrow inspiration, know-how, and beauty from others. A millionaire may pay a fortune for a gallery of paintings, and then the poorest among us may stamp them into his own heart and carry the most valuable treasury away with him. Without cost we may keep these masterpieces as our own, to enjoy and to instruct us throughout life. Similarly, the accomplishments and determinations of others can be printed upon *our* minds and hearts so that we may never lose possession.

The memory of our cherished friends may also be kept close by to strengthen and support us. When a loved one is absent from us, he writes us letters telling us about himself,

what he is doing and what his hopes and ambitions are.
Then, memory brings his face before us. We see his smile.
We feel his love. We can almost hear him speak. As we
read his letter we find lovely, inspiring things written between the lines.

We are *always* memorizing the things we hear, the
sounds of the ocean, the wind rustling in the trees, the
ideals that we hold in our hearts. We memorize the things
that we feel, the ocean spray on our face, the cool night air,
the smell of the salt. We memorize the ambitions that we
love and the determinations and godliness that we store in
our hearts. Each one of our senses is storing away memories that can be brought back at will. We can bring back
the feelings of harmony and relaxation that we knew on the
beach, or we may recall the ideals and spirituality of the
teachings of others, or we may rerun again and again our
own faith and gratitude.

James M. Barrie said, "God gave us memories so that
we might have roses in December." Memory can also give
us strength in temptation and courage in weakness. Probably the most thrilling exercise of memory lies in the realm of
religion. We can memorize and retain faith, righteousness
and Godliness. One of the most oft-repeated injunctions of
the Bible is "Remember." The Holy Scriptures are filled
with admonitions and suggestions for remembering: Remember the Sabbath day. Remember the commandments.
(Num. 15:39) Remember thy Creator in the days of thy
youth. (Eccl. 12:1) Paul said, ". . . I put thee in remembrance
that thou stir up the gift of God which is in thee . . ." (II Tim.
1:6)

The Sacrament of the Lord's Supper is primarily to help
us remember. Jesus said, ". . . this do ye in remembrance of
me." (Luke 22:19) One of the main functions of the Holy
Ghost is described as ". . . he shall . . . bring all things to your
remembrance, . . ." (John 14:26) On the other hand, many of

our greatest sins are those that are centered in forgetfulness. Everyone complains of his poor memory. We can't remember names, we can't remember faces, we can't remember ideas. But our situation becomes far more critical when we forget God, or the eternal welfare of our family. God commanded the ancients to keep a written Book of Remembrance. (Mal. 3:16) That is also an excellent idea for us. Ideas, plans, objectives and ideals can be preserved forever by writing them down.

God instituted another very interesting custom among ancient Israel to help them remember. Inasmuch as there are certain passages in the scripture that must not be forgotten, God had the Israelites write these memorable passages down on pieces of parchment. Then they were enclosed in little leather tubes and called phylacteries. These the Israelites bound across their foreheads, and between their eyes. They tied them upon their wrists, and hung them about their necks, and attached them to conspicuous parts of their clothing where they would always be in view. In this way they hoped to remember what God had forbidden them to forget.

The ideas on one of these phylacteries is as follows: "And thou shalt love the Lord thy God with all thy heart, and with all thy soul, and with all thy might." Then God said, "And these words, which I command thee this day, shall be in thine heart: And thou shalt teach them diligently unto thy children, and shalt talk of them when thou sittest in thine house, and when thou walkest by the way, and when thou liest down, and when thou risest up. And thou shalt bind them for a sign upon thine hand, and they shall be as frontlets between thine eyes." (Deut. 6:5-8)

The writer of Proverbs also refers to this interesting custom by saying, "Bind them continually upon thine heart, and tie them about thy neck. When thou goest, it shall lead thee; when thou sleepest, it shall keep thee; and when thou awakest, it shall talk with thee." (Prov. 6:21-22) We sometimes make a modern adaptation of this idea when we tie a string on our finger as a visual aid to memory, or when we get married we put a ring on the third finger of the left hand to make sure that certain promises will not be forgotten. When we enter the army we take the Pledge of Allegiance and put on the uniform of our country. The flag waving in the sky is also to remind us not to forget.

Out of the depths of his heart Kipling sang, "Lord God of Hosts, be with us yet, lest we forget, lest we forget." We ought to tie that same string firmly on our own fingers.

The secret of a good memory is attention. And attention depends upon interest. We rarely forget that which we are greatly interested in, and we can make our minds more hospitable to good ideas by writing them down, then memorizing them and stamping them deep into our minds and muscles. There are some great ideas that must *never* for a moment be allowed to grow dim in our minds.

The general term for loss of memory is amnesia. A French soldier once forgot who he was. When he was picked up at a railroad station all he could say was, "I don't know who I am." That is also one of our greatest spiritual hazards. We forget sometimes who we are, and what manner of men and women we ought to be. (James 1:23-25)

It is so easy to forget. We forget the dead. One can even forget his own family if he stays away from them long enough. And we forget our Creator by the same process. Then we become amnesia victims in a world of spiritual shell shock. And so to help us to remember we set aside this one day of a year and call it Memorial Day.

We make the day live with flowers and dedicate it to memory.

May God help us on this special day that we might greatly enrich our own minds and hearts as we pay our special homage to the past.

Mother's Day

W E HAVE AN interesting and very helpful custom among us of setting aside special days to think about special things.

And one of our most *special* days is the second Sunday in May. This is the day that we designate as Mother's Day. This is traditionally a day of family unity and solidarity. This is a day when we put on our best clothes and live at our best. With flowers and music, prayers and expressions of love we gather around our mother to honor her and try to make her happy. From some points of view Mother's Day represents more important events in our lives than any other day with the exception of Sunday. That is, our mothers have had more influence in determining our lives than anyone else and should therefore stand next to God in the appreciation and the honor that we manifest. Napoleon was once asked what was the greatest need of France and he answered "mothers." He said, "Let France have good mothers and she will have good sons." By the very act of thinking about and honoring our mothers we lift ourselves up. That is, the human mind has some of the qualities of the tendrils of the climbing vine. It tends to attach itself and draw itself upward by what it is put in contact with. Putting our minds in contact with the noble qualities and high ideals that have actuated our mothers' lives is one of the most pleasant and constructive of any of the activities in which we may engage. In President David O. McKay's great book, *Gospel Ideals*, there is one paragraph in which he says, "Last night I dreamed about my mother." And then he says, "I would like to dream about my mother more often." That is, in his dream his mind went back and relived those wonderful days spent at his mother's knee while he was learning from her the lessons of life which brought him to his present high station. Those important lessons were the lessons he learned in his youth. They were the lessons of honor and truth and Godliness. After reliving this experience in his dream, he awakened in the morning with these thrilling lessons freshly relearned. In his dream he had reabsorbed the original good.

This mental power enabling us to relive and revitalize the great experiences of our past lives is one that we should take greater advantage of. Our lives can be greatly benefited by remembering mother, her teachings, her love, her sacrifices, and her concern for us.

It has been said that one of the greatest gifts ever given by God to man is an imagination. In the imagination we may go back and relive the past while we reabsorb the original lessons, or we may go forward and prelive the future, while we make decisions about important events yet to be. Suppose that on this Mother's Day we go back in memory into our own past and relive the blessings that we have received from our mothers. As I read some sentiments entitled "Mother," let your imagination go wherever these words may take them. The poet has said:

MOTHER

Your hair has faded, mother dear,
From gold to silvery gray,
Yet, in your eyes, that little spark
Of love, I see today.

It means that you are proud of me;
You're glad for what you've done;
And in your heart I never see
A shame for me, your son.

Oh, I remember very well
When first I learned to pray,
Each night beside my little bed
You taught me how to say—

God bless my mother that she may
Protect and care for me,
And guide me right with truth each day
An honest man to be.

The days flew by; the years came on.
You led me all the while and
Through the trials that break with dawn
You held me with your smile.

The waves were strong that tempted me
To plunder wrongly
But with your love I could not go
Adrift far out to sea.

The darker ways that beckoned me
To lie, to steal, to cheat,
I might have gone, could you not see
My life lay at your feet.

And all through life you toiled away
And struggled just for me
To make me what I am today,
And what I'm proud to be.

Then God, it seems has answered them,
Those prayers we used to say,
And in my heart that mighty theme
An honest man will stay.

And when alone at times, dear heart
You ponder o'er the past
And wonder will I think of you
As long as life shall last—

Remember that I love you still.
You linger ever near,
And in my heart and soul I pray
God bless you, mother dear.

Then from the past and the future we move back into
the present to establish a more adequate place in our lives
for her, whose body nourished us, whose loving arms sustained us, whose every thought was to help us to do and to
become. She is our wisest counselor, our most effective
teacher, our most faithful supporter, our best friend, our

mother. Abraham Lincoln may well have been representing all of us when he said, "All that I am or ever hope to be I owe to my angel mother."

One of the beautiful stories of our literature appropriate to this day is Nathanial Hawthorne's story of *The Great Stone Face.* In the white mountains of New Hampshire there is a natural stone image on the mountainside. Each day a little boy in the village below looked up to the kindly features and noble traits pictured there, and every day he became more and more like the image that he loved, not only in personality qualities but also in actual physical characteristics. But Nathanial Hawthorne's story is the story of every man, for every man becomes like that which he habitually loves and admires. The ancient Romans used to capitalize this idea of transferring greatness by making statues of their most noble heroes and setting them up in their homes. Then when they looked at the statue they thought about the great qualities possessed by the one whom the statue represented, and they tended to become like the one that they continually looked up to and thought about.

But God has given us a better plan. It was he who organized the family in the first place and taught us that under the right circumstances the family group may maintain its identity and unity throughout eternity. Certainly God was not thinking only of the few years of mortality when he said, "It is not good that man should be alone," and so he set up in each home a mother fitted by him to perform a particular service for us, and as we look up to her in love and admiration, we tend to make her ideals and ambitions our own. These great qualities may then be ours forever. Whatever may have been said about "the sins of the fathers" it has also been *written* that the virtues of the mothers shall be visited upon the children.

Thirty-four hundred years ago out of the lightnings and thunders of Sinai, God said "Honour thy father and thy mother." And the prophets have pointed out that the human family can best be perfected together; that parents cannot receive their highest eternal glory without the children. Just so, our mothers cannot receive their greatest happiness either here or hereafter unless *we* have lived Godly, upright lives.

Sometimes we can learn best by thinking a little bit on both sides of an idea. Here then are some stimulating negative Mother's Day thoughts written by Lillith Schell under the title "The Other Woman." It is a part of the story of the Crucifixion. It pictures the agony and suffering that took place upon the cross. It tells of the thirst, the parched lips, the vinegar, then came the bitterness of that last outcry followed by the earthquake, the darkness, and the dreadful fear. From the cross Jesus had indicated his beloved apostle and had said to his mother, "Woman, behold thy son." Then to John, he said, "Son, behold thy mother." After the end had come, John took Mary and Salome and the other women to his own home. Later that night in the midst of their weeping, a knock came at the door. John opened the door to see standing before him a strange woman. He said to her, "Whom seekest thou?" The other woman said, "The mother of him who was crucified." John said, "She is within, but I cannot suffer thee to disturb her now." The woman said, "Thou must," and she pushed by John and made her way to the lighted door beyond which sat this little group of sorrowing women. She paused momentarily in the doorway while her eyes became accustomed to the light, after deciding which woman it was that she sought, she made her way to Mary and said to her, "I bring thee compassion." Mary replied, "I give thee my gratitude, O woman, whoever thou art. I give thee my thanks." Then the other woman said, "O thou happy one." Stirred by the *strangeness* of the words, Mary, the mother of Jesus, lifted her sodden eyes and looked sharply into the face of the stranger. What she saw there made her forget the bitterness of her own grief. "My sister," she said, "rather would I give thee compassion. *Thy* loss, *thy* sorrow, how great it must be. Wilt thou tell me of it? Wilt thou tell me who thou art?" "My name is Judith," answered the other woman. "I come out of Kerioth of Judea." Mary said, "My friend, canst thou not tell me of thy sorrow? Perchance I may be able to help thee. I will gladly share it with thee." "*My* sorrow," said Judith, "is such that thou canst never know." Her hand stole up to her forehead and brushed aside a lock of iron gray hair. Then clutching her throat as if to relieve the terrible choking there, she said in a shrill whisper, "I am the mother of Judas Iscariot."

I close with the words that come to each child this day from the heart of his mother.

> Do you know that your soul is of my soul such a part
> That you seem to be fiber and core of my heart,
>
> None other can please me as you dear can do;
> None other can please me or grieve me as you.
>
> Remember the world will be quick with its blame
> If sorrow or shame ever cover your name.
>
> Like mother like son is the saying so true,
> The world will judge largely of mother by you.
>
> Be yours then the task, if task it must be,
> To force the proud world to do homage to me.
>
> Be sure it will say when its verdict you've won,
> She reaped as she sowed, lo, this is her son.

May God, our Heavenly Father, give us his blessings that we may do proper honor to our mothers this day and every day throughout our lives by making our own lives acceptable before him.

Perspective

ONE OF THE most prominent of the teachings of Jesus had to do with the difficulty that most of us have in keeping the right kind of ideas operating in our lives. Jesus pointed out that there are some who have eyes but who cannot see and ears that cannot hear. The natural consequence of course is that our hearts do not understand. Our eyes and ears are two of the most important entrances by which understanding can get into our minds. When either of these fail in any degree, or when they function improperly, our welfare may be adversely affected.

As the old proverb says, "Where there is no vision the people perish." (Prov. 29:18) But many other people perish because of a distortion in vision caused by perspective.

Every day we see a repetition of the experience of the blind men from Hindustan who went to see the elephant. Each of the blind men came away with an entirely different concept of an elephant because of the limitations that blindness had placed on their point of view. If a blind man could get the idea that an elephant was like a rope, what might some other blind man whose perspective had been similarly distorted think about the purpose of life.

From this viewpoint it is an interesting experience to go into the mirror room at the circus and look into the glasses that have been provided especially to produce optical illusions. One mirror shows a fat man to be slender; another shows a slender man to be fat; a tall man is made short in his own eyes; and a short man sees himself very tall. But life also has some deceptive mirrors. So frequently we complain that we cannot always see ourselves as others see us.

We are sometimes like a desert traveler being troubled by a mirage. We may see a beautiful lake in the distance which is actually not there. Unless we are able to make proper allowances for some of the deceptions in life, we may cause ourselves injury even to the point of losing our eternal life.

For example, there is an interesting part of the law of perspective that makes everything in the distance seem small and unimportant, while everything close by looms very large and impressive. That is, if you look down a long row of telephone poles, the telephone pole by which you are standing seems very large, but the telephone pole on the distant horizon appears to be a mere pinpoint in comparison. That seems to be true; your eyes tell you it is true; and yet it is not true. If you will get into your automobile and drive to that exact point on the horizon and have another look, you will find that some almost unbelievable changes have taken place. The telephone pole which once had such great importance in your eyes has now become small and insignificant, whereas the telephone pole that you thought of no consequence has now doubled in size and importance by a million times, What a few miles back appeared to be the least of the telephone poles has now become the most important one of all.

Recently I flew over the city of Chicago and with my perspective elevated to 18,000 feet I could not detect one building in the entire city that seemed to be over one inch in height. Fortunately for me I had been warned in advance about the deception and was able to make the proper allowance. But then I realized how necessary to our success in life is the ability to compensate for our illusions and differences in perspective.

Suppose you try this interesting experiment. If you will put a nickel over your eye it will blot out the biggest star a few hundred million miles away. A quarter will blot out the sun. Of course, that does not mean that the quarter is larger than the sun—it is just closer to your eye.

This deception which applies to space also applies to time. If you have a six-year-old son who has a financial problem, test his perspective by asking him which he would rather have a quarter today, or a dollar next month. Unless he is a very unusual boy, the quarter right now will loom far larger in his eyes than the dollar will appear when placed thirty days in the future.

If you would like to try a little bigger experiment ask your wife which she would rather have—a new gown, today, or a new refrigerator today, or mansions in heaven twenty-five years from now. Of course, I don't know what your wife's answer will be, but that is a very interesting experiment.

I once heard of a colored boy who was about to steal a watermelon. Someone cautioned him by saying, "Rufus, if you take that watermelon you will have to pay for it in eternity." Rufus said, "If I can have that much time, I'll take two." Of course, everyone of us has present *wants* that are tremendously important, and in which we have a big chance to err. All of us have some difficulties with perspective and in its various applications to our welfare it carries some problems that are sometimes very hard to solve.

You will remember that this is the situation that got Esau into trouble. One night Esau came home hungry and Jacob said to him, Esau, if you will assign over to me all of the lands, cattle, barns, goods and properties contained in your birthright, I will give you a mess of pottage. From the perspective of one who has just had a good dinner, that proposition seems a little bit ridiculous. But Esau was hungry, and hunger can change one's perspective and make even a mess of pottage seem very desirable.

I suppose Esau thought, what difference does it make what happens tomorrow, if I am hungry right now. It is possible that almost any small unimportant want can be held so close to the eyes that it will blot out the entire future landscape. I don't even know what "a *mess* of pottage" is. It doesn't sound very appetizing to me, but Esau gave up his entire birthright to obtain it.

But that kind of situation is not at all uncommon among us today. It is very likely that during this coming week a great many of us will make that same kind of bargain. Almost every day we trade off some valuable future good for a mess of present pottage. Looking through this optical illusion of perspective, even one's birthright can appear small and unimportant.

The people of Noah's day were all drowned because they held their present evil pleasures so close to their eyes that they could not see their own future good, or hear Noah's warning voice, or understand his logic about repentance. The very carpenters who helped Noah build the ark could not see far enough ahead to save themselves in it.

But what do most of us do, when someone talks to us about education, or righteousness, or God, or eternal life. These things frequently seem so distant and unimportant, and we are victimized by this peculiar kind of shortsightedness where the present pottage of pleasure or sin has a bigger pull on our appetite than our future birthright of Godliness and accomplishment. The pleasures of today frequently loom tremendous in our eyes, whereas our eternal happiness is so small that it has no standing.

Jesus said, "In my father's house are many mansions." In speaking of these mansions Paul said that we cannot even conceive the magnificence of the things that God has prepared for his faithful children. Yet when we look at them through the little end of the telescope, they seem so small and insignificant that we lose all interest. Someone has said, "Heaven is all right, it is just too far away." And unless we carefully train ourselves to make sufficient allowances, we may not only lose our birthright but our souls as well.

I would like to retell the story of one who sold his soul. This is the ancient legend of Faust. You may say that this is only a story, and yet it actually happens in principle a million times a year.

The legend has it that Dr. John Faust died in Wittenberg, Germany, in 1540. But 24 years before he died he sold his soul to Satan. He said to Satan, "If you will serve me for 24 years, punishing my enemies and aiding my friends, at the end of that period I will forever deliver up my soul." That probably appeared to be a very good bargain to Faust. Twenty-four years of pleasure can seem very important under some circumstances. But *beyond* 24 years everything seemed so little and unimportant to Faust as to be of no possible consequence. But Satan with better perspective said, "I will wait on Faustus while he lives, and he shall buy my services with his soul."

During the next 24 years, Faust had every kind of experience good and bad. But almost before he was aware, it was said to Faust as it must be said to every one of us, "Thine hour is come." Then for the first time Faust knew that he had cheated himself. Then he said to himself, "Ah, Faustus, thou hast now but one bare hour to live and then thou must be damned eternally." Then he wanted to cancel his agreement, but he knew that was impossible. Then he prayed and said, "Oh, God, if thou canst have no mercy on my soul, at least grant some *end* to my incessant pain. Let Faustus live in hell a thousand years or even a hundred thousand, but at last be saved." But he knew that according to his own bargain even this could never be.

Then Faust watched the clock tick off the seconds and just as the hour struck, the last words of Faust before he died were, "Faustus is gone to hell." Faust, like Esau and Noah's carpenters, had been deceived by a faulty perspective, and what a terrible penalty each had to pay as a consequence. Twenty-four years is a long time, but it will not last forever, and someday each one of us will stand on the horizon of life and look back. Then we will discover an amazing thing, that many of those interests that previously loomed so gigantic in our eyes have now forever lost all of their importance.

One of the abilities we need most in life is the ability to get close enough to eternal things that we may see them clearly in their full dimensions. Unless we keep close to God and his work, we may unintentionally cheat ourselves out of our greatest blessings.

When an astronomer studies the stars he puts a powerful telescope to his eyes. A teacher writing on the blackboard writes in very large letters so that those in the rear of the room can see. We should follow these good examples and look at our spiritual goals through a magnifying glass and think about them in capital letters written large enough that the things of God may be able to compete successfully in our minds. We also need some kind of spiritual hearing aid so that we may turn up the volume of the still small voice to compete with the loud noisy clamor of present attractions.

Faust desperately *wanted* to be saved, but he didn't think about it soon enough. His deathbed repentance was intense because by then death was close by. But there was then nothing that Faust could do about it because by then his life had already been lived.

If we can put the telescope to our eyes and see death while it is yet a lifetime away, then we can repent in advance, so that no wrong will be committed. The man of vision is the one who can see the telephone poles on the horizon in the same scale as they will appear to him when he actually gets there.

Developing vision is not only the concern of the eyes; it is also a function of the brain. In the parable of Jesus the foolish man built his house on the sand because the picturing power of his mind could not see ahead to the rainy season.

The house built on the sand may have served very well as long as the good weather lasted. When the rains descend and the floods come in our own lives, our house will not cave in on us if we have developed a clear vision that can see beyond the good weather season.

Whereas those who hear the great judge of the universe say, "The harvest is past! the summer is ended! and your souls not saved," (D. & C. 56:16) will be those who could not judge the importance of things 24 years in the future.

It seems important that we keep in mind the tendency in our human nature to be a little nearsighted. We live most of our lives in very limited visibility spiritually speaking. It will help us, however, if we remember that every one of us lives constantly under a death sentence that has already been pronounced. Every day that we live we are marching toward death and while only the last day actually comes to it, yet each day contributes something to our final score. And each day should bear its own part of an adequate preparation for our eternal life.

Rededication

The Twenty-fourth of July is the day set apart to honor the Utah pioneers. On this day we recount their hardships, relive their faith, and rejoice in their accomplishments. It has now been well over a century since this little group of hardy men and women completed their long, slow, difficult journey from Nauvoo, Illinois to the Salt Lake Valley. In 1847 the Church was only seventeen years old, but those seventeen years had been very eventful as well as extremely difficult.

The members of the Church had been gathered from many lands. They had left their own homes in response to one of the most important announcements ever made in the world, that God the Father and his Son, Jesus Christ, had again appeared upon the earth and had opened the greatest and last of all of the gospel dispensations.

The pioneers brought with them into these valleys three great volumes of new scriptures which gave a great deal of information concerning the past and the future of the land on which we live. These scriptures make clear that *God's* hand had been instrumental in the establishment of this nation. Centuries before Columbus, God had dedicated this land as a sanctuary of freedom and had decreed that dictators should not prosper here, that God would direct our destinies if we would live righteously and serve him. These great volumes of scripture explained in detail the simple principles of the gospel as taught by the Master in Palestine over 1900 years ago. Now after the long night of apostasy, that once-familiar phrase "thus saith the Lord" was again heard upon the earth.

Even in these first seventeen years, under divine command the Church had sent missionaries throughout the world. This little religious band made up of many nationalities with no material wealth to begin with had built several cities including two temples—all in the face of many kinds of difficulties, including a tempestuous and murderous persecution. On more than one occasion they had been driven from their homes and forced to re-establish themselves anew. In this process their crops had been wasted, their property had been destroyed and many of their lives had been lost. Joseph Smith, the Prophet and founder of the Church, together with his brother Hyrum, the patriarch, had been shot by a mob with painted faces.

Finally this homeless refugee band turned their attention toward finding a permanent home in the far distant and forbidding regions of the Rocky Mountains which was then one of the least attractive of homesites. To many of this group, however, this was one of its greatest advantages, for the thing that they sought was not climate nor comfort nor political advantage nor food supply nor gold. They sought a place where they could carry out the commandments of God who had directed them to organize his Church and carry his message to the people of the world. They only asked for the freedom to do as they had been commanded and to worship God according to the new light which they had received. They desired to build temples to God and erect homes that they could call their own, where they could establish their families and rear their children according to the instructions of God.

Under divine inspiration, their new leader, Brigham Young, led these pioneers across the plains and into these desert valleys, thereby fulfilling the prophecy of Isaiah made some 2500 years previously saying, "And it shall come to pass in the last days, that the mountain of the Lord's house shall be established in the top of the mountains, and shall be exalted above the hills; and all nations shall flow unto it.

"And many people shall go and say, Come ye and let us go up to the mountain of the Lord, to the house of the God of Jacob; and he will teach us of his ways, and we will walk in his paths: for out of Zion shall go forth the law, and the word of the Lord from Jerusalem." (Isa. 2:2-3)

In the years that have passed since then, thousands of missionaries have gone forth from this place at their own expense, bearing the message of the restored gospel to all who would listen. And God has poured out his blessings upon us in our mountain home in a way that reminds us of the word of the Lord to Solomon, after he had erected and dedicated a temple to the Lord. In the Old Testament book of Chronicles we are told that "the Lord appeared to Solomon by night, and said unto him . . . . If my people, which are called by my name, shall humble themselves, and pray, and seek my face, and turn from their wicked ways; then will I hear from heaven, and will forgive their sin, and will heal their land." (II Chronicles 7:12, 14)

Here is a formula for prosperity and happiness of God's own making which will insure for *any* people the blessings of the Lord, not only upon their land but also upon themselves. On the 24th of this July we express our appreciation to God that he has healed our land. These mountain valleys have become wonderfully productive in many ways. The earth has yielded its treasure and the desert has been made to "blossom as the rose." We love our mountain home as we love this great free land of America of which it is a part. On this 113th anniversary, it seems appropriate to express our appreciation in the words of Kipling who said—

> God gave all men all earth to love,
> But since our hearts are small;
> Ordained for each *one* spot should prove
> Beloved over all.

But while we express our appreciation, we should always keep foremost in our minds the particular reasons that brought us here to begin with. When the pioneers arrived in these valleys they were lean and hungry. They had been starved, persecuted, plundered, and driven. But now in our peace and prosperity we are better fed, and that always carries with it the possibility that some may become complacent and thereby lose the blessings for which the pioneers came here.

Some time ago John W. Gardner, in discussing whether or not America had lost the sense of its divine mission, said that "a part of our problem in America is how to stay awake on a full stomach." That is also one of the problems that we have most to fear individually. Since the beginning of time most human beings have been forced to work hard, either because the need for subsistence demanded it, or because some taskmaster required it. Now when our chief economic problem is how best to dispose of our surplus, we are relieved of the necessity for hard labor merely to stay alive. Today we have no taskmasters and no food shortages or even persecution to force industry and diligence upon us. With this release from the outward pressures, we may as free men and women make the fatal mistake of thinking that vigorous effort is now unnecessary.

Through the ancient prophet Amos the Lord said, "Woe unto them that are at ease in Zion, . . ." (Amos 6:1) The world's greatest need has always been and still is for someone who can carry a heavy load and stick to his job over a long period. There must be no piecemeal surrenders of our faith, and there must be no partial discarding of our ambition. For neither our spiritual nor our material prosperity can long be maintained without continuous, vigorous, purposeful effort. The great mountains that encircle these valleys have maintained themselves with very little change in the past years. But the prosperity of the mind and the excellence of the spirit do not, like the mountains, go unchanged when they are unattended and left to themselves. Our faith must feed on continual accomplishment. There must be constant exercise and revitalization. It takes constant steering to keep an automobile on a straight course. The fact that the desert has been made to blossom does not insure the survival of our devotion to God, nor that we will fulfil our assignment. Nor does it guarantee a continuation of our blessings. If as Americans we continue to live in a free society, we must be worthy to live in a free society. If we continue to live in the favor of God, those blessings must be continually won.

Probably one of the things most appropriate to Pioneer Day would be to check up on ourselves to make sure that we are carrying out the purpose for which our pioneer forefathers brought us to this place. Sometimes we get so involved in the side issues that we forget the main purpose of our lives.

The story is told of a young man making preparation to go to college. One of his concerns was how he would support himself financially. Then someone suggested that if he would chop their firewood, he would give him enough money to pay for his room. Some neighbors across the street agreed to let him chop their wood to pay for his board; another neighbor was found who would pay certain of his school expenses if he chopped their wood. Soon the prospective student had so much wood to chop that he had no time left to go to school.

Sometimes we become so engrossed in the process of earning a living that we forget to live. There is a story about one man with large holdings of land who fell down and hugged the earth as though that were the purpose of life. It is possible that we may become so interested in building up our possessions that we may fail to build up ourselves. Edwin Markham has reminded us that—

> We are all blind until we see,
> That in the human plan
> Nothing is worth the building
> That does not build the man.

> Why build these cities glorious
> If man unbuilded goes,
> In vain we build the world
> Unless the builder also grows.

The reason the pioneers came to these valleys was to be free to worship God and build character and Godliness in themselves and others. What would it profit us if by coming here we obtained freedom from persecution only to enslave ourselves with the side issues of life? Probably the most important thing that we can do on Pioneer Day is to rededicate ourselves to those ideals and objectives that brought us here.

The dictionary says that to "dedicate" is to set apart for a definite use. Each individual life must be set apart to reach its highest possibilities. It is very unlikely that our mountain community will ever excel in financial power or as a center of world trade, or as a great political capitol. But we *can* become a center of education, a center for real religion and spirituality. We can excel in honor; we can excel in faith in God; we can excel in carrying the message of salvation to the rest of the world. Jesus has pointed out that a man's life consisteth not in the abundance of the things that it possesseth. That is, wealth is not so much what we have as what we are. We don't labor merely to acquire, but to become. The purpose of life is not just what we can get out of it, but what we can become by it, and what we can help others to become.

In order for one to be worthy of the highest blessings, he must live by the highest principles. It is of course a mistake to think of our dedication to God as a sacrifice, except that kind of sacrifice mentioned by Brigham Young who told of a man giving up an old coat to get back a brand new suit. The Lord is trying to make us all wealthy and Godly and happy. This is the real purpose of life. To accomplish this we must know something of the exhilaration that always attends real dedication to a great cause. Purposeful work gives life a zest and an enthusiasm that always results in accomplishment. Great things are never achieved by aimless or listless men. We need something to dedicate our lives to. Fifty years ago William James said, "What America needs is a moral equivalent of war. We need a moral equivalent of persecution. We need a continual spiritual hunger and a great personal faith that will keep us aroused and aware of our great opportunities. We can live on less if we have more to live for." Mr. James pointed out that, "The purpose of life was to spend it for something that outlasts it." We should rededicate ourselves to that purpose.

The greatest of all values is eternal life. That is also the greatest gift of God. That is what we came here to obtain. National leaders speak of summit conferences. We came to the tops of these mountains where we could hold some summit conferences with God. Certainly we should live by his every word.

The leaders of the great Communist state who are so vigorously disputing our way of life have distinguished themselves as the leaders of the world in atheism. They have banished God from Russia. We should excel in the opposite direction. We should invite God to be with us and then to live so that he will be pleased to honor us. As he has said, "righteousness exalteth a nation, but sin is a reproach to any people."

This pioneer anniversary is a good time to make some individual commitments to serve God. We should not be content merely to live in the house built by the Pilgrims and the pioneers. We must make even greater history ourselves. But when we choose greatness we automatically choose effort. Socrates once said, "If the Almighty should come to me with complete success in his right hand and eternal struggle in his left, I would take the left." That's also the one that we have taken.

May God help us to rededicate ourselves to him and to the purposes for which we have been established in this great land.

The Religious Talent

ONE OF THE most important and one of the most challenging of the parables of Jesus is the parable of talents. Jesus said, "For the kingdom of heaven is as a man travelling into a far country, who called his own servants, and delivered unto them his goods. And unto one he gave five talents, to another two, and to another one; to every one according to his several ability; and straightway took his journey. Then he that had received the five talents went and traded with the same, and made them other five talents. And likewise he that had received two, he also gained other two. But he that had received one went and digged in the earth, and hid his lord's money. After a long time the lord of those servants cometh, and reckoneth with them. And so he that had received five talents came and brought other five talents, saying, Lord, thou deliveredst unto me five talents: behold, I have gained beside them five talents more. His lord said unto him, Well done, thou good and faithful servant: thou hast been faithful over a few things, I will make thee ruler over many things: enter thou into the joy of thy lord.

"He also that had received two talents came and said, Lord, thou deliveredst unto me two talents: behold, I have gained two other talents beside them. His lord said unto him, Well done, good and faithful servant; thou hast been faithful over a few things, I will make thee ruler over many things: enter thou into the joy of thy lord.

"Then he which had received the one talent came and said, Lord, I knew thee that thou art an hard man, reaping where thou hast not sown, and gathering where thou hast not strawed: And I was afraid, and went and hid thy talent

in the earth: lo, there thou hast that is thine. His lord answered and said unto him, Thou wicked and slothful servant,
thou knewest that I reap where I sowed not, and gather
where I have not strawed: Thou oughtest therefore to have
put my money to the exchangers, and then at my coming I
should have received mine own with usury." Then the Lord
said, "Take therefore the talent from him, and give it unto
him which hath ten talents. For unto every one that hath
shall be given, and he shall have in abundance: but from him
that hath not shall be taken away even that which he hath.
And cast ye the unprofitable servant into outer darkness:
there shall be weeping and gnashing of teeth." (Matt.
25:14-30)

This parable is very closely related in its meaning to the
one having to do with the unproductive fig tree. "A certain
man had a fig tree planted in his vineyard; and he came and
sought fruit thereon, and found none. Then said he unto the
dresser of his vineyard, Behold, these three years I come
seeking fruit on this fig tree, and find none: cut it down; why
cumbereth it the ground?" (Luke 13:6-7)

It would be pretty difficult to mistake the Lord's meaning. He expects man, the masterpiece of all his creations, to
make his life productive. He wants us to increase the tremendous investment that he has made in us. We might try
to figure out what the particular talents were that the Lord
had in mind.

Jesus made it clear that the measure of our success is
not found in the abundance of the material things that we
are able to accumulate. The riches that count are those things
that make us rich toward God. Jesus said, "My meat is to do
the will of him that sent me, . . ." (John 4:34), and Jesus is our
pattern of success.

Thomas Carlyle made an excellent statement applying
to this parable when he pointed out that a man's religion is
the most important thing about him. That is what he believes

in, and stands for, and works at, and aspires to, and sets his heart on. If religion is the most important thing about a man, then our religious talents are the ones that we should be most concerned about strengthening and who can think of a more splendid and worthwhile talent than the religious talent?

I thought about this some time ago when a stranger called on the telephone and asked if he and his wife might come in and talk with me about a great tragedy that had recently taken place in their family, when their only daughter had just met her death under the wheels of a speeding automobile. When they came they asked me if I would talk to them about religion and explain to them something about the meaning of life and the purpose of death, and what their relationship should now be with each other and with their daughter. They wanted to know, was there a God, and what was meant by eternal life, and what were the advantages of them trying to live on. So oppressive was this great calamity in their lives that they seemed as though they could not get their breath, that they were smothering. They had been more than ordinarily successful in their material efforts, but all at once material things had lost their importance. They were well-informed and very capable in a great many ways, but their most splendid and worthwhile talent had been buried in the ground.

For over two and one-half hours I tried as hard as I could to help them with their problem. But there wasn't very much that I could do because there wasn't any place to begin. To quote the word of the Lord didn't mean anything. It was not that they particularly disbelieved in God, their skepticism went much deeper than that. They just hadn't thought about him one way or the other. It wasn't that they particularly disbelieved in eternal life, up to that point they hadn't cared. And then death had stepped across their threshold and taken the best-loved personality there. And then all of a sudden, right now, they needed great faith in God and couldn't find it.

Everyone of *us* is also walking straight into death, but whether we are preparing for life or death, one of the most important lessons to be learned is that we must earn the right to a blessing before we receive it. One can't just snap his fingers and get great faith in God any more than he can snap his fingers and get great musical ability or great financial skill. The religious talent like all other talents must first be born, then developed in advance of the need. For example, if you would like to have a Doctor's Degree at age 26, you had better start going to school at about age 6. If you would like to be a great football player in college, you had better work at it a little bit in high school. For the same reasons, if you would like to have great faith to meet the crises of life, you had better earn the right to have it before the crisis arises, because you can't postpone a crisis while you prepare for it.

I was recently talking about some of these things with a friend of mine. He shrugged his shoulders and said, "But I am just not religious." The shrug meaning that "there is nothing I can do about it." In trying to help him I said, "Bill, I'm sure that what you say is true, that you are not religious. But have you ever thought about the circumstances that brought that situation about? How could you ever hope to be religious? You don't go to church; you don't study the scriptures; you don't pray to God; you don't think about him one way or the other. You have not earned the right to be religious."

I told him a story that I had heard about a little boy. Someone asked this little boy. "Who gave you that black eye?" The little boy said, "No one gave me that black eye; I had to fight for it."

Neither black eyes nor great talents ever just happen to people. Neither is the most productive and worthwhile of all the talents merely left on our doorstep free of charge without any effort on our part.

Probably the most vigorous censure ever expressed by Jesus is that recorded in the account of the parable of the talents, and it was directed toward the unprofitable servant who hid his lord's money in the ground. What will be God's attitude toward us if we are guilty of the same sin, and what should we do about it?

I told my friend about a little toy clown that I saw at Christmas time. It was a little plastic figure with a lead weight in the crown of his head that could always be depended upon to bring him to an upside-down position. That is, if you laid him on his back, he would immediately flip up on his head. If you stood him on his feet, he would promptly reverse the position and light on his head. But isn't that just exactly what we all do? We place weights on our interests and then we respond accordingly.

My unreligious friend was tremendously interested in athletics. He spent his Sundays and leisure time in reading about or participating in some kind of athletic event. He was very proud of the fact that he could quote the batting averages of every important major league baseball player in the United States. And then he confessed to me that he could not quote one single verse from the word of the Lord. He justified the situation by shrugging his shoulders and saying, "I am just not religious."

Someone said, "I never put religion out of my mind, I was so open-minded that it fell out." Like my friend, he had merely buried his most valuable talents in the ground. A terrible responsibility always accompanies this tremendous thing that we call our free agency. We ourselves are presently determining what we will become. If we choose we may build bars in our homes instead of altars. We may train ourselves to be more interested in a horse race or a prize fight than in God or the celestial kingdom. When we stand before the eternal judgment bar of God to find out what we have become, then we may better understand that what we think about, and work at, and believe in, and develop an appetite for, are the most important things about us.

Someone may argue that the loss of just *one* talent may not be very important, but that was all that the slothful servant had. And in the final analysis what will we have besides our religious talent when we stand before God? Is our most profitable course, therefore, to spend our time memorizing the baseball batting scores or the Dow-Jones' averages of the stock market, and hope that our religious talent will take care of itself? We are sometimes affected in matters of religion with the same kind of romanticism that frequently influences our courtship. Many people wait to fall into religion like some people fall in love. They wait for it to come like a bolt from the blue accurately aimed at them without any effort on their part. Then they may feel that when they have fallen in love, all of their worries are over, their problems are permanently solved, and their prayers have all been answered, and there is nothing left for them to do. This philosophy is like the old sectarian doctrine of being saved in one effortless swoop. Certainly the religious talent is not developed or increased that easily.

More than about anything else we need to understand that the development of our talents is in our own hands. We may multiply their number and power by exercise, or we may take the alternative and bury them in the ground. But we should remember that there is no growth in the grave. *Disuse* is as mortal a sin as abuse. For example, how long would it take for your business to go on the rocks if you continually neglected it? And when we persist in sending all of the sap and energy of our effort into our money-making glands, or when we invest our energies in the pursuit of pleasure and let our religious arteries lie flat and empty, we demonstrate our unfitness to possess, and use the Lord's money, and as a consequence we soon hear life say of us,

"Take the talent from him and give it to him that has ten talents."

Certainly we cannot expect a well-rounded, symmetrical life when we leave our most important talent inactive and unused. It is the undeviating law of life that only those faculties grow that are put to effective use. Only brain cells that are exercised develop power. Only the personality traits that are given attention are increased in value. By disuse we may assign our most splendid talents to their deathbed while our coarser instincts can be promoted to tremendous size and influence by being indulged, supported and given nourishment and encouragement. As eating increases the appetite, so our action enlarges our inclinations. Our destiny is not in the hands of fate, it is in our hands, and as Paul once said, "How shall we escape, if we neglect so great a salvation? . . ." (Heb. 2:3), and we might repeat and ask ourselves, How indeed? Someone once asked this question, "How would you like to create your own mind?" But isn't that exactly what we do? The mind is made up by what it feeds upon. What the serpent eats becomes serpent, what the tiger eats becomes tiger, and what we think about and work at and fight for is what we will become. We must not let the aspirations of our souls toward God wither and become extinct so that our faculties will cease to find relish in spiritual things. If we do, our minds will turn away and seek other interests and other attachments. When we hide our religious talent in the ground, we bring about our own downfall. This is the same procedure that has brought about the destruction of many of the world's great civilizations of the past. It is this procedure that causes innumerable apostasies from God and the consequent loss of our blessings.

The negation of this religious talent is one of the most common and destructive forms of idolatry. By this process of default we raise our own altars to the unknown God, not because we deny God, what we really deny is activity. We seal our own fate by the sin of our neglect.

By a vigorous program of religious activities we may keep from our hearts the spiritual loneliness of that dread confession, "I am not religious." Twice during the parable of the talents the Master said, "Well done, thou good and faithful servant; thou hast been faithful over a few things, I will make thee ruler over many things: enter thou into the joy of thy Lord." What a great blessing we may receive at the hands of our religious talent.

Repentance

IN APRIL 12, 1912, the great ocean liner, Titanic, set out on its maiden voyage from South Hampton, England bound for the New York Harbor with some of the most important people of both continents on board. This great ocean liner cost over 10 million dollars to build. It was an unheard of marvel of ocean-going construction, the finest vessel that had ever been built up to that time. It was called a "city afloat." Its great steel sides of unheard-of thickness caused it to be referred to as unsinkable. It was the herald of a new day when the Titanic started on its first voyage to America.

Somewhere in the vicinity of mid-ocean it passed a sister ship returning to England. From this passing friendly ship the Titanic received a wireless message that at a certain distance ahead, the Titanic would pass through a region where icebergs had been sighted. Calculating their present speed, it was determined that at 10:40 that night they would be in the vicinity of the ice. At 10:30 they were still going full speed ahead.

There was on the Titanic, as on all similar ships, a place high above the decks called the "crow's nest." Stationed in the crow's nest were look-outs whose duty it was to keep a constant watch of the surrounding waters to note the first approach of any danger or sign of trouble. Shortly after 10:30 p.m. the man in the crow's nest tried to signal to Officer Murdoch in the control room below that something loomed up in the blackness ahead that appeared to be an iceberg. Officer Murdoch was busy with other duties and let the bell go unheeded for the time being. When he finally picked up the message, it was certain that the Titanic was bearing down upon an iceberg. The engines were immediately thrown into reverse, but it was too late, and this great unsinkable ship, this veritable city afloat, crashed upon the ice. For some 2½ hours the Titanic struggled for its life, but its engines were flooded, a gigantic hole had been torn through the ship's steel walls. The insufficient lifeboats were loaded with women and children and put out to sea. In the early morning hours the ship's band sat on the tilting deck and played, "Nearer My God to Thee." And finally the great wounded Titanic gave up the fight, reared up on its prow, and plunged to the bottom of the ocean, with the result that 1400 men lost their lives.

It has been said on good authority that this awful tragedy could have been averted had those in the control room heeded the warning flashed down to them from the look-outs in the crow's nest.

The ill-fated Titanic furnishes us with a striking analogy for the world of our own day. The signals are presently flashing that there are icebergs ahead. We know that other civilizations have crashed and gone to their doom because they failed to heed the divine warning concerning the course they were pursuing.

The dispensation of Jesus opened with the official statement from John the Baptist saying, "Repent ye for the kingdom of heaven is at hand." But those to whom the warning was sent refused to respond to the message, and what could have been a reign of peace and progress with the Son of God at its head became an era of sin and destruction. The people themselves who were involved became a hiss and a byword for future generations, and their disobedience helped to touch off the long spiritual night known as the Dark Ages.

In our own day the Church has been established again upon the earth by divine command. The crow's nest high above the decks has been re-established and reoccupied and again the message is flashing there are icebergs in the darkness ahead and that unless we change our course and choose our way more carefully, we may expect some very serious future trouble. The answer to all of our problems is that we need to know more and do more about obeying the gospel of Jesus Christ.

One of the most important and one of the most wonderful principles of the gospel is the principle of repentance. Repentance is a wonderful term. It is a wonderful idea. It stands for the most praiseworthy action in all of existence. It indicates the discontinuance of a wrong course. It signifies a personal improvement and a turning upward toward things more worthwhile. Repentance is a forerunner of forgiveness. It indicates that under some circumstances the bad may be completely expunged from one's life and record.

The forgiveness that may follow genuine repentance says, ". . . though your sins be as scarlet, they shall be as white as snow; though they be red like crimson, they shall be as wool." (Isa. 1:18) Who can think of anything more wonderful than that? Repentance offers hope; it means a second chance and a new start on a clean page. In some way that we do not fully understand, Christ took upon himself the sins of the world upon conditions of repentance. He suffers for our transgressions. He takes over the liabilities and leaves us the assets free and clear. He personally pays the debt of our sins.

But in addition to repentance being one of the most wonderful ideas in the world, it is also one of the most misunderstood. Isn't it strange that the thing that we dislike to hear talked about more than about anything else is repentance, when that is the very principle by which most of our blessings may be brought about? When people mention repentance, we think they are scolding us and we close our ears. We don't like to have anyone point out to us that the course we are following is heading us into the icebergs. When someone tells us of our fault, we usually hug the fault even closer to ourselves while we take serious offense at the one that would have saved us from it. If we refuse the warning, then like the Titanic we soon come to the time when it is too late for repentance, and we must deal with disaster.

Suppose that we could not repent. Suppose that we think of that time when we will have passed the point of no return and will have lost the ability to make use of repentance as a means of getting rid of our sins. Speaking of this time the great Prophet Mormon said, "And then cometh the judgment of the Holy One upon them; and then cometh the time that he that is filthy shall be filthy still." (Mor. 9:14) Quite likely we will then think that the most delightful privilege in the world would be the opportunity to discuss repentance and put its fruits in force in our lives!

Sometime ago while touring the Northern States Mission, I found myself one hot August afternoon in Southern Illinois. The heat was very oppressive, the humidity was terrible, and I was sticky and dirty and sweaty and as generally uncomfortable as I ever remember of being. That night after the day's work was finished, I was taken to an air-conditioned hotel where a reservation had been made. I took a warm bath and put on fresh, clean clothing. A little later I got into a bed between cool, clean, fresh white sheets, and for a few moments before going to sleep I lay there and thought about repentance. And I thought that if it could be this pleasant to cleanse the body of a little sticky perspiration, what would it be like to cleanse the mind and the soul of guilt and stand clean and pure before God.

Then I tried to imagine what it would be like to lose the ability to repent. The Book of Mormon Prophet Alma asks this challenging question. He said, "Can ye imagine yourselves brought before the tribunal of God with your souls filled with guilt and remorse, having a perfect remembrance of all your wickedness . . . that ye have set at defiance the commandments of God?" (Alma 5:18) For most people the answer to that question is "No." We can't imagine that kind of a situation because we don't try. We think of repentance as unpleasant, and we don't like to think about unpleasant things, but they don't cease to exist merely because they are ignored.

There are *some* religious groups who have a wiser procedure for dealing with this situation. Instead of burying their heads in the sand and hiding from repentance they do what they call "whipping the flesh." That is, they torture themselves in various ways with the thought in mind that a little suffering now may so center their minds on repentance that it will help them to avoid a lot of suffering later on. That is a pretty good idea; it helps us to visualize a Godly sorrow for sin and gives us a great advantage in working out our eternal exaltation.

The scriptures speak of *many* unpleasant things that are all very important for us to understand. The inspired record tells us of outer darkness. It tells of weeping and wailing and gnashing of teeth. But that isn't the kind of reading that we like to do, and few teachers dare to talk to us about it for fear of giving offense. But by this means we lose what is probably the greatest opportunity of our lives. Repentance must be a wonderful thing or the Lord himself would not have spent so much time talking about it.

There are only two ways to get rid of sin. One is by repentance, and the other is by suffering, and we may have our choice. One of the greatest of all the scriptural passages is found in section 19 of the Doctrine and Covenants, in which the Lord himself said, "And surely every man must repent or suffer, . . ." He said, "For behold, I, God, have suffered these things for all, that they might not suffer if they would repent; But if they would not repent, they must suffer even as I; Which suffering caused myself, even God, the greatest of all, to tremble because of pain, and to bleed at every pore, and suffer both body and spirit—and would that I might not drink of the bitter cup, and shrink—" (D & C 19:4, 16-18)

We may not like to read or hear about unpleasant things, but it is a lot more pleasant to find out about the consequences of sin from the word of the Lord than from our own personal experience. Jesus probably talked about hell and suffering as much as he did about heaven and happiness. In discussing these things he is trying to help us to produce in our own hearts a Godly sorrow for sin that will lead us to a reformation of life.

One of the great men of the scriptures was King Benjamin, the Nephite prophet. Just before he died he preached a wonderful sermon. It was based on a message given to him by an angel. The angel told King Benjamin of the blessed and happy eternal state of those who keep the commandments of God. He also told of the unhappy condition of those who remained unrepentant. Among other things he said, "Therefore if that man repenteth not, and remaineth and dieth an enemy to God, the demands of divine justice do awaken his immortal soul to a lively sense of his own guilt, which doth cause him to shrink from the presence of the Lord, and doth fill his breast with guilt, and pain, and anguish, which is like an unquenchable fire, whose flame ascendeth up forever and ever." (Mosiah 2:38) Continuing he said, "And if they be evil they are consigned to an awful view of their own guilt and abominations, which doth cause them to shrink from the presence of the Lord into a state of misery and endless torment, from whence they can no more return; therefore they have drunk damnation to their souls." (Mosiah 3:25)

King Benjamin closed his famous sermon by saying, "O man, remember, and perish not." (Mosiah 4:30)

Alma describes what the pains of sin may be like even in this life. He says, "And . . . Zeezrom lay sick at Sidom, with a burning fever, which was caused by the great tribulation of his mind on account of his wickedness . . . and his many other sins, did harrow up his mind until it did become exceeding sore, having no deliverance: therefore he began to be scorched with a burning heat." (Alma 15:3)

What then might it be like if we were required to endure the pains of hell throughout eternity? Someday we must give an account of our lives.

Alma says, "For our words will condemn us, yea, all our works will condemn us; . . . and our thoughts will also condemn us; and in this awful state we shall not dare to look up to our God; and we would fain be glad if we could command the rocks and the mountains to fall upon us to hide us from his presence." (Alma 12:14)

Repentance is the way to avoid evil consequences. It is the gateway to all good. It is the beginning of happiness. On one occasion the Lord said, "Say nothing but repentance to this generation." And the prophets have always made this great principle the burden of their cry. Alma says, "O, that I were an angel and could have the wish of my heart, that I might go forth and speak with the trump of God with a voice to shake the earth and cry repentance unto every people." The Prophet Mormon said, "And I would that I could persuade all ye ends of the earth to repent, and to prepare to stand before the judgment seat of Christ."

Forty-nine years ago this week, 1400 men lost their mortal lives because those in the engine room of the Titanic failed to respond to the signals of those in the crow's nest. Other thousands are going to their doom every year because they fail to heed the warning of those servants of God who tell us to repent of our sins.

May God touch our hearts and help us to hear and understand his great message of repentance that we may not repeat the tragedies of the past.

Retribution

THE STORY is told of a group of the ancients who had a very interesting way of punishing crime. For example, if one became a murderer, his punishment was to be chained to the corpse of his victim. There was no way that he could possibly disentangle himself from the result of his evil deed. Wherever he went forevermore, he must drag with him the dead body of the one whose life he had taken. If at a later date he should kill again, another corpse would be added to his oppressive burden. Such a punishment would be immediately dreadful, but its horror would increase as time passed. The murderer would therefore have to endure a far more serious torment and a greater loss of freedom than if he were incarcerated in the most confining dungeon. He would never be able to get away from his crime, nor could he ever qualify again for the society of other people, for even the worst criminals would not now tolerate his presence as he came dragging his awful load behind him.

Such punishment seems so severe that it is difficult to imagine, and yet life has a plan of retribution that is exactly akin to it. That is, we are always chained to the wrong that we do. For example, if one violates the laws of temperance, a ruinous, driving thirst attaches itself to push him farther and farther down the road to despair. Everyone has seen the pitiful struggles of some poor alcoholic trying to free himself from the monstrous thing that has fastened itself upon him. By his own act he chains himself to his fate as he sentences himself forevermore to endure the unimaginable terrors of alcoholism. His sin then robs him of his material resources, alienates his family, drives away his friends, destroys his will, and throughout his life he must drag behind him the putrefying corpse of his own wrong.

This horrible law of retribution operates in every field. The punishment of one who doesn't study is that he is chained to his ignorance, and he must drag this embarrassing burden with him whenever he goes. He cannot lay it aside even for one hour of freedom and as "no man can be saved in ignorance" so his sin will eventually destroy even his eternal exaltation.

The sentence of one who tells lies is that he must eventually become a liar, and everyone will be able to tell him for what he is. The moment any sin is indulged the habit begins to bury itself in the personality, and it is not long before it cannot be dislodged, cast aside or ignored.

The sentence of one who engages in immoral practices is that he becomes immoral. This poisonous sin imbeds itself in its practitioner and exudes its vile odor wherever he goes. The decaying corpses that were dragged behind the ancients were not more dreadful than the immorality that may eat into our very souls. Yet it is the law that every evil that we commit becomes a part of us. One of the biggest problems confronting any murderer comes in getting rid of the body. This problem is far more difficult for the sinner, as every sinner is chained to his sin. It becomes more and more difficult to win in the race for success as we load ourselves heavier and heavier with the dead bodies of our accumulating sins.

The Apostle Paul was probably thinking of this ancient custom when he cried out to the Romans, "O wretched man that I am! who shall deliver me from the body of this death?" (Romans 7:24) And we might echo the cry and ask, who indeed? Who can free us from the undesirable personality traits that we ourselves develop? Who can free us from our poisonous thoughts and our negative attitudes once we have securely chained them to ourselves? The governor can pardon the murderer, but who can restore the dead to life? God can forgive us our sins, but who can separate us from our sloth, our disobedience, our bad habits and our despair? The chains of habit are too light to be felt until they are too strong to be broken. They may begin as cobwebs, but they always end as iron chains.

We have seen the ravages of lung cancer as it has wrecked its havoc upon those who have embraced the cigarette habit. Our first association with nicotine seems like just a bad habit. But as it is indulged, the chains begin to form, and soon we find that we are chained together often until death do us part. Every sin sticks; bad habits stick. Not only does the nicotine stick to the lungs, the discoloration sticks to the fingers, the smell sticks to the breath, the craving sticks, the damage sticks, the cough sticks, and the disobedience sticks.

As the indulgence is continued the chains get stronger, the burden gets heavier, the patient gets weaker, the smell gets worse, and soon in accordance with this ancient law of retribution one finds himself chained to the loathsome corpse of his evil. The law never fails. It is never set aside. The only way to avoid the result is to stay clear of the cause.

The results of this natural law operate even beyond the boundaries of this life. In his *Christmas Carol*, Charles Dickens tells about the partnership of Ebenezer Scrooge and Jacob Morley. Both partners were stingy, money-grubbing old men who had thought negatively on some of the important issues of life until they had become what they thought. One Christmas Eve Jacob Morley died and exactly seven years later, on the Christmas Eve anniversary of his death, his spirit paid a visit to his former partner, Scrooge. Morley's spirit came up the stairs dragging behind him the fetters with which he had encumbered himself before his death. In explanation he said to Ebenezer, "I wear the chains I forged in life."

But that is exactly what everyone does, and he need not wait until he dies to feel the burden of their oppressive weight. Our chains are forged in the position in which they are to be worn so that we get used to them gradually. Before we become aware of any discomfort they have become too strong to be broken. Then after we are unable to free ourselves they begin their fearful oppression. If you don't think a bad habit can get power, just try to break one sometime. Our experience with this law should teach us caution. For example, it has been said that there are only two classes of liquor drinkers, those who *could* quit if they would, and those who *would* quit if they could. We should be particularly careful in selecting the chains we wrap ourselves in, for we will probably be wearing them for a long time; in many cases even reaching throughout eternity.

It is a little bit startling to realize that we ourselves continue to court the very things that oppress, punish and enslave us. These habits are not something that we are born with, nor do they come upon us unaware. The evil that we do must be courted before it can get power over us. We can easily learn in advance the dreadful control that nicotine, alcohol, or dope can get over us. Yet we deliberately choose that which will bring destruction upon us. The same principle operates against us as we bind ourselves with the chains of dishonesty, disobedience, lethargy and spiritual disease. We can fashion the strongest chains very quickly. We can fasten them upon ourselves almost without realizing what we are doing. But one of the responsibilities of every human being is to understand this terrible law of retribution that continually watches over the world of men like an unseen avenger to make sure that no sin shall go unpunished.

The dictionary says that retribution is the impartial infliction of punishment. This natural retribution is like a great invisible police force. It never quits. It never makes a mistake. It always gets its man. No guilty person ever gets away. This relentless, sleepless, merciless unseen policeman accepts no gifts and hears no prayers. It is not deceived. There is no court of appeals and no one to soften the verdict. The only law it knows is that every sentence must be carried out according to the law that every wrong of which one is guilty shall be incarnated in the doer. Then from its place of vantage the sin carries out a terrible vengeance against the perpetrator. The penalty is always far out of proportion to any benefit or satisfaction received. We tell ourselves that crime does not pay, and yet we sometimes live as though it was our most profitable enterprise. Every crime that we commit is against ourselves. The thief always steals most from himself. He robs himself of his peace of mind, his self-respect, and his own freedom.

One man spent a total of 34 years in Ohio State Penitentiary for robberies which he had committed. Yet the most money he ever obtained at any one time was $60.12. But in addition to his loss of freedom, he was also punished by his loss of associations, his loss of opportunities; and his crimes continued to punish him even in the periods while he was outside of the penitentiary where he was robbed of his prestige, the trust of his fellow men and the pride and respectability of his family. Most of the goods that thieves steal are insured, and the losses to the one robbed are insignificant, but the losses to the robber are always tremendous.

Sometime ago the press announced the arrest of a kidnapper who had held his victim a prisoner for 18 days in an old abandoned house. But the kidnapper was sentenced to serve 30 years in a federal prison in addition to the other more serious losses.

A soldier who sleeps at his post for 15 minutes may be sentenced to a lifetime of disgrace, imprisonment or even death. He may cause an untold loss of life to his fellow soldiers and disaster to his country. No conceivable satisfaction gained for 15 minutes of sleep could compensate him for the penalties that he initiates. There is a small chance that a criminal may never be caught by the law, but there is no chance at all that he will be able to evade this natural retribution. We are not only punished *for* our sins, we are also punished *by* our sins, and we are punished in so many ways, including penalties that are physical, mental, social, spiritual and financial. And in addition, we are punished over and over again. In fact, in her accounts with men retribution never closes her books. This law is not just interested in those guilty of *great* crimes, evil is still evil even when taken in small doses. Jesus said, "For every idle word that man shall speak, he shall give an account thereof in the day of judgment." We are even punished for the evil thoughts we think, as every thought incarnates itself and then proceeds to carry out its terrible vengeance against us, giving us negative minds, depraved minds, split personalities, guilt complexes, nervous breakdowns, and even insanity.

Shakespeare's Lady Macbeth thrust a dagger into the heart of the sleeping King Duncan while he was a guest in her home. No one knew of her evil deed, yet immediately Lady Macbeth was chained to her sin. The thoughts of her crime lodged themselves in her mind and a dreadful punishment began. It was continued without mercy until it sent her insane. She washed her hands a thousand times trying to get Duncan's blood off her hands, but the uncleanness was not on her hands, it was on her conscience and in her heart, where it is far more difficult to get at.

But that is the pattern of punishment followed whether the sin is great or small. No one needs a recording angel to look over his shoulder to take note of our sins, because everything that we do and everything that we think becomes a part of what we are. Then when the X-ray is turned on anyone will be able to recognize us for what we have become.

Just think of the terrible consequences inflicted upon us when indifference, indecision and sloth imbed themselves like a lot of poisonous wood ticks in our flesh to take away our success, ruin our health, destroy our happiness, rob us of our prestige, self-respect and even our place in the presence of

God. The state makes laws to prevent us from injuring other people, but who can ever stand between us and ourselves?

Someone prayed, "Great God, I ask thee for no meaner pelf than that I may not disappoint myself."

Shakespeare said, "To thine ownself be true, and it must follow as the night the day, thou canst not then be false to any man." The gospel is a program for being true to ourselves. It counsels us against every evil. God cannot look upon sin with the least degree of allowance. (D & C 1:31) And God, himself, has advised that no unclean thing can dwell in his presence. This gives us the basis for real success in our lives. The law of the ancients is still in force and its punishment has lost none of its dreadfulness, for who can imagine the horror of dragging our foul load of sin into the presence of God? May our Father in heaven help us to keep all evil out of our lives.

Serendipity

MANY YEARS ago Horace Walpole wrote an interesting story entitled "The Three Princes of Serendip." Serendip was a part of the ancient kingdom of Ceylon, and in their travels the three princes were always finding important things for which they were not directly in search. As a result of this story a new word came into existence called "serendipity." Its purpose was to convey to our understanding this interesting idea that many of the most worthwhile things of life come to us through a kind of indirection. That is, Columbus started out to find the East Indies, and he discovered America instead. Horace Mann said, "If any man seeks for greatness, let him forget greatness and seek for truth, and he will find both."

Happiness itself is in large measure a kind of by-product and is very seldom obtained by direct pursuit. We may find happiness indirectly in our work, but sometimes when we quit our work to add to our happiness, we frequently lose that which we already have. The sweetest friendships are usually those that are not deliberately courted, but rather the ones that come as a result of something else. Often when we woo a thing too conscientiously or make our attack too direct, we seem to frighten it so that it escapes us.

We see the operation of this principle in many places. It appears in our personal affairs, in our work, in education, and in our lives generally. Sir Alexander Fleming, the discoverer of penicillin recently spoke of "serendipity in science." He pointed out that most of the wonder drugs were discovered while the discoverer was looking for something else.

It is interesting that one of the best ways to rest, is to

work harder and more effectively. Someone once remarked to Abraham Lincoln that he looked tired and that he should take things a little easier. The President replied that it was his heart that was tired, and in order to rest his heart he must go on at an accelerated pace. A job is always the hardest when we work at it the easiest. An automobile uses much more gasoline per mile when running at four miles per hour than at 40 miles per hour. When you are ahead of your job you love it, when your job is ahead of you you hate it. No one ever seems to get tired while he is ahead. No athletic team ever loses interest while it is winning.

On the other hand, work soon becomes a drudgery to anyone when he begins to drop behind in his accomplishment. It has been said that the tired businessman is the one whose business is not successful. Weariness is often increased as one begins to slow down, and the most tiresome thing in the world is complete inactivity. Constructive, worthwhile work does not produce weariness, rather it makes us more buoyant and vigorous.

In harmony with this idea Jesus said, "Take my yoke upon you and learn of me . . . and ye shall find rest unto your souls." To take his yoke upon us in the best sense is probably the most stimulating, energizing restful experience in our lives. In fact the most important manifestation of this process of indirection is what we might call "serendipity in religion." The classical statement of which was made by Jesus himself when he said, "He that findeth his life shall lose it: and he that loseth his life for my sake shall find it." (Matt. 10:39) To forget one's self and lose one's self in the work of the Lord is the most likely way to find one's self and one's real success and happiness. Henry Van Dyke put one phase of this idea into verse saying:

> He who seeks heaven alone to save his soul
> May keep the path but will not reach the goal.
> But he who walks in love may wander far;
> God will bring him where the blessed are.

It may sometimes be a little hazardous to make a direct assault upon the gates of heaven for the sake of the reward itself. And one who spends too much time in self-seeking, trying to find his life, frequently loses it. The shortest distance between two points is not always a straight line. We may reach heaven sooner, if with hearts full of love we go out of our way and work in the interests of others. As someone has said, just "tow your brother's boat across and lo, your own has reached the shore."

James Russell Lowell gives an interesting expression to this idea in his story of the vision of Sir Launfal. There was an old tradition in King Arthur's time that Joseph of Arimathea had brought to England the cup from which Jesus and the apostles drank at the last supper. The tradition had it that to whoever this holy vessel was revealed was given power to bring great blessings upon himself and country. Sir Launfal, one of Arthur's most chivalrous knights, made a vow that he would never cease his search until he had seen the Holy Grail. Then mounted on his most beautiful charger, clad in his richest mail, wearing his golden spurs, with his heart filled with ambition, he set out to search in all climes for the Holy Grail. As he passed over the drawbridge, he was aware of a leper who crouched by the gate asking alms. Sir Launfal tossed him a piece of gold in scorn.

That night Sir Launfal had a vision in which he spent his life in a fruitless search. But during this long period he learned humility, purity of heart, and the meaning of unselfish service. Years passed, and when he finally returned, old and gray, it was winter and Christmas time. As he was turned away from what had once been his own castle, he saw another leper lying at the gate.

> To the leper Sir Launfal said "—I behold in thee
> An image of him who died on the tree;
> Thou also hast had thy crown of thorns,
> Thou also hast known the world's buffets and scorns,

"And to thy life were not denied
The wounds in thy hands and feet and side;
Mild Mary's Son, acknowledge me;
Behold, through him, I give to Thee!"

The heart in Sir Launfal was ashes and dust,
He parted in twain his single crust.
He broke the ice on the streamlet's brink
And gave the leper to eat and drink.

'Twas a mouldy crust of course brown bread,
'Twas water out of a wooden bowl,
Yet with fine wheaten bread was the leper fed
And 'twas red wine, he drank with his thirsty soul.

As Sir Launfal mused with a downcast face,
A light shone round about the place;
The leper no longer crouched at his side,
But stood before him glorified.
And with a voice that was calmer than silence, said
"Lo, it is I, be not fraid!

In many climes, without avail,
Thou hast spent thy life for the Holy Grail;
Behold it is here—this cup which thou
Didst fill at the streamlet for me but now."

Sir Launfal found the Holy Grail only after he had lost himself.

There are many things that we might learn from this idea of losing ourselves. The right spirit in which to pay our tithing is not merely that of a good businessman seeking a greater return, but rather to help others, to be obedient, and to serve God. Then the windows of heaven are opened, and a blessing is poured out, overflowing our ability to receive it. (Mal. 3:10) By this same kind of indirection we find character, Godliness, and God himself. The princes of Serendip themselves didn't discover so many unexpected worthwhile things as does the honest seeker after truth who loves to serve God and keep his commandments.

One of the best illustrations of this interesting idea is given in the fourteenth chapter of Matthew. On one occasion many people had gone into the desert to hear Jesus. The record said, "And Jesus went forth, and saw a great multitude, and was moved with compassion toward them, and he healed their sick. And when it was evening, his disciples came to him, saying, This is a desert place, and the time is now past; send the multitude away, that they may go into the villages, and buy themselves victuals. But Jesus said unto them, They need not depart; give ye them to eat. And they say unto him, we have here but five loaves, and two fishes. He said, Bring them hither to me. And he commanded the multitude to sit down on the grass, and took the five loaves, and the two fishes, and looking up to heaven, he blessed, and brake, and gave the loaves to his disciples, and the disciples to the multitude. And they did all eat, and were filled: and they took up of the fragments that remained twelve baskets full. And they that had eaten were about five thousand men, beside women and children." (Matt. 14:14-21)

The people came seeking instruction, but in addition their bodies were healed and their hunger was satisfied. But even after all had eaten they had more food left over than when they began.

This miracle points out the wonder of religion. We not only receive many blessings that we do not expect, but they come to us multiplied, some ten, some a hundred, and some a thousandfold. Those who swear allegiance to Christ only for the sake of the loaves and the fishes are not really true to him. After feeding the 5,000, large crowds followed Jesus, but he said to them, "Verily, verily, I say unto you, Ye seek me . . . because ye did eat of the loaves, and were filled." (John 6:26) Then he pointed out this divine law of success saying, "Labour not for the meat which perisheth, but for that meat which endureth unto everlasting life, . . . (John 6:27) By this procedure God has not only promised us spiritual blessings but has also said that the fulness of the earth may be ours. (D & C 59:16)

In many ways religion reacts upon our lives like an

atomic breeder which produces more fuel than it consumes. The harder we work, the easier our work is, and the more vigorous *we* become. Like a self-winding watch, we wind ourselves up by our own motion. Even life itself is involved in a kind of "serendipity." That is, we live to die, and then we die to live. Jesus suffered death that we might have life. We spend our lives that we might have it more abundantly. The more we give of ourselves, the more we have left. Jesus fed the multitude and had more food when he finished than when he began.

But that kind of result is not peculiar to this particular miracle. Every service in the church re-enacts the miracle of the loaves and the fishes. When one gives of himself in teaching others, he always ends up with more than he had before. When one renders any worthy, uplifting service without thought of reward, he always finds a greater reward than he would have expected; and in addition, he takes up his twelve baskets full of both spiritual and material blessings. When anyone undertakes to develop the abilities of others, he himself becomes more capable. When one labors to promote a brother's spiritual welfare, he finds his own feet more securely planted upon the roadway of eternal life.

In King Benjamin's last great discourse he pointed out that God had created us and therefore we were indebted to him. Then when we keep his commandments, he immediately blesses us so that our debt is greater than before. Therefore, how can even the most valiant fail to receive more than he deserves?

Serendipity works best when the traveler keeps himself on the right road. It was the particular course that Jesus followed that made his life so productive. Then to help his disciples to qualify for these same blessings, Jesus said to them, "Are ye able to drink of the cup that I shall drink of?" That is also our question. Are we able? Are we able to lose ourselves in doing good? Are we able to serve effectively?

Are we able to maintain the right spirit in ourselves? Are we as willing to drink of his cup as we are to eat of his loaves?

The most wonderful surprises are reserved for those who are "able" to *drain* the cup. What could be more thrilling than to travel the straight and narrow way of duty which God himself has marked out. Then we will find the happiness of a well-spent life and the riches of eternity in addition.

Apostle Paul indicated that this principle of serendipity continues beyond this life. He wrote this thrilling line to the Corinthians, "Eye hath not seen, nor ear heard, neither have entered into the heart of man, the things which God hath prepared for them that love him." (I Cor. 2:9) We can imagine some wonderful things. We can imagine elegance, comfort, convenience, beauty and luxury costing billions of dollars, but we cannot even imagine the things that God hath prepared to delight us upon our arrival in his kingdom. Here is serendipity at its best.

In imagination I can see the three princes of Serendip as they go happily on their way, constantly discovering valuable things and finding pleasant situations for which they did not seek. But who can even imagine the joys of traveling on that royal highway of eternal progression to qualify as princes of the kingdom of God and be crowned with endless happiness and eternal life.

The Seven Days before the Tomb

URING THE last few weeks of the Savior's life the antagonism of his adversaries became so severe that he withdrew from Jerusalem and went some twenty miles north into an isolated place called Ephraim, and there he instructed the disciples upon whom the full burden of the ministry was soon to fall. (John 11:54)

When he emerged again into the public notice, it was to begin his solemn march toward Jerusalem and the cross. He said to his disciples, "Behold, we go up to Jerusalem, and all things that are written by the prophets concerning the Son of man shall be accomplished. For he shall be delivered unto the Gentiles, and shall be mocked, and spitefully entreated, and spitted on: And they shall scourge him, and put him to death: and the third day he shall rise again." (Luke 18:31-33)

Jesus arrived in Bethany a short distance from Jerusalem on Friday evening, the beginning of the Sabbath. He was to spend the last week of his mortal life in the home of his good friends, Martha, Mary and Lazarus. Over this last Sabbath of the Lord's life the gospel writers have drawn a reverent veil of silence. Saturday evening after the Sabbath was over, a supper was spread for Jesus and the Twelve. This was an event never to be forgotten. From among her treasures Mary had brought forth an alabaster cruse containing a pound of costly ointment. She poured its fragrant contents upon the head and feet of her Lord, wiping his feet with her loosened tresses. When Judas objected to this apparent waste, Jesus rebuked him and said, "Let her alone: against the day of my burying hath she kept this." (John 12:1-7)

Early the next morning on Sunday, the first day of the week, Jesus with his disciples, started toward Jerusalem. A colt was obtained on which Jesus rode in the midst of his followers. They were joined along the way by other groups of travelers going into the holy city for the Passover. Soon a great crowd was following, and the people were jubilant over the spectacle of Jesus leading this multitude toward the holy city. They spread out their garments and cast palm branches and other foliage in his path, thus carpeting the way as for the passing of a king, and for the time being he was their king. The voices of the multitudes sounded in reverberating harmony, "Blessed be the King that cometh in the name of the Lord: . . ." (Luke 19:38) But amidst all of this jubilation Jesus was sad. As he came in sight of the great city wherein stood his Father's house he wept because of the wickedness of the people. (Luke 19:41-44)

When he rode through the massive portal and actually entered the capital, someone inquired who he was, and the multitude shouted, "This is Jesus the prophet of Nazareth of Galilee." (Matt. 21:11) Dismounting he entered the temple enclosure where shouts of adulation greeted him. But this was no accidental happening, no meaningless pageantry, it was the actual advent of the King into his royal city as the prophets had foretold. (Zech. 9:9) He came riding on an ass in token of peace, acclaimed by the hosanna shouts of the multitudes.

On that particular first day of the week many interesting things happened in the temple, crowded as it was with the Passover multitude. Certain Greeks came seeking an interview saying, ". . . we would see Jesus." (John 12:21) To them Jesus testified that the hour of his death was near at hand. They were surprised and pained at the Lord's words. Jesus himself sorrowed deeply saying, "Now is my soul troubled." Then he prayed and said, "Father, glorify thy name. Then came there a voice from heaven, saying, I have both glorified it and will glorify it again." (John 12:27-28) The people who were standing by heard the voice and gave it various interpretations. Some said an angel had spoken unto him. To those who heard, the Lord said, "This voice came not because of me, but for your sakes." (John 12:30)

Sunday night Jesus returned to Bethany to lodge with this humble family that he loved so much. (Mark 11:11) On Monday, the second day of the week, Jesus and the Twelve returned to Jerusalem and sepnt the greater part of the day teaching in the temple. His time was short, it was now only four days until he would hang with outstretched arms above Calvary. It was on this last Monday that he cleared the temple courts of those who sold merchandise. He overthrew the tables of the money changers and upset the seats of them that sold doves. He said, "Is it not written, My house shall be called . . . a house of prayer? but ye have made it a den of thieves." (Mark 11:17)

In clearing the temple he had greatly increased the anger of the chief priests. They had previously decreed his death and had made repeated efforts to take him. And here he was disputing their authority in the very area over which they claimed supreme jurisdiction.

On Monday evening Jesus left the city and again retired to Bethany to lodge. On Tuesday he came again to the temple with the Twelve, and taught the people for the last time. It was on Tuesday that the Lord's public ministry came to its solemn end. It was probably in the late afternoon when he took his final departure from the temple. Whatever of discourse, parable, or ordinance was to follow would be directed only to the further preparation of the apostles.

The course of his last walk from Jerusalem back to Bethany took him across the Mount of Olives. He rested at a convenient spot near the summit from which he had a commanding view of the great city and the magnificent temple, illumined as it must have been by the rays of the declining sun of that eventful April afternoon. He saw before him in fullest splendor a scene made dear to every Jewish heart by the sacred memories of this place. The temple stood upon the spot where ten centuries earlier David had been commanded by an angel to build an altar to Jehovah. It was here that Solomon had built his magnificent temple which had been burned to the ground by the invading hoards from Babylon. It was here that the temple had been rebuilt by Zerubabbel. It was here that the temple of Herod now stood. It was to this place that the Son of God himself had come, and he was now leaving its sacred courts forever. As he rested he was asked some questions concerning the future. He then foretold the destruction of the great temple, the fate of Jerusalem and the end of the world. He foretold his own glorious second coming. (Matt. 24) As he gazed out upon the sacred scene before him he gave with undying eloquence his memorable farewell to Jerusalem saying: "Oh Jerusalem, Jerusalem, thou that killest the prophets, and stonest them which are sent unto thee, how often would I have gathered thy children together, even as a hen gathereth her chickens under her wings, and ye would not! Behold, *your* house is left unto you desolate." (Matt. 23:37-38) But yesterday while clearing the temple he had called it "my house," now their chance had gone and he pronounced their awful doom saying, "Your house is left unto you desolate."

Continuing their journey back to Bethany, Jesus again reminded the Twelve of the fate awaiting him and specified the time of his betrayal and the manner of his death. He said, "Ye know that after two days is the feast of the passover, and the Son of man is betrayed to be crucified." (Matt. 26:2)

While the chief priests were trying to design some way to get him into their hands, Judas Iscariot, sought an audience with them and offered to betray the Lord. He said, "What will ye give me . . . And they covenanted with him for thirty pieces of silver." (Matt. 26:15)

On Thursday evening Jesus sat down with the Twelve for the Last Supper. He said, "I have desired to eat this passover with you before I suffer." It was during this meal that he administered the Sacrament and instituted the washing of feet. (John 13:4-10), Mark 14:22)

After Judas had left the room on his errand of betrayal, Jesus gave an impressive discourse to the Twelve followed by a prayer such as only he could give. (John 13:19-34) Then when they had sung a hymn, Jesus and the Eleven went out into the night. They crossed the ravine of the Cedron, and entered an olive orchard on the slope of Mount Olivet, known as Gethsemane. (John 18:1) He left eight of the apostles near the entrance with the instruction: "Sit ye here, while I go and pray yonder." Accompanied by Peter, James, and John, he went a little farther and was soon enveloped in a sorrow, which appears to have been surprising even to himself, for we read that he "began to be sore amazed, and to be very heavy." Then he said to the three, "My soul is exceedingly sorrowful even unto death: tarry ye here, and watch with me. Then he went a little farther, and fell on his face, and prayed, saying. O my Father, if it be possible, let this cup pass from me: nevertheless not as I will, but as thou wilt." (Matt. 26:38-39)

Later in this agony of his soul he returned and found his most trusted followers asleep. Momentarily aroused from their slumber the three apostles saw the Lord again retire and heard him pleading in agony, "O my Father, if this cup may not pass away from me, except I drink it, thy will be done." Luke tells us that, "There appeared an angel unto him from heaven, strengthening him"; but not even the presence of an angel could dispel the awful anguish of his soul. "And being in an agony he prayed more earnestly: and his sweat was as

it were great drops of blood falling down to the ground."
(Luke 22:43-44)

Christ's agony in the garden is unfathomable by the finite
mind, both as to intensity and cause. His suffering was not
because of any fear of death. Death to him was preliminary
to resurrection and a triumphal return to the Father from
whom he had come, but he groaned under a burden that no
other man could even conceive. It was not physical pain nor
mental anguish alone that caused him to suffer, but a spiritual agony of his soul such as only God was capable of experiencing.

In some manner, incomprehensible to us, the Savior took
upon himself the burden of the sins of mankind from Adam
to the end of the world.

When for the last time Jesus came back to the disciples
left on guard, he said: "Sleep on now, and take your rest:
behold, the hour is at hand, and the Son of man is betrayed
into the hands of sinners." (Matt. 26:45) There was no use
now for further watching; for already the torches of the enemy were observable in the distance. Soon this nocturnal
company intent on his destruction were at hand with Judas
at their head. Jesus surrendered himself voluntarily. Seeing
that resistance was useless the eleven turned and fled. Then
began that long, awful night of trial and sentence.

Pilate finally surrendered to the mob's clamorous demands and issued the order of death by crucifixion between
two thieves. It was nine o'clock on that fateful Friday morning that spikes were cruelly driven through his hands and
feet, securing him to the cross, and over his head was placed
the title, "Jesus of Nazareth, the king of the Jews." (Matt.
27:35-37)

At noon the light of the sun was obscured and darkness
spread over the land. This terrifying gloom continued for a
period of three hours. Then at the ninth hour or at about

three o'clock in the afternoon, a loud voice, surpassing the most anguished cry of physical suffering came from the cross, rending the dreadful darkness saying, "My God, my God, why hast thou forsaken me?" What human mind can fathom the significance of that cry? It seems that in addition to the fearful suffering incident to crucifixion, the awful agony of Gethsemane beyond any human power to endure had recurred. In that most bitter hour the dying Christ seemed alone, in terrible reality. The Father seems to have withdrawn the support of his immediate presence, leaving to the Savior of men the glory of complete victory over the forces of sin and death. His mission in the flesh had now been carried to its glorious consummation and he exclaimed in holy triumph: "It is finished." (John 19:30) Then in resignation, and relief he said, "Father, into thy hands I commend my spirit: . . ." Luke 23:46) Then he bowed his head, and Jesus was dead.

His death was accompanied by other terrifying phenomena. There was a violent earthquake; the rocks of the mighty hills were disrupted, and some said, "Truly this was the Son of God." (Matt. 27:54)

It was now late on Friday afternoon, just seven days from the time he had returned from his temporary retirement. At sunset the Sabbath would begin. Joseph of Arimathea, a secret disciple of Christ, hurriedly removed the body from the cross and laid it in his own tomb, and the earthly ministry of Jesus Christ, the Savior of the world, was at its end.

The Star of Bethlehem

ONE OF THE most important texts in the New Testament is found in the second chapter of Matthew which reads as follows:

"Now when Jesus was born in Bethlehem of Judea in the days of Herod the king, behold, there came wise men from the east to Jerusalem, Saying, Where is he that is born King of the Jews? for we have seen his star in the east, and are come to worship him." (Matt. 2:1-2)

And that is what wise men have been doing ever since. Ever since that day when wise men from the east followed the star that lead them to the manger in Bethlehem, other wise men have also been asking, "Where can we find Jesus? How can we know the Savior?" It is a small wonder that this should be so, for as Luke says, "Neither is there salvation in any other: for there is none other name under heaven given among men, whereby we must be saved. (Acts 4:12)

The journey of the wise men was over when they had found the king, and so is ours. His life represents the main objective in our lives. In our own day the objective has been renewed and the Lord has said, ". . . seek me diligently and ye shall find me . . ." (D & C 88:63) Certainly the greatest tragedy of the world of 1900 years ago, as well as our own world, is found in the large number of people who fail to find the king. Jesus said, "He that seeketh me early shall find me . . ." (D & C 88:83) We fail to find only when we fail to seek. Certainly the greatest discovery ever made is when man discovers his Redeemer.

A great many people have found Jesus at this period of the year when we set aside a whole season in which we open our hearts to commemorate his birth. It is our custom at Christmas time to go back and relive those important events that began 19½ centuries ago when the Angel Gabriel came from God to a virgin in Galilee named Mary. The angel said to her, "The Holy Ghost shall come upon thee, and the power of the Highest shall overshadow thee: therefore also that holy thing which shall be born of thee shall be called the Son of God." (Luke 1:35)

Just before Jesus was born, a decree had gone out from Caesar Augustus that all the world should be taxed. (Luke 2:1) And because everyone was required to go to his own city, Joseph took Mary and traveled some 65 miles from Nazareth in Galilee to Bethlehem of Judea. When they arrived, there was no room available in the inn, and so an improvised lodging was arranged for them in the stable, where Jesus was born.

The announcement of the birth was made by an angel to some shepherds who were tending their flocks upon the neighboring Judean hills. The record says: "And there were in the same country shepherds abiding in the field, keeping watch over their flock by night. And, lo, the angel of the Lord came upon them, and the glory of the Lord shone round about them: and they were sore afraid. And the angel said unto them, Fear not: for, behold, I bring you good tidings of great joy, which shall be to all people. For unto you is born this day in the city of David a Saviour, which is Christ the Lord. And this shall be a sign unto you; Ye shall find the babe wrapped in swaddling clothes, lying in a manger. And suddenly there was with the angel a multitude of the heavenly host praising God, and saying, Glory to God in the highest, and on earth peace, good will toward men." (Luke 2:8-14)

The announcement was also made in several other places to people living greater distances away from Bethlehem. Among these were the wise men from the east mentioned in the text. I would like to present their story which someone has written in verse under the title of,

THE THREE KINGS

Three kings came riding from far away,
Melchior and Casper and Balthazar.
Three wise men of the East were they,
And they traveled by night, and they slept by day,
For their guide was a beautiful, wonderful star.

The star was so beautiful, large and clear
That all the other stars of the sky
Became a white mist in the atmosphere.
And by this they knew that the coming was near
And the Prince foretold in the prophecy.

Three caskets they bore on their saddle bows
Three caskets of gold with golden keys.
Their robes were of crimson, with rows
Of bells and pomegranates and furbelows,
Their turbans like blossoming almond tree.

And so the three kings rode into the west,
Through the dusk of night, over hill and dell,
And sometimes they nodded with beard on breast.
And sometimes they talked, as they paused to rest
With the people they met at some wayside well.

"Of the Child that is born," said Balthazar,
"Good people, we pray you, tell us the news.
For we, in the East, have seen his star,
And have ridden fast and have ridden far
To find and worship the King of the Jews."

But the people answered: 'You ask in vain,
We know of no king but Herod the Great,"
They thought of the wise men as men insane,
As they sped their camels across the plain,
Like riders in haste who could not wait.

And when they came to Jerusalem,
Herod the Great, who had heard this thing,
Sent for the Wise Men and questioned them;
And said, "Go down unto Bethlehem,
And then bring me tidings of this new king."

So they rode away; and the star stood still,
The only one in the gray of morn.
Yes, it stopped—it stood still of its own free will
Right over Bethlehem on the hill
The city of David where Christ was born.

And the three kings rode through the gate and the guard
Through the silent street, till their camels turned
And slowed as they entered the great inn-yard;
But the windows were locked, and the doors were barred,
And only a light in the stable burned.

And cradled there on the scented hay,
In the air made sweet by the breath of kine,
The little Child in the manger lay
The child that would be King one day,
Of a kingdom, not human, but divine.

His Mother, Mary of Nazareth,
Sat watching beside his place of rest,
Watching the even flow of His breath
For the joy of life and the terror of death
Were mingled together in her breast.

They laid their offering at His feet;
The gold was their tribute to a King;
The frankincense, with its odor sweet,
Was for the Priest, the Paraclete;
The myrrh, for the body's burying.

And the mother wondered, and bowed her head,
And sat as still as a statue of stone;
Her heart was troubled, yet comforted,
Remembering what the angel had said
Of an endless reign of David's throne.

Then the kings rode out of the city gate,
With a tramp of hoofs in proud array,
But they went not back to Herod the Great,
For they knew his malice and feared his hate,
So they returned to their homes by another way.

Not only the wise men but the shepherds also went to
see and worship the new-born king. Luke says of the shepherds, "And it came to pass, as the angels were gone away
from them into heaven, the shepherds said one to another,
Let us now go even unto Bethlehem, and see this thing which
is come to pass, which the Lord hath made known unto us.
And they came with haste, and found Mary and Joseph, and
the babe lying in a manger. And when they had seen it, they
made known abroad the saying which was told them concerning this child. And all they that heard it wondered at

those things which were told them by the shepherds. But Mary kept all these things, and pondered them in her heart. And the shepherds returned, glorifying and praising God for all the things that they had heard and seen, as it was told unto them. (Luke 2:15-20)

What an interesting and important picture for us to contemplate at this Christmas season. We might ask for more information about this particular event. How many were present in this visiting company of the heavenly host who came praising God and singing *Glory to God in the Highest?* We might also ask who these visitors were.

We know that the word *angel* as used in the New Testament came from a Greek word meaning "messenger." Angels of God were of course messengers of God. We have learned a great deal about angels from latter-day revelation which tells us that all of God's messengers to this earth are those who *do* belong or *have* belonged to it. (D & C 130:5, 129:1, 130:4-5, 130:67) For example, we know that Gabriel was one of the great prophets who had lived upon this earth some 2,000 years before Christ. But all of that great multitude were children of God, and whether they *had* lived or were yet to live upon the earth they were all dependent for their salvation upon the atonement of Christ. Some of *us* who are now living upon the earth may have been present that night on the Judean hills. Since the resurrection of Christ some of God's messengers are resurrected personages who have bodies of flesh and bones just as Jesus has had since his resurrection. (D & C 129:13) Of course, those who came to announce the birth of Christ had not yet had the privilege of resurrection inasmuch as Christ was the first fruits.

We also might ask ourselves why the birth of this one baby was so important as to call forth this great celebration even in heaven? In order to get a full answer we need to go back behind the scenes. The birth of Christ had been ordained in the grand council of heaven, it had also been foretold many generations before it actually took place in Bethlehem. Some 700 years B.C. the Prophet Isaiah gave a partial account of a vision which he had had of that ante-mortal council. It had to do with the time when the first begotten Son of God in the spirit was being chosen as the Savior of what was as yet an unborn race of mortals. He was ordained to redeem a world, yet in its formative stages of development.

Isaiah said, "And I heard the voice of the Lord, saying, Whom shall I send, and who will go for us?" (Isaiah 6:8) Modern revelation tells us that there were two who responded. One was the first begotten Son of God in the spirit who was particularly qualified for this special mission. He answered and said, "Here am I, send me, . . . Father, thy will be done, and the glory be thine forever." (Moses 4:1-2)

But another also spoke. It was Lucifer, the brilliant son of the morning. And he said, "Behold, here am I, send me, I will be thy son, and I will redeem all mankind, that *one* soul shall not be lost, and surely I will do it; wherefore give me thine honor." (Moses 4:1, D & C 76:26, Isaiah 14:12-14)

Here we see initiated these two opposing philosophies which have continued with us ever since. The first begotten son of God offered to come to the earth in the interests of our redemption. Lucifer offered to come in the interests of his own glory. And God said, "I will send the first." And the record says that "The second was angry, and kept not his first estate." (Abraham 3:27-28) Because Lucifer did not get his own way to serve his own interests, he became rebellious and ever since he has fought against the work of God. Lucifer was cast out of heaven and one-third of the hosts of heaven were cast out with him. They became fallen and were deprived of the privileges that all of us who did not follow Lucifer receive, that of mortal life upon this earth.

In the pre-existence Jesus was known as Jehovah and was a personage of great power. He was associated with Elohim, his Father, in the creation of the world. Just before his death Jesus said in his prayer to his Father, "I have glorified thee on the earth: I have finished the work which thou gavest me to do. And now, O Father, glorify thou me with thine own self with the glory which I had with thee before the world was." (John 17:4-5)

Jesus came to the earth under the commission from God and the council of heaven to redeem the world and save us from death on condition of our repentance. The song says:

> There was no other good enough to pay the price of sin,
> He only, could unlock the gates of heaven and let us in.

But those who had lived upon the earth and those who would yet live upon the earth had an equal interest in the mission of the Savior. Jesus broke the bonds of death and initiated the resurrection. He also serves as the pattern for us to go by.

In foretelling the life of Jesus, Isaiah said, "For unto us a child is born, unto us a son is given: and the government shall be upon his shoulder: and his name shall be called Wonderful, Counseller, The mighty God, The everlasting Father, The Prince of Peace." (Isa. 9:6) Someone has suggested that we remove one comma so that the line would read, "and his name shall be called 'Wonderful Counsellor.'" Our lives depend on following his counsel. He was a wonderful counseler in the pre-existence and he has been a wonderful counseler here. We need to follow that counsel more closely.

May God, our Heavenly Father, who by the shining of a star did guide the eastern wise men to behold his Son and our Redeemer, may he by the light of his inspiration guide us to find and follow the Savior of the world. And as the wise men of old laid at his feet gold and frankincense and myrrh, may we present the offering of a humble heart, an adoring spirit and an obedient will.

The Sunflower

IT HAS BEEN said that most things are not important for themselves alone, they are sometimes even more important for what they are a sign of, or for what they stand for, or for what they make us think about. The ancients communicated to each other by means of pictures, but we *still* think in pictures. For example, if someone tells us about a glass of water, we *see* a glass of water. If he tells us about having done some particular thing, there comes a picture into our minds, and we see him doing that particular thing Mostly we use words merely to represent the pictures that we hold in our minds. If someone has a picture in his mind that he wants us to see, he describes it for us in words. We receive the words and then reconstruct the picture in our own minds so that we can *see* it as he does. The comparative values of some things may fluctuate, but *one* picture is still worth a thousand words, and the degree of our understanding depends largely upon our picturing power or the ability to translate words, ideas and ideals into pictures. Books and magazines are made more interesting and understandable with pictures. The printed story gives way before the movies; the radio is forsaken for the television.

Ideas, virtues and ambitions are invisible, and so in our thinking we provide visual aids by painting pictures to represent the ideas or virtues that otherwise could not been seen. For example, the parables of Jesus are word pictures of ideas. It is more easy to understand waste if we see a moving picture of the prodigal son in our minds. What word can present "compassion" and neighborliness more clearly to our minds

than does a mental picture of the Good Samaritan? The
parables make up a great mental picture book of ideas.

We have another helpful procedure of developing tangi-
ble symbols to represent intangible ideas, ideals and ambitions. The symbol may not be important for itself alone, but
it may be tremendous for what it stands for and makes us
think about. The music of a symphony orchestra is invisible,
yet we are able to capture every tone and preserve it in
visible form by notes on a musical score sheet. A flag waving
in the sky above the capital or on the battlefield may be
unimportant for itself alone, yet who can adequately express
the importance of what it stands for? The mere thought of
what it represents sends a thrill of pride and gratitude
through millions of hearts. How many books would it take
to convey the significance and meaning of a ring on the
finger? A light kept burning in the window may be a beacon
of love to draw one home from foreign battlefields across
oceans and continents. Such a simple thing may be vested
with a lifetime of devotion and sacred promise.

Over the centuries in the minds of millions, the cross
has stood as the symbol of Christianity. The Savior himself
gave us the bread and wine as emblems of his sacrifice and
death. Symbols not only make ideas visible, they also make
them memorable. We make the marriage ordinance impressive to our minds and sacred to our memories by a particular
kind of dress, flowers, and ceremony. We try to be at our
best for this particular occasion and thereby set a standard
that we hope will last throughout our lives. In various ways
we give visual expression and impressiveness to the invisible
and the intangible.

As we use parables and figures of speech to represent
ideas, we use other symbols to represent virtues and ambitions. For example, it has been pointed out that the sunflower following the sun across the sky is the symbol of
loyalty. There are many flowers that open their petals to the

sun, but only the sunflower follows. A recent moving picture showed a ship that had been torpedoed at sea. The lifeboats had been launched, and the passengers had abandoned the sinking ship. But there were two who remained aboard the stricken vessel. The commanding officer who had been blinded by the explosion had made known his intention to be true to the tradition of the sea and go down with his ship. The other was the personal attendant and faithful friend of the captain, who had helped to load the lifeboats and then had gone to stand silently by the side of his blind master without making his presence known until all of the lifeboats were filled and well out to sea.

When his presence was known, the captain urged his faithful aid to save himself. But the servant told his master the story of the sunflower, the symbol of loyalty. The sunflower follows the sun, not only in the early morning hours when the day is young, but also continues throughout the zenith of the day, when the heat is great. The sunflower looks directly into the face of the sun in the morning and is constant and steadfast throughout the long afternoon. And as the sun declines in the west, the face of the sunflower still follows the sun, until evening when the sun finally disappears into the sea. But the next morning when the sun arises again it is greeted by the face of the ever loyal sunflower.

For the two men in the captain's cabin, the water rose from their ankles to their knees to the waists, and just before the great ship gave up its life to plunge its two occupants to the bottom of the ocean, the servant said to the master, "The sunflower follows the sun. You go down with your ship. I go down with you." Every captain who meets such an experience likes to do so dressed in his smartest uniform, with all of his personal qualities at their best, in full loyalty to his ship.

There was a similar custom common to many early battlefields requiring that when the commanding officer was slain in battle, those who attended his person fought it out until they had all died with him. That is, even men are not only important for themselves alone, they are also important for what they stand for and believe in and fight for and are willing to give their lives to. And one of the most thrilling thoughts that I know of is that the most humble among us may give his life to the greatest cause.

At age 21 Nathan Hale was sentenced to be shot as a spy. But dressed in his best character qualities he said, "I regret that I have but *one* life to give for my country." Nathan Hale will live forever in the hearts of his countrymen, not only because of his own service and personal importance. but he also serves as a symbol of loyalty, freedom and unselfish love for his country.

How different from some who live in America posing as respectable members of society, enjoying all that this great nation has, while their loyalties are pledged to Russia or China, whose chief purpose is to enslave and destroy. Their lives are symbols of treachery, evil and disloyalty. The dictionary says that to be loyal is to be constant and faithful in every relationship; if requires one to be worthy of the trust and confidence of others. Certainly one of the brightest and most beautiful of all human character traits is a genuine loyalty. If one is loyal he is almost everything; if he is not loyal, his other traits have little value. To be disloyal is to be faithless or false to one's obligations. Loyalty gives us a kind of personal possession to those things to which we are loyal. And disloyalty removes them from our reach and use. Even if disloyalty could be kept a secret from others it still has a damaging effect upon all who practice it. Supermen are men with super loyalties. These loyalties belong to one's work, his friends, his family, his country, the Church and to God.

One of the most important religious commandments has to do with our work. God said, "By the sweat of thy face shalt thou eat thy bread." That is not a command of punishment but a command of opportunity. But all kinds of work are not equally honorable, and if our work is not uplifting, then we should quit it; but if it is in the best interests of all concerned, then we should be loyal to it. Elbert Hubbard said, "If you work for a company, in heaven's name work for it." He said, "Business is the process of ministering to human needs; therefore, business is essentially a divine calling." If our work qualifies under this heading then we ought to get excited about it and learn to be loyal in everyday things. If any success "an ounce of loyalty is worth a pound of cleverness." But our work is not the only way we get our bread, it is the way we learn to overcome difficulties, and develop abilities and build character, and carry out our part of the work of the world.

Think how brilliantly this quality of loyalty shows itself when applied to one's family, his country, and to God. One who is loyal develops a kind of radioactivity. He radiates enthusiasm. His loyalty lights up his whole personality, it puts sparkle in his eyes, a light in his expression, conviction in his voice and success in his accomplishments. Loyalty provides a far greater incentive for accomplishment than money. It has been said that you can live on less "if you have more to live for," and if you would know happiness and inspire confidence in others, be loyal and constant to every trust. Don't be like the weathercock whose loyalty changes with every passing breeze, or like the chameleon that changes its color in every environment.

The damaging effect of disloyalty is seen in a story told of a student of one of our great American universities. He first became negative by overemphasizing the shortcomings of this fine institution that he attended. He developed a bad attitude toward some of those who conducted its affairs. He always listened to and sided with the disgruntled students. He accumulated and hoarded in his own personality the negative reactions of others. As a consequence he lost confidence in the university, but at the same time the university lost its power to help him. Because of his experience many were hurt, but the greatest damage was not done to the university, nor the loyal, enthusiastic students, the greatest harm came to the one who smeared his own life with disloyalty.

One who is looking can always find faults in others. There are no perfect people; there are no perfect institutions; there are no perfect situations; but we should not allow imperfections in others to make us sour or bitter. We might add something to the Ten Commandments and say, don't be a griper, don't bear tales, don't feel too sorry for yourself and your situation, don't allow the seeds of disloyalty to take root in your heart, don't do anything that may turn into this damaging disloyalty trait—it is too dangerous. Learn to see things as they are and find good things to say and do.

A kind of sunflower loyalty is one of the finest attributes anyone could develop. The great state of Kansas has adopted the sunflower as its state emblem, that might also serve as an effective individual emblem for us. Of course, our greatest loyalty belongs to God, God created us to begin with. He gave us life. He lends us breath. He enlightens our minds and quickens our understandings. Every days he sends us food, energy and vitality from the sun. We do not live on an independent earth. If the sun's rays were turned off for just a few hours, no life could survive upon this earth. Because the most important human need is for God, that has become the first and greatest commandment. It says, "Thou shalt love the Lord thy God with all thy heart, and thou shalt serve him with all thy strength." This is also our greatest opportunity for only as we keep *this* commandment does God have *his* maximum power to help us.

But just as there are many flowers that open their petals to receive the rays of the sun while only one follows him, so there are many children of God who open their hands to receive blessings, but a much smaller number really serve him.

The greatest benefits that we can bring into our own lives are obtained only by developing our unquestioned loyalty to God.

Of the thirteen Articles of Faith which summarize the beliefs of the Church, twelve of them begin by saying, "We believe" It gives us strength to believe in great principles. It is a lot of fun to believe in people, to have confidence in them, to support them. But the greatest satisfaction comes when we harmonize our lives with the beginning of the first Article of Faith which says, "We believe in God." What a tremendous situation is thereby brought about. When we say that we believe in God, we mean that we know the kind of being he is. We believe that he is our Father. We believe that we have inherited his potentialities. We believe that his interests are our interests. But when we say we believe in God, we also mean that we *believe* in him, that we trust him, and that we will follow him by doing what he says, not only when it suits our fancy but at all times. Job said, "Though he slay me, yet will I trust in him: . . ." (Job 13:15)

In the great hymn, "How Firm a Foundation," we sing:

> In every condition, in sickness, in health,
> In poverty's vale or abounding in wealth,
> At home or abroad, on the land or the sea.
> As thy days may demand, so thy succor shall be.

And the Lord says to us,

> When through the deep waters I call thee to go,
> The rivers of sorrow shall not thee o'erflow,
> For I will be with thee, thy troubles to bless,
> And sanctify to thee thy deepest distress.

> When through fiery trials thy pathway shall lie,
> My grace, all sufficient, shall be thy supply.
> The flames shall not hurt thee; I only design
> Thy dross to consume and thy gold to refine.

In developing our own super-loyalties toward God we might well say in the words of Socrates, "Whatsoever place thou assigneth me, sooner would I die a thousand deaths than to forsake it." Then we ourselves may stand for the greatest things in the world. As the sunflower follows the sun, may we open our lives to God and always follow him.

"Take Ye Away the Stone"

(John 11:39)

Some two miles in a southeasterly direction from Jerusalem is the little city of Bethany in which once lived Mary, Martha and Lazarus. It was to their humble home that Jesus often went when he felt a special need for a measure of rest and relaxation.

Near the end of his ministry, the antagonism of the Jews had become so pronounced that he had taken his disciples and gone into the comparative seclusion of the region of Bethabara beyond the Jordan. While he was away, his friend Lazarus became seriously ill, and the sisters sent word to Jesus saying, "Lord, behold, he whom thou lovest is sick." Jesus received the message, but continued where he was for two more days. Then he startled his disciples by saying, "Let us go into Judea again." They reminded him of the recent attempts that had been made upon his life. But Jesus said to them, "Our friend Lazarus sleepeth; but I go, that I may awake him out of sleep." When they did not understand, Jesus said to them plainly, "Lazarus is dead."

When Martha and Mary heard that Jesus was returning, Martha went out to meet him and said, "Lord, if thou hadst been here, my brother had not died." Jesus said to her, "Thy brother shall rise again." Martha said, "I know that he shall rise again in the resurrection at the last day." Jesus said, "I am the resurrection, and the life: he that believeth in me, though he were dead, yet shall he live: And whosoever liveth and believeth in me shall never die. Believest thou this?"

Martha said unto him, "Yea, Lord: I believe that thou art the Christ, the Son of God, which should come into the world."

Then Jesus said, "Where have ye laid him?" And they replied, "Lord, come and see." And they led him to the cave in which Lazarus had been buried. The entrance of which had been closed with a stone. Jesus said to those that were present, "Take ye away the stone." Martha, probably in protest, reminded Jesus that Lazarus had now been dead for *four* days. Jesus said unto her, "Said I not unto thee, that, if thou wouldest believe, thou shouldest see the glory of God."

When the stone had been removed, Jesus lifted up his eyes to his Father in heaven. And after he had prayed, he cried with a loud voice, "Lazarus, come forth." And he who had been dead for four days came forth from the tomb bound hand and foot with grave clothes, and his face was bound about with a napkin. Then Jesus said unto them, "Loose him, and let him go." (See John 11:4)

It is an interesting point to consider why it was that Jesus, who could look into men's souls and who knew so many things that others did not know, should have bothered to ask where Lazarus had been buried. After Jesus had conversed with the Samaritan woman at Jacob's well in Sychar, she said to the men of her city, "Come, see a man which told me all things that ever I did." (John 4:29) Yet this same Jesus said to Martha and Mary, "Where had ye laid him?"

Jesus had previously indicated that he could command the service of twelve legions of angels. He was endowed with the power of God. Then why did he not *hurl* away the stone from the sepulchre's mouth without enlisting the aid of puny human hands saying, "Take ye away the stone." Certainly he who could raise the dead and control the tempest could have stricken the grave clothes from the body of the risen Lazarus instead of saying to his mortal associates, "Loose him, and let him go."

It may be that the Lord was trying to teach us that there are many things that we are required to do for ourselves. That is, why should it be necessary for us to get an education or be compelled to earn a living, when God could provide for us as easily as he does for the lilies of the field or the birds of the air? Yet he says to us, "By the sweat of thy face shalt thou eat thy bread."

Not only are we required to provide our own bread, but we must also build our own characters and develop our own faith, and work out our own salvation in fear and trembling before God. The gospel is the greatest do-it-yourself project ever known in the world. No one can do our growing for us and no one can do our repenting for us. No one can exercise our priesthood for us, and no one can do our thinking or our working or our praying for us.

There are, of course, some things that we cannot do for ourselves. We cannot redeem our own souls. We cannot atone for our own sins. We do not have power over death, and we cannot bring about our own resurrection. But it is a part of the plan that we must do what we can for ourselves, then the Redeemer will do for us those things that we cannot do alone. But even in saving our souls, there are many important things that we can and must do for ourselves if we are to qualify for divine assistance.

No one in Bethany could have raised Lazarus from the dead, but there were some things that they could do, and so Jesus said to them, "Where have ye laid him?" "Take ye away the stone." "Loose him and let him go." When they had done their part, then Jesus did what they were unable to do: to call his friend back from the dead.

This great idea has many applications in our lives. There are a lot of grave clothes that need to be loosed. There are a lot of stones that need to be cleared out of the way. Many of these stones are stumbling blocks which if unmoved make progress impossible. We can best serve our own eternal in-

terests if we get these obstructions identified and then one
by one say to ourselves about them, "Take ye away the stone."

Some time ago a mission president told me that there
were over 300 people in his mission who wanted to be baptized. They believed the Lord when he said, "He that believeth and is baptized shall be saved, and he that believeth
not shall be damned." And yet they could not eliminate from
their personal lives those stumbling blocks that had so long
been standing in their way.

One of the important parts of this idea is that no one
can do these important things for us, no one can get rid of
our bad habits for us. We cannot buy freedom from sin. The
court cannot decree it to us. The doctor cannot remove sin
by surgery. The mission president cannot repent of *our* sins,
and I suppose that even God cannot make of us what he
desires us to be unless we do our part in removing our own
stumbling blocks. God can raise us from the dead, but who
can rid us of faults or develop our ambition? The resurrection
from the dead is God's business, but the housecleaning and
motivation of our lives is our business. God can regulate the
planets but who can control our sloth, or wipe out our lethargy, or unwind the grave clothes of bad habits by which
we have bound ourselves?

Over in Japan they grow some ornamental oak trees by
taking the young shoots before planting and wrapping cop-
per wire around the roots. A tree so bound is stunted so
that it will never grow more than 16 to 18 inches in height.
In a similar way we wrap ourselves up in evil, thereby we
stop our own growth and destroy our own success unless we
effectively say to ourselves, "Loose him and let him go."

In his youth King David was called a man after God's
own heart. But he wrapped himself with the wires of sin
which immediately cut off his opportunities. It was one of
the greatest desires of David's heart to build a temple to the
Lord, but he disqualified himself by his own evil deeds. The

Lord wanted a temple built; the people needed a temple. Four hundred and sixty years after being established in their promised land they were still using the little portable tabernacle that they had carried with them during their wandering in the wilderness in the days of Moses. Since then they had become a great nation and badly needed a temple. But David's sins stood in their way. The Lord could not accept a Holy Temple built by unholy hands. David had made plans for the temple, and had accumulated much of the building material, but still the Lord said that construction must wait until David was dead.

By this same kind of process we wrap ourselves in limitations. If we ever find ourselves worrying a little bit about doing too much for the Lord, suppose that we put ourselves in David's shoes and imagine that the Lord would not accept any service at our hands. Just suppose that he would not permit us to enter the temple or pay our tithing, or repent of our sins, or say our prayers. We don't always keep the Sabbath Day holy, but suppose that God took away the Sabbath and forbade us going to the house of prayer, or partaking of the sacrament, or worshiping him. What a thrilling sound it would then be to hear the Lord's command, "Take ye away the stone," knowing that thereby spiritual progress would again be made possible for us. At all costs we must keep the lines of communication open between God and ourselves. This can be done only by our own righteousness and industry.

At one time an angel appeared to King David and told him that the Lord desired that he should build an altar on which to offer sacrifice. The angel specified the exact spot of ground on which the altar should stand. It was an elevated area in the center of a wheat field owned by one of David's wealthy subjects whose name was Ornan. This was destined to be the spot on which Solomon would later build the magnificent temple of God.

David told Ornan what the angel had said and asked if he could obtain the land to do with as the angel had commanded. Ornan replied that not only would the land be made available, but David could also have it free of charge. In addition, Ornan agreed to furnish the materials out of which the altar should be built, and also to supply the wheat, the oil, and the cattle which should make up the sacrifice.

Then David said something profound no matter to what department of our lives it may be applied. He said, "I will not offer burnt offerings unto the Lord my God of that which doth cost me nothing." (II Sam. 24:24) David had already deprived himself of some of his greatest possible blessings. He was not going to lose any more if he could help it, and he knew that next to actual sin itself, the easiest way to lose eternal blessings was by inactivity.

There are many among us who get a little weary in doing the work of the Lord. Some try to get out of as much church work as possible. Just suppose that we could get someone else to do our church work for us. Suppose that we could get someone to take over our welfare work, and pay our tithing for us, and do our teaching, and our studying, and our praying, and worshiping for us. Of course he would also get our blessings. These heavy stones of inactivity and wrong thinking can become mountainous in size and isolate us from God. Work is our greatest blessing. It is impossible to grow strong physically or spiritually without it. As the poet has said:

> The tree that never had to fight,
> For sun and sky and air and light;
> But lived out in the open plain
> And always got its share of rain,
> Never became a forest king,
> But lived and died a scrubby thing.

The best way to develop ourselves is to remove the obstacles that bar our progress, and so we should frequently say to ourselves, "Take ye away the stone."

There is another interesting obstruction that frequently tends to thwart our eternal happiness. That is a conscious or subconscious feeling that God should do our work for us. For a long time we have been familiar with the fact that there are some who feel that the world owes them a living. But there are a far greater number who by their action show their feeling that God owes them an eternal life. Think of the large number who fully expect mansions in heaven, yet year after year they remain spiritually unemployed.

We make long prayers asking God for every conceivable thing, while we ourselves do very little toward bringing them about. Frequently we say, "Let George do it." But even more frequently our attitude is to let God do it. We ask God to make us good and wise and successful without giving him the necessary cooperation. So much of our religion tends to be the "verbal christianity" mentioned by James. When someone needs help we sometimes merely ask God to help him.

As in the days of James we pray, "Depart in peace, be ye warmed and filled; . . ." (James 2:16) Then James asks, "What doth it profit?" We should not ask God to do both his work and ours. Most of our prayers we can answer ourselves. For example, we don't need to ask God to forgive our enemies. We can forgive them ourselves. We don't need to ask God to make us faithful or industrious, for we are the only ones that can really answer those prayers.

The gospel places the greatest possible emphasis on works and activity as the most effective means of obtaining every blessing temporal or spiritual, including our eternal exaltation. We say that we believe in prayer, and yet so frequently we fail to recognize its answer when it comes.

> We ask for strength and God gives us difficulties to
>   make us strong.
> We pray for wisdom and God sends us problems,
>   the solution of which develops wisdom.
> We plead for prosperity and God gives us a
>   brain and brawn to work.
> We plead for courage and God gives us dangers
>   to overcome.
> We ask for favors and God gives us opportunities.

As the women were going to the sepulchre on that first Easter morning they asked themselves, "Who shall roll us away the stone?" That is also our question, "Who will remove the obstructions that are stopping our progress?" The very best answer in almost every case is the "Do-it-yourself" answer, and I would like to close with the challenging philosophy of Cannon Farr who said:

> I am only one, but I am one.
> I can't do everything, but I can do some things;
> What I can do that I ought to do,
> And what I ought to do
> By the grace of God,
> I will do.

May God help us to help ourselves.

Temptation

I WOULD LIKE to say something on a subject about which people generally have more information than on any other. The subject is temptation. Our age is noted for its temptations. Temptations are all around us. They are in the movies and the magazine. About everything we read, hear, or think is likely to have some lurking temptation to draw us downward. Every crime, every sin, every unhappiness started from a temptation.

This is a subject with which many people have also had a good deal of personal experience. Even the Apostle Paul said, "When I would do good, evil is present with me." When we *speak* of temptation we almost always have in mind the temptations of evil. They are the temptations of ignorance, the temptations of sin, the temptations of sloth. They are the temptations which entice us downward.

Some time ago I looked up this interesting word in the dictionary, and it said, "To tempt is to arouse a desire for." Of course, desires can go in either direction. They can go up just as well as down. William James, the great Harvard psychologist said, "That which holds our attention determines our action." But for some reason most of us pay more attention than we should to the things down. And of course where our attention goes is where we are pretty certain to follow. For example, when one thinks too many negative thoughts, his mind becomes negative. If he thinks depraved thoughts, he gets a depraved mind. We know what happens to those who think damned thoughts. We always follow the lead of the mind. The Apostle James said, " . . . every man is tempted, when he is drawn away by his own lusts. . . ." (James 1:14) The beast goes down on all fours, which tends to throw his vision upon the ground. By different means our temptations accomplish about the same end.

John Bunyon's "Pilgrim's Progress" tells the story of a man with a muckrake who could look in no direction but down. His interest was in material things and he spent his life raking unto himself the muck and chaff of the earth. There was an angel standing over his head with a celestial crown in his hand, offering to exchange the crown for the muckrake. But the man could look in no direction but down. Therefore, he regarded not the offer of the angel, but continued to rake unto himself the muck and waste of the earth. When we look down for too long, we lose the power to do anything else.

In Dante's *Inferno,* a group of hell's inmates explained their situation by saying, "As our eyes intent on earthly were never lifted up to heaven, so now doth justice *fix* them down upon the ground. And even as greed destroyed our love for good whereby the labors of our lives were lost, so now doth justice hold us captive here fettered in close restraint." That is a natural consequence, and how we handle our temptations probably more than anything else determines our lives.

The best way to judge a person is by what tempts him. That is, a doctor judges health by the appetite, and the quality of our lives may be judged the same way. Henry Ward Beecher once said, "temptations without imply desires within. We ought not to say how powerfully the devil tempts, but how strongly I am inclined."

Recently I heard of a woman saying that she could read murder mysteries all night without tiring. But if she read the Bible for ten minutes, she went sound asleep. Physical or mental appetite responds readily to training. One can easily train himself to become more interested in a horse race or a prize fight than in the celestial kingdom. We are pointing the directions for our temptations to follow when we build bars in our homes instead of altars. A muckrake can become more important to us than a celestial crown. It is pretty easy to ruin one's appetite for the things of God when he feels he must personally try out every sin and investigate every temptation.

It may be a pretty good idea to give a little more thoughtful consideration to our temptations. It can be very helpful to make some written inventories of temptations. One should consist of our "desires down" and the other should catalog our "desires up." If one can muster enough courage actually to list his temptations down, he will be surprised what an unattractive assortment we generally have.

Some time ago a mission president told me that there were three hundred people in his mission who wanted to be baptized, but they were prevented from doing what God had commanded because they were not strong enough to overcome the temptation of tobacco. To one who has never formed the tobacco habit, such a situation is difficult to understand, especially if he shares an airplane seat about every week with a chain smoker. A few hours each week of that sick, dizzy, nicotine intoxication will always produce a feeling of amazement that anyone should be attracted to such a habit. Yet many people go out of their way to form an attachment for tobacco and then cling to it for all they are worth. I heard of one heavy smoker who was very much disturbed by reading about all the new discoveries concerning lung cancer, and so he gave up reading.

One of the most attractive temptations of our day, and one that drags more people down than almost any other is the temptation of alcohol. This is also a little difficult to understand. About this temptation Shakespeare said, "Oh, thou invisible spirit of wine. If thou hast no name to be known by, let us call thee devil. Oh, God, that men should put an enemy in their mouths to steal away their brains, that we should with pleasure transform ourselves into beasts."

Robert G. Ingersoll had this to say, "Every man who touches whiskey is demoralized. It demoralizes those who make it, those who sell it, those who drink it. I believe that from the time it issues from the coiled and poisonous worm of the distillery until it empties into the hell of crime, dishonor and death, this liquid crime demoralizes everybody that touches it. Think of the human wrecks, of the deaths, of the suicides, of the insanity, of the poverty, of the ignorance, of the distress of little children tugging at the faded dresses of weeping and despairing wives asking for bread, of the genius it has wrecked, of the millions struggling with the imaginary serpents produced by this devilish thing. Then think of the jails, of the almshouses, of the asylums, of the prisons and of the scaffolds. I do not wonder that every thoughtful man is prejudiced against the damn stuff called alcohol."

Isn't it peculiar that among the strongest desires that some people have, are to fill their lungs with nicotine and their blood with alcohol. Some have their desires aroused to keep their mouths filled with profanity, their minds with immorality, and their hearts with disobedience to God. These are some of the things about which God has given us a stern "Thou shalt not." Yet sometimes our desires actually seem to be increased by the fact that God has forbidden it.

A young man driving down the highway with his father was explaining what he did not like about the Ten Commandments. In the first place, he said, they were negative. In the second place he said he did not like anyone telling him what not to do. He thought that the Lord made a serious mistake in giving the Ten Commandments a negative form. Soon the father and son came to an intersection in the highway. The signboard told them where each fork in the road would take them. The father took the wrong road. The son was very upset. He could not understand why his father should make such a ridiculous mistake. Then the father admitted that he had read the signboard, but he said he just did not want any signboard telling him where to go.

The "Thou shalt nots" are among the most important instructions of the Holy Scriptures and they are in the best possible form. There are some things that we just must not do. They should be settled first. It is a lot easier to do what we should do, if we first make some definite decisions about what we should not do. There is no mistake about what God meant when he said, "Thou shalt not kill," "Thou shalt not commit adultery," "Thou shalt not steal." If once and for all we could definitely settle the "thou shalt nots" then many of the most destructive temptations would no longer arouse our desires. It is only when we maintain these temptations within ourselves as possibilities that they are able to pull us down to their level.

Sometimes even the smallest temptations can get power over us because they are made so easily available to our minds. But we should not go through life with our heads down for it is much easier to shun the bait than to release ourselves from the snare, once we are caught. "Greater is he who lives above temptation than he who being tempted overcomes." "No person ever fell into a mud puddle who didn't get too close to it." But still we hear till we are weary about the temptations of our day, the temptations downward. But what about the temptations upward? Suppose that we trade in our muckrakes so that we can see some of the thrilling temptations upward. The temptations of culture, the temptations of learning, the temptations of character, the temptations of faith, the temptations of industry, the temptations to become like God. Incidentally, these are the temptations that make us strong and happy.

A small community in Tennessee recently built a church. It looked to me as though they had spent half of their money on the spire. The front end of the church was made into a steeple that looked like a giant finger pointing up to God, and I thought of what Mr. James said about "that which holds our attention determining our action." One of the most thrilling things to me about any church is its spire. I hardly ever come within sight of the Salt Lake Temple, particularly at night, but that I stop for a few minutes to look at the spires. They point us up to God and eternal life. They represent the most satisfying of all the temptations. Then it is pleasant to think of the hymn that says:

> Look up my soul, Be not cast down,
> Keep not thine eyes upon the ground.
> Break off the shackles of the earth,
> Receive my soul, the spirit's birth.

Some time ago a young man came to see me who seemed to be a patron of all of the temptations downward. As a consequence he had been dishonorably discharged from the army. His friends were ashamed of him. His life was reeking with sin. I asked him why he had done these things. He said, "I wanted to have a fling at life." I tried to point out to him that he was flinging in the wrong direction. Life is up, death is down. He was flinging at death. Much of the best that was within him had already died. His eternal life itself was in serious jeopardy. I tried to persuade him to take a fling at repentance. What a thrilling temptation it ought to be to him to take a fling at cleansing his mind and soul and destroying within himself his strong affinity for evil things.

Herman Melville wrote a great whaling story entitled, "Moby Dick." In choosing his crew to go out to harpoon this killer whale the captain said, "I will have no man in my boat who is not afraid of a whale." He wanted men who could recognize danger, and he knew that there would be no success if a spirit of careless bravado rode in his boat.

Similarly a wise man should never underestimate the power of evil. We sometimes wrestle unsuccessfully with the most trivial temptations. Even a cigarette can get dominion over some people. My friend had not been afraid of the right things. With devastating heedlessness he had walked straight into the danger zone where sin and failure had laid him low.

I tried to point out to him some of the advantages of the temptations upward. The temptations of honor, the temptations to look up to God, the temptations to keep the Sabbath Day holy. Or think what a realm of inspiration and delight is opened to us through the pages of the Holy Scriptures where we may fill our minds with the thoughts of God himself. In the scriptures we may go with Moses to the top of Mt. Sinai and receive with him the law of the Lord.

Through the scriptures we can cultivate an association with such towering figures as Abraham, the father of the faithful, and learn the secrets of his life that gave him such favor with God.

Or suppose that we go out onto the hills of Judea for that first Christmas and learn to understand the significance of the birth of the Son of God. Or, we might go with Jesus to Bethabara for his baptism and hear his Fathers's voice out of heaven saying, "This is my beloved Son in whom I am well pleased." Then suppose that we go with him into the wilderness for his forty days of fasting and testing and see how the Master himself handled temptations. What a thrill to see him come off the field glorious and triumphant. His victory will stimulate us to follow his examples. Then we might even go in the scriptures to spend a few hours upon the Mount of Transfiguration where in shining garments, Jesus with Moses and Elias was transfigured before Peter, James and John.

One of the greatest opportunities of our lives is to trade in our muckrakes and develop an affinity for the thrilling temptations upward.

> I raised my eyes to yonder heights,
> And longed for lifting wings;
> To bear me to their sunlit crests
> As on my spirit sings.

And though my feet must keep the path,
That winds along the valley's floor;
Yet, after every upward glance
I'm stronger than before.

Man was created upright in the image of his maker that he might look up to God. Let's trade in our muckrakes, stand erect, and look up to him whom we resemble.

The Testament of Jesus

ONE OF OUR biggest problems is the difficulty we sometimes encounter in getting the right kind of ideas into effective operation in our lives. I thought about this the other night as I was re-reading Shakespeare's great literary masterpiece, "Julius Caesar." And inasmuch as Jesus referred to Caesar on several occasions, I would like to make a reference to him now in developing a text for what I would like to say.

Caesar had been stabbed by a group of conspirators, but no one seemed very concerned about it, probably indicating that human nature doesn't change very much. So frequently we don't get greatly aroused even about the most important things. A prophet speaks, eternal opportunities present themselves, the gospel is restored, or even the Savior is crucified, but more or less we insist on business as usual. Nero fiddled while Rome burned. The soldiers diced while Jesus died. The disciples slept while their Master suffered, and so frequently our attention is centered on secondary considerations while our eternal exaltation is being lost.

Caesar's friend Mark Antony was very much disturbed about this lethargy in the Romans, and he tried to stir them up to sense of the wrong that had been done. At the funeral he held up Caesar's mantle rent as it now was with dagger wounds and stained with Caesar's blood. Mark Antony recounted the times that Caesar had worn this mantle in their service. Finally he read to them Caesar's last will and testament as an evidence of Caesar's love. Caesar had left them his money, his private arbors, his newly planted orchards, and his places of recreation. He had made the greatest nation in the world.   After recountng all of these things, Antony said, "Here was a Caesar. Whence cometh such another?"

Antony planted the seeds of some new thought in the minds of the Romans. And then he kept adding emphasis until the thought had taken root; and as it began to accumulate power in their minds, Antony stood aside and said, "Now let it work." At first these Romans had only possessed an idea, but now the idea possessed them.

Tonight if I had the gift of speech or power of words of Mark Antony, I would plant in our minds those great ideas having to do with that important relationship that we bear to God, our Heavenly Father. The reason that we are asked to live the first and great commandment is because that is our greatest need. God created us to begin with. He gives us our daily breath. He enlightens our minds and quickens our understandings.

Jesus was ordained to be the mediator between God and us.   (I Tim.2:5) Paul refers to Jesus as "the mediator of the new covenant." (Heb. 12:24) Jesus called it the "new and everlasting covenant."   It contains the specifications for our eternal salvation. The testament of Caesar was a covenant made between Caesar and the people of Rome regarding the disposition of Caesar's property. The testament of Jesus is a covenant made between God and us which indicates how God's blessings are to be distributed.   And if I could, I would stir up our minds to a point where gospel ideals and ambitions would possess our lives and impel us to an action so vigorous that we would never stop until we had safely arrived at what Paul described as "the glory of the sun."

Solomon said, "Fear God and keep his commandments, for this is the whole duty of man."   Only a faithful compliance with the ideals and attitudes stated in the testament of Jesus can mold us into what God desires us to be. If we can put sufficient power behind these ideals, then we might well stand back and say, "Now let it work."

Mark Antony began his funeral oration by saying, "Friends, Romans, nobles and countrymen, lend me your ears." I would like to make a similar request except that I would like to borrow your imaginations for an important mental journey. Each of us is given a mental "picturing power" which when properly developed and focused can put the most powerful ideas in force in our lives. The creative power of the imagination, is one of the greatest gifts that God has ever given to man. By its proper use we may build our lives to the most magnificent specifications.

But every great accomplishment must first take place in the mind. Shakespeare said, "All things are ready if our minds be so." The mind can master anything it can conceive. In the mind we can go backward or forward across time or space. We can revitalize our lives by reliving the greatest experiences of the past, or we can establish our greatest objectives by effectively preliving the future. The research and the presearch of the mind can also make the most worthwhile experiences of others available to us.

In trying to stir up those potentialities within ourselves, suppose that we borrow the technique used by Charles Dickens in his *Christmas Carol.* You may remember that Scrooge had some bad attitudes. He had some bad attitudes about life. He had some bad attitudes about Christmas. He needed to have his point of view refocused and his better self revitalized. And so the spirit of Christmas took him back into his own past and let him relive his own Christmases of long ago. Scrooge was given time to rethink the thoughts of his youth before his present bad habits and selfish attitudes had crowded so much good out of his life.

Then Scrooge was taken up into the future and allowed to see and think about those things which were yet to be, where events were yet subject to change. After some important truths about Christmas, and life, and people had been restamped into his mind, Scrooge was brought back into the present. And as he began putting his new appreciation into action he said, "I am not the man I was."

Making improvement within ourselves is one of the most important of life's processes. William James said, "The greatest discovery of my generation is that we can change our circumstances by changing our attitudes of mind." Before anyone can change his circumstances he must first change himself.

Therefore, suppose that we follow the example of Scrooge and get what we can from our own past. Suppose we go back to the first thing that we knew about ourselves, when as spirit children of God we were gathered together in the grand council of heaven before this world was created. Then we lived with God. We knew him. He is our Father. Then we walked by sight. We discussed, and helped plan for our own earth life. We saw Lucifer, the brilliant son of the morning, expelled from heaven because of his rebellion against God. We sustained the first Begotten Son to be ordained the Savior of the world.

We had come to a place in our progression where young people always come, where it is desirable for them to move away from the homes of their parents, and establish a life of their own. God wanted us to have the opportunity to see good and evil side by side. This was not possible while we were living with God, for no sin is permitted in his presence. It was necessary that we learn to walk a little way by faith The consequences of our free agency as well as our opportunities were fully explained to us. We knew that we were going to have these wonderful, beautiful, mortal bodies, endowed for a brief period with the miraculous power of procreation. We were so delighted at the wonderful prospect of earth life and its opportunities that ". . . all the sons of God shouted for joy." (Job 38:7)

Suppose we try to understand how tremendously we wanted to succeed when we walked by sight and fully understood the consequences of good and evil. Then as the importance of our present privileges began to take hold of our minds we might well stand back and say, "Now let it work."

For the second stop in this imaginary journey of thought, suppose that we go out onto the hills of Judea for that first Christmas morning, and join that heavenly host who came from God to announce the birth of him who was ordained to take upon himself our sins and redeem us from death. Jesus said, "For God so loved the world that he gave his only Begotten Son, that whosoever believeth in him should not perish, but have everlasting life. For God sent not his Son into the world to condemn the world; but that the world through him might be saved." (John 3:6-17) (I Cor. 15:22)

Jesus is the Son of God, the Savior of the world. Next to the Father, the greatest intelligence of heaven. He is our example. He is the administrator of the new and everlasting covenant given in our interests. Suppose therefore that we follow him for those 33 short years while he trod the dusty roads of this earth as our model of righteousness. Even at age twelve we see him in the temple faithfully going about "his Father's business." Suppose that we go with him to Bethabara beyond Jordan where he was baptized of John "to fulfil all righteousness." We listen enthralled to the voice of his Father saying in approval, "This is my beloved Son, in whom I am well pleased." (Matt. 3:17)

Then suppose that we follow him into the wilderness and share his fasting and temptations. What a thrill to see him meet the adversary and come off victorious on every count! (Matt. 4:1-11) And what an inspiration for us to follow him in his triumph.

One of the first events after the beginning of his public ministry was the miracle at the marriage feast in Cana. On that occasion his mother said to the servants, "Whatsoever he saith unto you, do it." (John 2:5) What a thrilling motto that would make for our individual lives.

Suppose now that we go with him to Gethsemane where under the burden of our sins he sweat great drops of blood at every pore. To share his suffering might help us to learn something about the great principle of repentance which was the burden of his ministry.

His dispensation opened with John's call in the wilderness saying, "Repent ye for the kingdom of heaven is at hand." That has been the continuing message from the beginning of time to our own day. Repentance is still our most needed message. It is that tremendous procedure by which we cleanse ourselves of sin.

Walter Malone says,

> Art thou an idler, then rouse thee from thy spell,
> Art thou a sinner, sin may be forgiven;
> Each morning give thee wings to flee from hell
> Each night a star to guide thy soul to heaven.

If we fail to repent, we may some day find that we have lost the power to repent. As we are stimulated by this all important idea of repentance, suppose that we again say to ourselves, "Now let it work."

Now for the last stop suppose that we go and stand before the tomb on that first Easter morning and watch the angels roll away the stone from the door of the tomb, and see the Son of God break the bonds of death and initiate the universal resurrection upon the earth. To see him come forth from the dead serves us as a preview of our own glorious resurrection. When we can get these ideas and enthusiasms established in our lives, then we will be able to say with even greater enthusiasm than Ebenezer Scrooge, "I am not the man I was."

The testament of Caesar left a few material possessions to the citizens of Rome, but through the testament of Jesus we have been promised every blessing that we are willing to live. God has created our spirit in his image, and has given us this beautiful, wonderful body to match, without which we could not receive a fulness of joy. He has endowed us with his attributes, including a wonderful mind that may eventually be developed to think like God. He has given us the unlimited use of this thrilling principle of repentance. He has atoned for our sins. He has initiated the resurrection. He has established the principle of eternal progression. He has prepared the celestial kingdom, and Jesus has promised, " . . . all that my Father hath shall be given unto him." (D & C 84:38)

What a tremendous accomplishment it would be to really get the great ideas of the gospel actively working in our lives with a power sufficient to mold us as God desires us to be. That is the greatest of all possible objectives, and when once our determinations are aroused in that direction, then we may well stand back and say, "Now let it work."

The Time Machine

MANY YEARS AGO Mr. H. G. Wells wrote an interesting fantasy about a man who invented a machine in which he could travel through time, much as we now travel through space. He could go thousands of years into the future in a period of just a few hours, and the speedometer of the time machine always indicated which year of time he was in. This time traveler studied peoples, civilizations and institutions as they would some day actually be. Then he would get back into his time machine and return to the present.

By pushing the lever in the other direction, this time scientist could with equal speed go back into the past. Being a historian he took great delight in witnessing the important events of history while they were actually taking place. He could personally verify the account of the Battle of Hastings by going back to the year 1066. By going still further back, he could visit the Golden Age of Greece and personally discuss philosophy with Socrates—400 years B.C.

While this story is only a fantasy, yet it contains the germ of a great idea. Actually our minds are equipped to serve us as a sort of mental time machine. In thought we can go backward or forward, across time with far greater speed than the fastest airplanes or guided missiles can carry us through space. This ability to see what is ahead we call foresight, vision and imagination. The process of looking back we refer to as reflection, meditation or consideration. We sometimes speak of one as being absent-minded. That is when one's thoughtful mind may have forsaken the present to focus either on the future or the past. When we desire to recall some important past experience, we let our minds go back to the time of its actual occurrence. Then as we relive this event, its vividness, and influence upon us is rewarded and revitalized.

God has sometimes given a kind of time traveling ability to the prophets which we call "revelation," and it may apply either to the past or the future. For example, the Lord took Abraham back into the pre-existence and let him see things as they had already taken place in the council in heaven before the earth was created. On the other hand, John the Revelator went in the other direction and saw a vision of the final judgment that has not yet taken place. But John saw it just the same. John went thousands of years into the future and saw the judgment exactly as it will someday actually be.

But the human mind has some wonderful powers to serve our more common needs. In an instant we may go back into the past and be restimulated by a rerun of our own greatest past experiences. Or by means of combining our reason, forethought, and imagination we may go up into the future and *preview* or *prelive* our lives.

A wonderful past experience, even though it may have happened 20 years ago can greatly benefit us by its influence upon our present. How many helpful applications can we make of this interesting idea? Suppose that occasionally we go back and *relive* our marriage vows. Or suppose that we relive the covenants we made at the waters of baptism, or the determination that we felt when under the stress of some great crisis when we promised God that we would be faithful. Now suppose that we push the lever for an easy trial run back into the past. Suppose that just for practice we relive last Sunday's dinner. We can renew and refeel and recall all that happened on that occasion.

Now that we have had this much experience in time traveling, suppose that we take a much more important trip back into the past. Suppose we get into our Time Machine and go back some 1900 years and place ourselves in thought at the feet of Jesus of Nazareth. Through the Holy Scriptures we may relive his life and reabsorb his inspiration. We may have a most thrilling experience by understanding his message and by living in harmony with his life and teaching. Mrs. C. H. Morris has written a great song entitled, "The Stranger of Galilee." Suppose that you let your imagination go where these words take it.

Mrs. Morris said

In fancy I stood on the shore one day
Of a beautiful murmuring sea,
I saw the great crowds as they thronged the way
Of the Stranger of Galilee.

I saw how the man who was blind from birth
In a moment was made to see;
The lame were made whole by the matchless skill
Of the Stranger of Galilee.

His look of compassion, His words of love,
Shall never forgotten be,
When sin-sick and helpless He saw me there,
This Stranger of Galilee.

He showed me His hands and His riven side
And he whispered it was for me;
My burden fell off at the pierced feet
Of the Stranger of Galilee

I heard Him speak peace to the angry waves
Of that turbulent, raging sea,
And lo, at His words are the waters stilled
This Stranger of Galilee.

A peaceful, a quiet, a holy calm
Now and ever abides with me;
He holdeth my life in His mighty hands
This Stranger of Galilee.

Come ye who are driven and tempest tossed
And His gracious salvation see;
He will quiet life's storms with his "Peace be Still."
This Stranger of Galilee.

Then He bids me to go and the story tell
What He ever to you will be,
If only you'll let Him with you abide,
This Stranger of Galilee.

Oh, my friend, won't you love Him forever
So gracious and tender is he;
Accept Him today as your Savior,
This Stranger of Galilee.

Edgar A. Guest has written a poem which takes us even farther back into the council in heaven where we were discussing the conditions under which we would live upon this wonderful new earth that was yet to be created as our home. We knew that we were going to have these wonderful, beautiful mortal bodies without which we could never have a fulness of joy. For the first time we would be endowed with this miraculous power of procreation and would have the privilege to organize a family, which under the right circumstances would continue throughout eternity. We were so *delighted* with these wonderful prospects that the Bible says that "All the sons of God shouted for joy." (Job 38:7) If we remembered now, as we walk by faith, what we clearly understood then when we walked by sight, I am certain that we would be willing to crawl on our hands and knees through life for this great privilege which we now enjoy. Mr. Guest's poem might represent a conversation which took place at the time you left the spirit world to participate in this wonderful mortal experience.

UNINSTRUCTED

"I'm going to send you down to earth,"
Said God to me one day.
"I'm giving you what men call birth,
Tonight you'll start away.
I want you there to live with men
Until I call you back again."

I trembled as I heard him speak,
Yet I knew that I must go.
I felt his hand upon my cheek
And wished that I might know
What on the earth would be my task,
And timidly I dared to ask,

"Tell me before I start away,
What thou wouldst have me do.
What message thou wouldst have me say?
When will my work be through?
That I may serve thee on the earth,
Tell me the purpose of my birth."

God smiled at me and softly said,
"Oh, you shall find your task;
I want you free life's paths to tread
So do not stay to ask.
Remember that if your best you do
That I shall ask no more of you."

And then Mr. Guest said:

How often as my work I do
So commonplace and grim,
I sit and sigh and wish I knew
If I were pleasing him.
I wonder if with every test,
I've really tried to do my best.

Everyone has thought that same kind of thoughts. Everyone would like to know whether or not he is pleasing God. And probably the best way to make sure that our lives will be what we want them to be is to get into this little mental taxicab of thought and go up into the future and learn to understand the important issues of life before they actually take place. God has told us what we can expect under given circumstances. By means of a little careful forethought we can pre-live our own success.

Suppose then that we go and stand, not on the shore of a beautiful murmuring sea, but on the shore of eternal life. Suppose that we had just sixty minutes of life left to live. What would be the things that would be important to us then? Then after we have securely made up our minds about the real values in life and have got as much good as possible from thinking about our own future, we can then reverse the lever and come back to the present and live by the standards that our forethought has set up for us.

SUPPOSING

Supposing today were your last day on earth,
The last mile of your journey you'd trod,
After all of your struggles, how much are you worth,
How much can you take home to God?

Don't count as possessions, your silver and gold,
For tomorrow you'll leave them behind,
And all that is yours to have and to hold,
Are the blessings you've given mankind.

Just what have you done, as you've journeyed along,
That is really and truly worthwhile?
Do you think that your good deeds would offset the wrong?
Can you look o'er your life with a smile?

We are only supposing—but if it were real,
And you invoiced your deeds from your birth,
And figured the profits you've made in life's deal,
How much are you really worth?

Suppose that in our last hour we were asked by the Creator to write a letter of recommendation for ourselves. How many items would we have to include? Of course, the last hour of mortal life is the key hour. The last hour judges all of the other hours. No one can tell how successful his life has been until his last hour. Final appraisal of the lives of Jesus or Judas or Nathan Hale would be impossible without their last hour. While you are thinking about this idea, let me give you the thoughts that one man had while living in his last hour.

This story comes from Shakespeare's *Henry the VIII*. Shakespeare's Cardinal Woolsey had been a man of great power and influence, but along the way he had done evil, thinking as most of us do that the end would never find him out. But in his final hour he found himself discovered, discredited, and discarded. His commission had been withdrawn by his church, his property had been confiscated by the king. And in that humble place where he went to die, he said in substance, the last hour of my long and weary life has come upon me. I have done not well and may God have mercy on my soul. Farewell, a long farewell to all my greatness. This is the state of man. Today he puts forth the tender leaves of hope; tomorrow blossoms and bears his blushing honors thick upon him. The third day comes the frost, the killing frost and then he falls, as I do, never to hope again. I have ventured many summers in a sea of glory far beyond my depth. I have sounded all the depths and shoals of honor but I have missed the way. My highblown pride at last broke under me and left me weary and old in service to the mercy of the rude stream.

Then he said to his servant, the only one who had not forsaken him, "Oh, Cromwell, Cromwell, I charge thee, fling away ambition. By that sin the angels fell. Corruption wins not more than honesty. Be just and fear not. Let all the ends thou aimest at be thy country's, thy god's and truth's. Then if thou diest, thou diest a blessed martyr." Then he said, "Oh, Cromwell, Cromwell, had I but served my god with half the zeal I served my king, he would not in mine age have left me naked to mine enemies."

Think how the great cardinal could have improved the quality of his life by a more effective use of his time machine.

Charles F. Kettering, the great mechanical wizard who made many wonderful machines, once said, "My interest is in the future because I am going to spend the rest of my life there." Today will be gone forever, in just a few hours, but the future will continue throughout all of eternity.

May God give us the *ability* as time travelers to draw strength from the past and then develop the necessary *vision* to make our eternal future glorious is my humble prayer.

This Is the Day

THERE is a great line which makes up the twenty-fourth verse of the 118th Psalm. It says, "This is the day which the Lord hath made; we will rejoice and be glad in it." This sentiment is an important part of the philosophy of great success and happiness.

There are many who cling to the idea that *tomorrow* is the big day. Tomorrow is the day that we have always talked about. What a wonderful time we will have tomorrow. Then we do all of the things that we have always promised ourselves to do.

"Tomorrow" things will be different. Then we will be prepared. Then we will live at our best. Tomorrow is the day when we will get the breaks. Then we will really do great things. One of the most popular ideas in our world is that things will be better tomorrow.

But in spite of the stories that we may tell ourselves, deep down inside we know that we will never see that day of myth and mystery that we talk so much about. "Tomorrow" is the day when idlers work, when fools reform, and when mortal men lay hold on heaven: Tomorrow is a snare and a delusion. Tomorrow is an impostor. There is no tomorrow. Today is *the day,* and it is a wonderful day. It is a day of wonders and miracles and workers. It is a day of opportunities and blessings. It is a day of progress and accomplishment. "*This* is the day that the Lord hath made; we will rejoice and be glad in it." We will also get the maximum benefit out of it.

A great man once said:

> With every rising of the sun,
> Think of your life as just begun.
> The past has cancelled and buried deep
> All yesterdays. There let them sleep.
>
> Concern yourself with but today,
> Grasp it, and teach it to obey
> Your will and plan. Since time began
> *Today*, has been the friend of man.
>
> You and Today! A thought sublime
> With your great heritage of time,
> And God himself to bind the twain.
> Go forth, brave heart! Attain! Attain!

To start *this* day off suppose that we get up to watch the dawn, and see the light of God's sun break over the earth. It will fill us with the glory of today. If the sun only came up once every ten years, we would certainly be on hand to witness that great event. Then we would really *see* its light and *feel* its warmth and *absorb* its vitality. We ought to look at the sunrise every morning as if we had never seen it before.

Try to imagine what it must have been like prior to that first morning of creation. We can feel the brooding, unbroken darkness that moved upon the face of the deep. Then picture what it must have been when in the march of progress God first said, "Let there be light." Why not make that kind of experience out of the beginning of each wonderful new day, as we see God's light again flood over the earth as on that first morning of creation. It is small wonder that some people who don't know God worship the sun.

In some parts of the world people worship the "good earth." God not only gives us the sun, but he has also covered the earth with sixteen inches of a miraculous substance called topsoil. Here is another of the wonders of wonders. A good farmer who understands the sun and the rain and the soil can get 400 sacks of potatoes per acre out of his sixteen inches of topsoil. He can then repeat the operation every year for forty years and still have his sixteen inches of topsoil left undiminished. Instead of potatoes, he could get strawberries or onions or peaches or watermelons as he himself may choose. Think how lavishly God rewards us in everything that we do. One potato carried to England by Sir Walter Raleigh in the sixteenth century multiplied itself into food for millions. If a farmer plants one kernel of wheat, he gets a hundred kernels in return. One tomato seed will multiply itself a million times in one year. Ten forests come out of one acorn.

Some of life's other benefits are given us in even greater proportions. If a few of the right kind of ideas are put into the mind of a great human being there come out ambition, courage, enthusiasm, faith and other productive qualities beyond imagination. Or plant a few seeds of righteousness and love in the human heart, and they multiply and blossom into invaluable benefits.

William James once said that "the greatest use of life is to spend it for something that outlasts it." The real purpose of life is that we might *spend* our lives to secure eternal life and exaltation. The final destiny of man is to become like God.

In the days of Job it was said that "All that a man hath he will give for his life." There is no expense we would avoid or no inconvenience that we would not suffer to prolong life even for a week or a month even though we knew that that period would be filled with pain and unhappiness. If mortal life is worth so much, how much is eternal life worth? What effort should be spared in bringing it about. The most valuable thing in life is life, none of which should be lost. Anyone can take a day off, no one can put a day back. And "Today" is the most important section of life. We should rejoice and be glad in it.

A little while ago during a refreshing spring shower I met a friend and asked him how he was. He said, "Terrible.

Who could feel good on such a miserable day?" My friend was not joking. It was a miserable day to him. He had taken some of the good qualities out of the Lord's day and made it over to match the gloom inside himself. His remodeling job was complete in its dreary dreadfulness. You can easily guess the amount and kind of his accomplishment in that wonderful day that God had given him. Anyone who desires success and happiness in his life should learn the 118th Psalm and get the spirit of the Lord's day inside of him.

Robert Loveman had a very constructive idea when he wrote:

> It isn't raining rain to me.
> It's raining daffodils.
> In every dimpled drop I see
> Wild flowers on the hills.
>
> The clouds of gray engulf the day
> And overwhelm the town,
> But it isn't raining rain to me,
> It's raining roses down.

The sunshine is wonderful, and so is the rain. They are God's gifts. Every life is given some of both. No life can be complete unless into that life there falls a little rain. Every life should also have a lot of sunshine. Both the rain and the sunshine are a part of this day. They must not pass unappreciated or unnoticed. For as the philosopher Thoreau wrote, "Only that day dawns to which we are awake." Elizabeth Barrett Browning has reminded us that—

> Earth is filled with heaven
> And on every foot there shines
> The glory of the burning bush
> But only he who see, takes off his shoes.

We must not send back to God any of these wonderful days only half used or half appreciated.

Think of all of the beautiful sights we have seen. Think of the great feelings we have felt. Think of the times we have gone before God on our knees. Think of the great blessing of fresh air in our lungs and food in our stomachs. Think of the energy and vision and enthusiasm we may have. Think of the refreshing rest every night, and the new opportunity to serve God every morning. Think how many souls we can turn from the broad road that leads to destruction by helping them to get their feet on the straight and narrow path that leads to eternal life. This is the day of our greatest opportunity. We must take full advantage of it.

"Many prophets and righteous men have desired to see the things which we see and have not seen them, and to hear the things that ye hear and have not heard them." We should allow no day to pass without rejoicing in its inspirations and participating in its blessing.

To miss a lifetime is only a multiplication of missing one day, and each day is increased in power as we develop the ability to appreciate and to live it.

After creation God himself looked out upon the world and called it "good." If we have the right spirit we will do the same thing—every day. With this spirit of appreciation Martin Luther said, "Not long since I beheld a sign in the heavens. I was looking out through my window at night and beheld the stars, and the whole majestic vault of God being held up without my being able to see the pillars on which the Almighty had caused it to rest. Some men say that they fear the sky may fall. Poor fools, do they not know that God is always there." Martin Luther's "sign" was to see the stars and the whole majestic vault of God—what wonders! But more important, what a thrill to know that God is always there. He is our father offering us his blessings at every turn. He has planned the world for our good—only one day of which we may have at a time and "This is the day."

We have the sun and the rain, the stars and the daffodils, and we have God giving us the most wonderful of all opportunities. We have the seeds of faith, ambition and determination. We have some of the good earth, a little rain and a lot of sunshine. We have a pair of willing hands, a productive mind, and an immortal spirit formed in the image of God. Who can fix any limits for our accomplishment? A little planning, a little enthusiasm, a little dedication, and we may entitle ourselves, our family and friends to the celestial kingdom of God. Every day can be utilized in doing some thrilling and worthwhile thing. We can plant the seeds of the wonders of the gospel to quicken other hearts. Each of us can be a better person, a better friend, a better member of the Church, a better example of righteousness.

We need never let one day go by without getting its blessing. Every day should bring us new benefactors and new beneficiaries. From the Sanskrit we hear:

> Listen to the exhortation of the Dawn!
>   Look to this day!
> For it is life, the very Life of Life.
> In its brief course lie all the
> Verities and Realities of your Existence;
>   The Bliss of Growth,
>   The Glory of Action,
>   The Splendor of Beauty,
> For yesterday is but a dream,
> And tomorrow is only a Vision;
>   But today well lived makes
> Every yesterday a dream of Happiness,
> And every Tomorrow a Vision of Hope,
> Look well therefore to this day!
> Such is the salutation of the Dawn.
>
> —From the Sanskrit

"This is the day which the Lord hath made; we will rejoice and be glad in it."

Trapped

A N AMERICAN naturalist was once walking along the seashore looking for interesting specimens of sea life. His attention was attracted to a large, strange-looking object lying ahead of him out a little way in the water. Upon examination he found that it was an immense bird, an American eagle, with a large steel trap snapped onto one foot.

Three hundred miles away on a rugged mountain slope, this great American eagle, the symbol of freedom, the emblem of power and courage, had soared down out of the skies to pick up an enticing piece of bait. In the process of getting the bait, the eagle had put his foot into the jaws of a vicious steel trap. Then the noble bird had struggled with all his might. He had jerked and pulled and fought until he had finally broken the chain and had flown away with the trap to which a part of the chain was still attached.

The eagle had regained enough of his freedom to fly three hundred miles away, but he was still fatally handicapped. He must continue to endure the torture of the trap's steel jaws relentlessly biting into his leg. In addition to the constant pain, he was now unable to maintain the old time association with his companions. He was also severely handicapped in obtaining his food and maintaining his spirit.

After weeks of suffering and exhaustion, this great eagle, worn out by struggle, famished by hunger, sickened by loneliness and tortured by despair, had fallen into the margin of the sea to die with the vicious teeth of the trap still biting into his broken, festering foot.

In the experience of the eagle is seen a close parallel of

human life. Many thousands of people are living a tortured
existence comparable to the eagle with the trap on his foot.
Attached to thousands of individuals is some galling, oppressive handicap which is sapping their energy, exhausting their
mental and spiritual resources and depleting their ambition
to live happy, productive lives. They are compelled to carry
their torment with them wherever they go, until exhausted
and defeated they give up the struggle and fall into the sea
of discouragement, failure and death. Many people go to their
graves with their tortures and sins still relentlessly biting into
their souls.

There are many different kinds of traps that wear out
the lives, wipe out the courage, exhaust the hope and destroy
the happiness of people. I recently conducted a funeral for
a friend of mine who died at age 58 with lung cancer. He
had been trapped by nicotine. This man had once been a
faithful member of the Church, and then he had been attracted by some cigarette bait, the danger of which did not
seem very serious at first. But once established, the nicotine
habit kept calling for the amount to be increased. After a
few years he had become a chain smoker. As the amounts
of nicotine grew larger, my friend's taste buds became im-
paired. As his appetite deteriorated his work load had to be
cut to correspond to his decreased vigor. Soon he wasn't
feeling very well. Over a period of months, his family physician didn't seem to be able to help much, and he was finally
sent to a specialized medical clinic in San Diego. They told
him that he must quit smoking immediately and get back to
regular, vigorous work in an attempt to recover his appetite
and normal body functions. But he couldn't get nicotine's
trap off his foot.

All bad habits that fasten themselves upon us in such a
way that we are unable to free ourselves are pretty dangerous.
If the eagle could have got the trap off his leg at any time
then, his situation would not have been so serious. But like

all of the traps of evil, once they are sprung or habits have been established, they are pretty difficult to get rid of.

In steady succession my friend had lost his appetite, his ambition, his health, his peace of mind, his income, and finally he developed lung cancer. No eagle ever endured a more agonizing, unhappy death struggle, and eventually, like the great eagle, he fell exhausted, disheartened and overcome. We buried him with this vicious forbidden habit still biting into his life.

I thought what a pity it is that we don't all accept the word of the Lord who said, " . . . tobacco is not for the body, neither for the belly, and it is not good for man, . . . " (D & C 89:8) It might have been added that it is also very expensive, time-consuming and causes considerable discomfort to others.

But there are some of us who, regardless of consequences, seem to have to try out every sin personally, and then before we know it we find that we have put our foot in the trap. My friend is just one example of what the result can be for one who tampers with evil. Frequently the consequences cannot even be stopped by death. In my friend's case the suffering was merely transferred to his family. His wife is now without a home or a husband; his young children are on their own without the direction and support of their father.

But if we could sufficiently look into all of our lives, we would find many similar situations. Many of us are dragging toward our graves the galling, wearisome traps of alcohol, immorality, ignorance and disobedience to God. These dangerous traps are usually concealed under some attractive bait to draw the attention of the intended victim. But when they are touched or stepped on, they hungrily snap shut on whoever sets them off.

If you want to catch a mouse, you just put a little cheese on the tongue of the trap. The mouse will be very anxious to get the cheese, but if he gets the cheese, he must also take the trap.

But by far the most important traps are not set to catch mice, but men and women. Military leaders set traps for their enemies. Criminals set traps for their victims. But Satan sets the most dangerous traps. They are spread over with various kinds of bait designed to appeal to every susceptible appetite. Before one has nibbled for very long on the bait, he is pretty likely to put his foot in the trap and then be forced to drag behind him this deadly instrument of torture painfully biting into his life, destroying his peace of mind and endangering his spirituality and his eternal life. But all of the possible logic, reason, and even the word of God himself seems ineffective once we have a foot in one of the traps of sin.

Each new generation continues to be trapped by the same kinds of bait. It has been said that, "There are no new sins, there are only new sinners." Each week brings new profanity users, new desecrators of the Sabbath Day, new tragedies in immorality, new violators of the Word of Wisdom, and each week a new group of God's children feel the terrible distress and heartbreaking penalties of the trap's steel jaws biting into their minds and hearts and souls.

Recently a young married man came in to talk about his troubles of which he had a large number, every one of which he had brought upon himself by his own voluntary violation of God's commandments. I talked with him about this fundamental law of consequences, that if one steps into the trap he must not be surprised if it snaps shut on his leg. I tried to point out how dangerous it was to try to get the cheese without also getting the trap. Certainly we can't expect anyone to keep putting on more cheese once the mouse has been caught. What a wonderful thing it would be if we could develop an ability to keep out of traps, a love to obey the gospel, and a hunger to please God.

Some time ago a friend of mine told me that he was

going to quit a certain bad habit. I asked him why, and he said that he was afraid to continue. I thought how much more wonderful it would have been if his motive for quitting had been to please God. In spite of the fact that God pleads with us to live righteously and in spite of the fact that every sin always brings unhappiness and suffering, yet we sometimes seem to hang on to our sins for dear life.

I told my friend with many troubles the story of Frank Buck of "Bring Them Back Alive" fame. Frank Buck captured monkeys in Africa without the use of guns or poisons. His secret was in knowing monkey psychology. Mr. Buck prepared a sweet-scented rice that he knew all monkeys were very fond of. Then he bored some holes in some coconuts just large enough to admit the monkey's empty hand when the fingers were extended. The coconuts were fastened to trees by small chains. The monkeys always followed the scent until they found the coconuts, then they would reach through the holes and get a handful of rice. But when the fingers were closed on the rice, the monkey could not get his hand out of the coconut. The monkeys would try every method of freeing themselves—except they would not let go of the rice.

There are a few chapters in the psychology book where we tend to resemble the monkeys. We get our fists full of bad habits. We load our minds with wrong attitudes. Then we sometimes refuse to let go, no matter what the cost may be. Many people become prisoners of their own thoughts because they will not let go of unworthy ideas. Frequently we will lose our lives or our eternal exaltation rather than open our fists.

We might have our own ideas about a monkey who would not let go of a handful of rice to maintain his freedom. But what about man, the masterpiece of creation who allows himself to be trapped by such disagreeable and hurtful things as dishonesty, drunkenness, immorality, ignorance, indifference, and disobedience to God? We ought to open not only our hands but our hearts to God. God is much wiser than we are, and if we will learn obedience he can save us from a lot of unnecessary trouble and pain both here and hereafter.

My young friend said that the reason he had got into so many difficulties was because he wanted to take a fling at life, but actually, like the eagle and the monkeys, he was really taking a fling at death.

In conclusion, I would like to paint three word pictures, that you may want to hang on the walls of your minds. The first is the picture of a beautiful American eagle, the symbol of power and courage, the emblem of freedom, with a vicious steel trap dangling from his broken, swollen, festering foot.

The second is a picture of great human being, who has allowed himself to be trapped by sin, one who has been pitted and pocked by the evil which he himself has initiated. The picture may show him to be unfaithful, disobedient to God and poisoned in his principles. He is tortured by guilt, worn out by discouragement and despair, and he drags himself toward eternity with an accumulation of Satan's traps still punishing his fretful, fearful soul.

The third picture is one of yourself, a child of God, formed in God's image and endowed with his attributes, heir to his kingdom, with an understanding of your own eternal potentialities. There is everything in knowing your origin and destiny and constantly reaffirming them in your life. You are an offspring of divinity; you have inherited the Creator's wisdom and power. Cling to your inheritance. Think of yourself as "a child of Omnipotence." Never let the thought escape you even for a moment. Never let evil destroy the picture.

To such Jesus has said, "Then all that my Father hath shall be given unto them," We all like to inherit from the wealthy father. What could be more desirable than to inherit from God.

Transfusions

SOMETIME AGO a friend of mine called and asked if I would come to the hospital and give him a blood transfusion. He was about to undergo a very serious major operation and without the revitalizing effect of new blood he would probably die. As I lay on the hospital cot and watched the blood run out of my arm, I asked the nurse how many blood transfusions I could safely give in the course of a year, and she said that it would be perfectly safe to give four. That is, if it were necessary, I could possibly save the lives of four people every year by a transfusion of my blood.

Then I thought about another *kind* of transfusion, and I remembered some of the people along life's way who had given me some transfusions of faith, transfusions of courage, transfusions of inspiration. And I thought that if someone should subtract from me that which properly belonged to someone else, there would not be very much of me left.

We have two main sources from which we draw our strength. The first and the greatest commandment has to do with our relationship with God, and the second great commandment has to do with our relationship with each other. What a thrilling thought that we may receive transfusions of strength from God; but John Greenleaf Whittier in his quaint Quaker style once pointed out a kind of personal vitalization that we get from each other. He said, "Me lift thee and thee lift me and we'll both ascend together." And while that may not be possible in the physical world, yet it is the very essence of mental and spiritual uplift. There is a personal stimulation that we may get from others that is very important to our success, as Jesus said, "Man does not live by bread alone." To his disciples, Jesus said, "I have meat to eat that ye know not of." (John 4:32)

In his play, *The Masque of Kings*, Maxwell Anderson said:

"If you'll go stop three tradesmen on the street, and ask the three what it is they live by, they'll reply at once, bread, meat, and drink, and they'll be certain of it; victuals and drink, like the rhyme in Mother Goose makes up their diet; nothing will be said of faith in things unseen, or of following the gleam—just bread and meat and a can of wine to wash it down, but if you know them well behind the fish-eyes and the bellies, if you know them better than they do, each one burns candles at some altar of his mind in secret; secret often from himself, each is a priest to some dim mystery by which he lives. Strip him of that and bread and meat and wine won't nourish him. Without this hidden faith he dies and goes to dust."

To supply this important need man may draw power and inspiration from God. But everyone around us may also make a contribution to our success. Ralph Waldo Emerson once said, "I have never met a man who was not my *superior* in some particular." That is, God gives each one of us some talent or some ability or some trait that we may develop whereby we are expected to excel everyone else in the world; and then we use our gifts to inspire each other, or said another way, we may draw from the available supply according to our own individual need.

Appelles, a Greek artist, who lived in the fourth century BC *borrowed* from many the features for his portrait of the goddess of beauty which enthralled the world. He devoted himself to painting the best in life. He searched out the fairest women and then reproduced the outstanding traits of each. On his canvas he painted the eyes of one, the forehead of another. He captured a particular grace here and a turn of beauty there. Finally he had a composite of a perfect woman that was able to win the admiration of mankind.

In a little different way this interesting procedure of Apelles is used by each of us. Oscar Hammerstein said, "A heart can inspire other hearts with its fire." Then he said:

> "Give me some men
> Who are stout-hearted men,
> Who will fight for the right they adore.
>
> Start me with ten
> Who are stout-hearted men
> And I'll soon give you ten thousand more."

Suppose that we take Mr. Hammerstein's suggestion and start ourselves with ten example virtues from which we may draw transfusions for our own success. Suppose that we take our first transfusion from a man whose leading virtue might be typed as "integrity." Our benefactor is the late Indian patriot, Mohandas K. Gandhi who did so many things for his people, including winning their political independence. Gandhi weighed 112 pounds. He went around four-fifths naked. He lived in a mud hut which never had an electric light or a telephone or running water. He didn't own an automobile. He never sought or ever held a public office. He had no armies, no diplomats, no statesmen.

His early life was characterized by some serious faults. But by what Louis Fischer calls the "miracle of personality" Gandhi deliberately built into himself the most worthwhile personal qualities and he later called himself a self-remade man. If you would like a good phrase here it is. By use of this idea Gandhi made himself the greatest power in India and probably in the world. Everyone understood the Gandhi was honest, that he could be trusted, that his motives were right. When Gandhi said something, everyone knew that that was exactly what he meant.

On one occasion he took a pledge from his mother to remain a vegetarian throughout his life. Many years after his mother's death Gandhi became very ill and the doctors tried to persuade him that if he would drink a little beef broth it could save his life.   But Gandhi said, "Even for life itself we may not do certain things. There is only one course open to me—to die, but never to break my pledge."

Transfusion number two is entitled "faith." Its donor is Joan of Arc, the maid of Orleans who put herself at the head of the French army in the early part of the fifteenth century. With her sacred sword, her consecrated banner and her belief in her mission, she sent a thrill of enthusiasm through the army such as neither king nor statesman could produce. She saved France from the British and then fell into the hands of her enemies. While the fires were being lighted around the stake at which this nineteen-year-old peasant maid was to be burned alive, she was given a chance to regain her liberty by denying what she believed. In choosing the fire above her freedom she said:

"The world can use these words. I know this now. Every man gives his life for what he believes. Every woman gives her life for what she believes. Sometimes people believe in little or nothing, and yet they give their lives to that little or nothing. One life is all we have, and we live it as we believe in living it and then it's gone. But to surrender what you are and live without belief is more terrible than dying— even more terrible than dying young."

Transfusion number three could well be entitled, "The will to win." We see it at its best in a man by the name of Winston Churchill. On May the 10th, 1940 Winston Churchill became Prime Minister of England. This was the time when the powerful German air fleet was making round-the-clock trips across the channel dumping plane load after plane load of bombs on England. England had already been beaten almost to a point of insensibility, and no one knew whether she could hold out for another week or a month. But everyone knew that if the British Empire was to survive, it must immediately find someone who could infuse courage and the "will to win" into the British people. If there was one man in England who could save the world from Nazi tyranny, that man was Winston Churchill, for nowhere did the fires of freedom burn with a brighter flame.

This is how Churchill responded to having the burdens of a giant groggy empire dumped on his shoulders. About that day of May 10, 1940 he said:

"As I went to bed at about 3 a.m., I was conscious of a profound feeling of relief. At last I had authority to give direction over this whole scene. I felt as if I were walking with destiny—that my past life had been but a preparation for this hour, for this trial. I could not be reproached either for having made the war or for lack of preparation for it, but I felt that I knew a good deal about it, and I was sure I would not fail."

Sure that he would not fail to do what? To save the world from the greatest mechanized might ever known in history, and this with a minimum of battle equipment and trained men.   But Churchill went on the radio, and his indomitable spirit went into the minds and hearts of his countrymen. He said:

"We shall not flag nor fail. We shall go on to the end. We shall fight in France. We shall fight on the seas and the oceans. We shall fight with growing confidence and power in the air. We shall defend our island whatever the cost of it may be. We shall fight on the landing grounds; we shall fight in the fields and in the streets. We shall never surrender. And if, which I do not for a moment believe, this island or a large part of it were subjugated and starving, then our empires beyond the seas, armed and guarded by the British fleet, will carry on the fight, until in God's own time the new world in its power and might steps forth to the rescue and the liberation of the old."

Transfusion number four is entitled "responsibility." Martin Treptow was killed in the battle of Chateau-Thierry in the year 1918. In the diary found on his body had been written these words: "I will work; I will save; I will sacrifice; I will endure; I will fight cheerfully and do my utmost as though the entire conflict depended upon me alone."

For transfusion number five we might charge ourselves with a little of the spirit of Edith Cavel, a British war nurse in occupied Belgium during the First World War. From her position in the hospital she helped some two hundred allied soldiers to escape across the border. Then she was sentenced to stand before a military firing squad. Just before the German bullets tore through her quivering flesh she said, "Patriotism is not enough."

Transfusion number six is from another great woman. It is typed "determination." Marie Skodowska was a Polish girl who married the French physicist, Pierre Curie. For many years they worked tirelessly without adequate equipment or funds in an old leaky shed trying to isolate radium from a low-grade uranium ore called pitchblende. In the play *Madam Curie*, after the 487th experiment had failed, Pierre threw up his hands in despair and said, "It will never be done, maybe in a hundred years, but never in our day." Then Marie confronted him with a resolute face and said, "If it takes a hundred years it will be a pity, but I will not cease to work for it as long as I live."

Transfusion number seven comes from our great Civil War President, Abraham Lincoln, who said:

"I am not bound to win. But I am bound to be true.

"I am not bound to succeed, but I am bound to live by the best light that I have.

"I must stand with anybody that stands right and part with him when he goes wrong."

Transfusion number eight comes from Grantland Rice, for many years the dean of American sport writers. He followed the great champions of sport and studied their lives. As Madam Curie isolated radium from pitchblende, Grantland Rice isolated the qualities that make men great in sports or in life. Then he wrote some 700 poems about these qualities, hoping to make these championship traits negotiable in the lives of others. One of his poems is entitled "Courage." Mr. Rice said:

"I'd like to think that I can look at death
And smile and say
All I have left now is my final breath.
Take that away,
And you must either leave me dust or dreams
Or in far flight
A soul that wanders where the stardust streams
Through endless night.

"But" said he,
"I'd rather think that I can look at life
With this to say
Send what you will of struggle or of strife
Blue skies or gray
I'll stand against the final charge of hate
By peak and pit
And nothing in the steel-clad fist of fate
Can make me quit."

Transfusion number nine is entitled "devotion." In the Galerie des Beaux Arts in Paris stands a beautiful statue. It is the work of a sculptor whose poverty compelled him to live and work in a garret. His clay model was nearly completed when one night a sudden frost fell upon Paris. The sculptor knew that if the water in the interstices of the clay should freeze, the beauty of the statue would be forever lost. So he wrapped his bedclothes around the clay image. The next morning they found him dead. He had frozen to death in the night, but his statue lived.

And finally as number ten, I would like to suggest an infusion from the greatest life that was ever lived, who in three words gave the greatest success formula that has ever been given when he said merely, "Come follow me." In the final analysis every life must be judged by how well it carries out that one single direction.

The Virtues of the Fathers

IN the year 428 B.C. a play was being presented in the ancient city of Athens entitled *Hippolytus*. This was a Greek tragedy written by Euripides. It was centered around Theseus, the old king of Athens and his son Hippolytus. Theseus had received from his father, Poseidon, the Grecian god of the sea, three gifts in the form of three curses. These curses not only had the power of temporal destruction, but they would also continue throughout eternity to punish anyone against whom they were invoked.

The first of these curses was directed by Theseus against his own son, Hippolytus. Hippolytus had done no wrong, but Theseus had been deceived and did not discover his error until Hippolytus was on his deathbed. And while Theseus had the power to invoke the curse, he did not have the power to set it aside once it was in operation. And so as the father sat by the bedside of his dying son he said through his tears, "I weep for your good heart, your true and upright mind. The gods have cheated me of my good sense." And as Hippolytus contemplated the eternity that he was about to enter, he said to Theseus, "Twas a bitter gift your sire gave." And then just before he died he said to his father that he could already see the gates of hell beyond which he would suffer his own father's curse throughout eternity.

If we had been seeing this tragic play in ancient Athens, we would probably have joined our tears with others not only in feeling sorry for Hippolytus, the victim of this dread curse, but more especially for his father who had set it in motion. But Theseus was not the first to possess this power to curse, nor is he the only one who has turned it against his own son.

Ten centuries before Theseus was born, God gave ancient Israel their law from the top of Mt. Sinai, and out of the lightnings and thunders of that holy mountain came the divine warning that " . . . the iniquity of the fathers shall be visited upon the children. . . . " (Exodus 20:5) The most effective way to set a curse in motion against one's own son is to develop the cause of the curse in his own life. And then as our children play with us this fateful game of "Follow the leader," it will not be long before the curse will begin to appear in their lives—that is the power to lead, possessed by every parent, is also the power to mislead. The power to mislead is the power to destroy; it is the power to cause eternal suffering.

It is a little bit startling to realize that this father and son tragedy is being enacted in real life in many of our own homes. Let me give you a more up-to-date Theseus and Hippolytus story.

A friend of mine recently called me on the telephone and told me that his young son had the habit of coming home from Sunday School each week and discussing his Sunday School lesson with his father. Sometimes the father was unable to answer adequately the son's questions, and it became necessary for him to get outside help. On this particular occasion he asked me if I would supply him with some answers. We discussed the question at some length and noted the scriptural references that were applicable.

But I suggested to my friend that it would be impossible to keep his son content for very long with the answers of someone outside the family. The son would want to know that the father knew the answers for himself. Before the son was very much older he would also discover that his father did not go to Sunday School, and he would want to know why. At Sunday School they would teach the son that some things that the father was doing were contrary to the commandments. Then this fine young son would be forced to make some decisions of his own. Should he follow his father or should he follow the Church? The father is the one who provides him with his food and his clothing and his love. He is the one who takes him on picnics and provides for his general welfare. It would be pretty difficult for the Church to win against that kind of competition. And it is pretty difficult to get the curse stopped once it is set in motion. If this splendid young son could see the end of his life from its beginning, he might say to his father as did Hippolytus, that he could already see the gates of hell beyond which he would suffer eternally for his father's bad example. This situation furnishes us with a little different setting for the statement of Jesus that ". . . a man's foes shall be they of his own household." (Matt. 10:36)

We are greatly disturbed whenever evil is brought upon one person by someone else; for example, we were upset when Russia closed her church doors by governmental decree. But what Russia has done officially, many of us are doing individually. That is, what good does it do if our churches are open if we are not in them? Or, how much better off are we than the Russians if we don't manifest our faith by our works.

In 1958 *The U.S. News & World Report* carried an interesting headline: "What 22 Years of U.S.-Soviet Talks Have Produced." The article pointed out that during this period 3400 meetings had been held between high diplomatic representatives of the United States and the Soviet Union. During this time fifty-two major agreements had been made, fifty of which had already been broken by the Russians.

Fortunately for us our eternal exaltation does not depend upon whether Russia keeps or breaks her international agreements. But we might ask ourselves if our upsurge in juvenile crime and delinquency is a satisfactory result of what 22 years of dealing with our own children and with God have produced. During the past twenty-two years we have attended many church meetings. We have made many major agreements with each other and with God. Some of these agreements have been made at the waters of baptism; others have been made as we have received, and been advanced in the priesthood. We have made some important agreements at the marriage altar. And each week we meet before the Sacrament table and witness unto our Heavenly Father that we will always keep his commandments. Wouldn't it be interesting if some impartial statistician could determine how many of these important agreements we have made and how our personal performance percentage compared with the Russians?

We should remember that any disobedience to God that we pick up in our lives is soon transmitted to others, particularly our children. That is, the power of example is the greatest power in the world. That is the way we learn to walk. That is the way we learn to talk. That is why we speak with the accent we do. That is how we learn to dress ourselves. That is why we have our hair cut and our clothing tailored the way we do.

I suppose that if I had seen you eat your breakfast this morning I would have discovered that most of you ate with a fork in your right hand. But I discovered the other day that in certain parts of Canada people eat with the fork in their left hand. I suppose the reason is that they have seen somebody else do it that way. Probably if we had been born in Japan we may not have eaten with a fork at all.

The other day I went to a meeting attended by about twenty-five people. During the meeting one man in the front of the room yawned. Then I watched that yawn go all over the audience. The people who were yawning in the audience were not even aware of why they were yawning. Unconsciously they were following the example of someone else.

That is also the way we get many of our manners, our morals, and our attitudes.

Thomas Carlyle said, "We reform others when we walk uprightly." And it is just as true that we destroy others when we walk unrighteously. Even Jesus said, "The Son can do nothing of himself, but what he seeth the Father do: for what things soever he doeth these also doeth the Son likewise." (John 5:19) That is also true of our children. They may not follow our advice, but they will follow us.

One of the important functions in the life of Jesus was to serve as a pattern for us. And we reach our highest rank while serving as a pattern for our children. It has been said that the first question that God will ask every parent is, "Where are your children?" The responsibility of parents is not just to be mothers and fathers of bodies, we are also appointed to be mothers and fathers of blessings.

Fortunately the lesson from Sinai did not end with the decree that " . . . the iniquity of the fathers shall be visited upon the children." (Ex. 20:5) It is also true that the *virtues* of the fathers are visited upon the children. Theseus received from his father, Poseidon, three curses. We have received from our Father in heaven some great blessings which we may direct as we choose.

Nancy Hanks directed one of her blessings into the life of her nine year old son, Abraham Lincoln when on her death bed she said "Abe go out there and amount to something." Later in his life Lincoln said, "All that I am or ever hope to be I owe to my angel mother." Jesus conferred a blessing upon Simon Peter and raised the life of this humble fisherman to one of great spiritual worth.

We may confer as many blessings as we like on whomever we like by first developing the inspiration in our own lives. We speak a great deal about our right to receive inspiration from God, and what a tremendous blessing that is.

But the thing we don't always understand is our equal right to *give* inspiration.

Some time ago I listened to a great Sunday School teacher recount the thrilling story of creation. "So God created man in his image." (Gen. 1:27) As I listened to this story unfold, I closed my eyes and wished that I could have been there to have seen this great event take place. Then I remembered something that I have tried not to forget, and that is that the creation of man is not something that was finished and done with in the Garden of Eden 6,000 years ago, the creation of man is still going on, and we are the creators. That is, we are creating the faith and the enthusiasm and the attitudes which will determine what men and women will be throughout all of eternity.

God has also left the world of men unfinished. He has left the character unformed, the lessons unlearned, the testimonies unacquired, and the determination undeveloped. Then as an effective means for our accomplishment he has given us this basic, fundamental law of the harvest that says, "We reap as we sow." But that is only a part of the law. Mostly we reap as others have sown for us. We reap as our teachers have sown. And one of the most thrilling ideas in the world is that our children will reap as we sow. This is a part of that divine law "that the virtues of the fathers shall be visited upon the children."

Each of us has been given a set of the most wonderful blessings, which we may confer upon whomever we choose. May God help us to use wisely this power that he has placed in our hands.

Vision

I WOULD like to tell you what to me is one of the most thrilling stories of the New Testament. It has to do with a blind man by the name of Bartimaeus, who sat by the roadside just outside of the city of Jericho begging for his living. And when he heard that Jesus of Nazareth was about to pass by, he began calling to him. And Jesus heard Bartimaeus and asked that he be brought, and the blind man stood before Jesus.

Jesus said to Bartimaeus, "What would you that I should do unto you?" This blind man had asked for a great many things from a great many people as they had come down this road from Jericho. Probably none of these things had any very great value, but this time he didn't ask for some small thing. When Jesus said, "What would you that I should do unto you?" the blind man replied, "I would that I might receive my sight." And that is the thing that most of us need more than anything else. Almost more than anything else we need vision, we need appreciation, we need understanding. We don't see things clearly enough, and we don't see them soon enough, and we don't see far enough.

The thing that bothers me more than anything else as I go about a little bit, is to see the very large number of people, particularly young people, who are running the risk of losing their blessings because they take a negative view of things, and are so easily discouraged by the very problems that were intended to make them strong. Of course, a discouraged person is always a weak person. To me discouragement is one of the great sins inasmuch as it causes so many people to lose their blessings. I am not trying to say that there are not a lot of serious problems in the world, because there are. There is a great deal of unrighteousness among us. There is the threat of war and destruction that constantly hangs over the world. No one knows whether or not he will be permitted to carry out his plans even if he makes them. Many brood about the future and what it holds for us. But try to think of a time when there were no problems, or when people had any guarantees that they would be permitted to carry their plans to completion. There have always been trouble and sin and death in the world. But it has been pointed out to us that "Even the crash of the universe could only kill us once."

But too many of us suffer too many things that never happen. Paraphrasing Shakespeare, "The fearful die a thousand times before their deaths. The brave man never tastes of death but once." Historians tell us of the dark day that once took place in Connecticut when some strange darkness came upon them in the middle of the day. The legislature was in session, and considerable confusion arose concerning what should be done. Some thought it was the end of the world. One legislator moved for adjournment. Then another legislator arose and addressed his colleagues. He told them that if it was the end of the world, he for one, wanted to be found doing his duty when the end came. He moved that the lamps should be lighted and that they proceed with their business. This was done. Soon the darkness passed and with it their fear.

Whether the reason may be good or bad, discouragement always leads toward failure. To counteract this evil suppose that we count our blessings. Suppose that we do at least an equal amount of thinking on the positive side of our problems. At least, I would like to offer for your consideration a point of view of our times.

1. You live in the greatest age that has ever been known in the history of the world. Your forefathers lived on a flat, stationary earth and plowed their ground with a wooden

stick, whereas you live on an earth of power steering and jet propulsion, and you must have courage and other character qualities to match.

2. You live in the greatest nation that has ever been known since creation. With some 6% of the world's population, we have 50% of all of the washing machines, television sets, automobiles and other devices for civilization. In a material way you live better than any king lived just a hundred years ago. There are very few people in America who would not count it an incredible hardship to have to live as Solomon lived even in all of his glory.

A great flood of knowledge has been released in the world in our day, and we may have as big a share as we like in this great age of wonders and enlightenment. What a thrill it is to live now. Many ancient prophets looked down to our day and desired to live in our times. Someone referred to the wonder of our day and said, "All of this I have seen, a part of it I was."

3. You live in a day when the gospel of Jesus Christ has been restored to the earth in a fulness never before known in the world. You may secure for yourself and family the blessings of the celestial kingdom no matter what may happen in Washington or Peiping or Moscow. Anyone who in our day gets off the straight and narrow path that leads back to God does so because of his own choice, because the pathway to eternal life is now perfectly marked and brilliantly lighted. From this point of view and by way of contrast, think of living in the ignorance, superstition, and uncertainty of the dark ages.

4. We live in a day when the knowledge of medicine gives us strong bodies and clear minds. You may be interested to know that had you lived in Jerusalem 2,000 years ago, your life expectancy at birth would have been 19 years. If you had lived in George Washington's day in America, it would have been 35 years. When I was born, the life ex-

pectancy in the United States was 48 years. But the baby
that was born in an American hospital this morning has a
life expectancy of 70 years. Even in my lifetime God has
given us 22 more years of life in which to get ready for those
thrilling experiences which lie beyond mortality, but all of
our years are now lived under infinitely better circumstances.
I am very grateful that I did not die at 19 or 35 or 48.   As
someone once said, "I'm not afraid to die, but I'm afraid that
I will die before I accomplish the things that I would like to
accomplish."

5. You live in a day in which pain has largely been eliminated. How would you like to have a tooth pulled, or an
appendicitis operation performed by the methods of a hundred years ago? I suppose that everyone some time ought
to have the privilege of telling about *his* operation, and so
I am going to tell you about *my* operation.

Some time ago I lay on the operating table for about
two hours while a friend of mine chiseled out the boney partition in my nose. I think you call this complaint a deviated
septum. The partition in the nose gets out of line and ob-
structs the air passage. The doctor laid me on the operating
table and put a cloth over my eyes. Then he gave my nose
a little bath in cocaine hydrochloride. Then he got his instruments inside the nostril and cut the cartilage and tissues
loose. (This is a little bit gruesome here for a few minutes,
but I will hurry over the worst part.) But he took out the
tissues and the bone, cut the bone up in little strips, straight-
ened it out and then put everything back, and sewed the
whole thing together again. And in all of this process I had
not the slightest sensation of any pain.

I was especially interested in this because I had just
finished reading a book written by a French surgeon who
accompanied the French army in the year 1600. He told
about some of his operations. In the most simple one that
I can remember, he told about curing a man of a simple

gunshot wound in the fleshy part of his leg. That is an operation that I suppose might be handled in our day by a doctor with not much more than a little mercurochrome and a bandaid. But here is what this doctor did. First, he laid the patient on the operating table and had ten men sit on him. Then he cut and sawed and hacked until he got his leg off. Then he disinfected what was left of his leg with a white-hot searing iron by cooking the first inch and a half of the fleshy stump. Then he told of the screaming and terror that always accompanied those situations, and that 75% of all of the patients that he cured of their disease, died of the remedy in the next 24 hours.

Now I am not trying particularly to save you the thought of any pain. But how would you like to have your children live with the mutilation, distortion and terror of those days, being constantly ridden by disease, and suffering untold tortures throughout their lives. Someone has said that it costs more to live now than it used to. And somebody else said, "Yes, and it is worth a lot more, too." And we should keep that in mind.

6. You live in a day when you may have all the education that you desire. One of the first things that Adam and Eve were asked to decide when they were placed in the Garden of Eden was whether or not they would eat the fruit from the Tree of Knowledge of Good and Evil. And after they had eaten God said, "The man is now become as one of us, knowing good from evil." And I would just like to point out in passing that the right kind of knowledge still tends to have that effect upon people. It still tends to make men and women become as gods.

There was a flaming sword placed in the Garden of Eden to guard the Tree of Life. But fortunately for us there is no flaming sword guarding the Tree of Knowledge of Good and Evil, and everyone of us may eat till his heart's content.

When you tend to get a little discouraged or feel sorry for yourself, suppose that you ask yourself these questions.

a. When would you rather live than in this great age of wonders and enlightenment which the prophets looked forward to and called "the dispensation of the fulness of times"?

b. Where would you rather live than in this great free land of America?

c. Who would you rather be than who you are?

I don't know why it is that we are so favored as to be permitted to live in the greatest age in the greatest country, under the most favorable circumstances that have ever existed in the world. But inasmuch as that is the fact, we ought to appreciate it, and we ought to make the most out of it. And we can't do that if we are continually in some kind of mental depression and are being shot through with several kinds of discouragement merely because we lack vision.

One of the most important secrets of success comes in recognizing our blessings and getting sufficiently excited about them. The story is told of a man who was enjoying the great beauties of the earth, the glory of the landscape, the beauty of the mountains and the forests, the color of the blossoms and the miracle of the growing things around him. Then he was startled by hearing on the sidewalk behind him the tap, tap, tap of a blind man as he felt his way with his cane. Then he was sad, his blind friend was missing all of these wonders that so delighted him. Then he remembered what Jesus had said, that there were some who had eyes and yet could not see. Then he wondered if probably he was one of these. Then he wrote some verse which concluded with these lines. He said:

> I pitied him in his blindness,
> But can I boast I see,
> Perhaps there walks a spirit close by
> Who pities me.

> Some spirit who hears me tapping,
> That five sensed cane of mind.
> Amid such unguessed glories
> That I am worse than blind.

And I suppose one of the most thrilling lines in all of the scripture was spoken by blind Bartimaeus, who after his contact with the master said, "Whereas I was blind, now I see." That should also be our experience. Certainly it is one of the greatest accomplishments in life—to develop the ability to see clearly those considerations that have to do with our salvation. Sometimes we don't do that and consequently our blessings are lost.

John Milton who wrote the great epic poem *Paradise Lost* was blind for some twenty years before his poem was written. Someone said that "Milton never saw paradise until he lost his eyes." Milton's first wife died and he married again. He lived with his second wife for many years but never saw her face. He tried to imagine what she looked like. One night he dreamed that he saw her. She was dressed all in white. He had never imagined anyone or anything so beautiful. But as he was about to embrace her, he was awakened and he said, "Day brought back my night." That is, when he was asleep he could see; but when he was awake he was blind. Then he prayed that inasmuch as he had been denied this great gift of physical vision, that God would give him spiritual sight that he might see and understand the things of God. In his prayer he said:

> So much the rather, thou celestial light,
>   Shine inward;
> And the mind with all her powers irradiate.
> There plant eyes, all mists from hence
>   Purge and disperse.
> That I may see and tell of things
>   Invisible to mortal sight.

Sometimes we have to close our eyes upon some things, that we may see the more important things more clearly. The author of the song *The Blind Plowman sang,* "God took away my eyes that my soul might see."

Now in conclusion I would like to take you back once more to the roadside just outside the city of Jericho and join blind Bartimaeus in his prayer to God in which he said, "I would that I might receive my sight." May God help us to open our eyes, to obtain understanding, and the spiritual vision that will guide us to him, is my humble prayer.

Waging War

THE CHURCH and every individual member in it should be constantly waging war, *not* a war against anyone—it should be a war *for* everyone; a war for God and peace and righteousness, a war for our children, for the Church and for our country. We should wage a constant war against ignorance, for no nation or individual can be ignorant and free at the same time.

In the battle of life we have many antagonists that come in many shapes and sizes. All of his days Abraham Lincoln fought against melancholy and despair. Others are harrassed by inertia, lethargy, sloth and sin.

Someone has said that, "There is nothing the devil loves so much as peace." He is the inspiration of those who are satisfied to let well enough alone. For years Hitler, the assassin and trouble maker, cried out to the nations, "Let us alone. We want peace." The communist dictator wants to be let alone while he enslaves the world. He continually talks of peace while he murders helpless peoples and tries to deprive them of their God-given free agency. The liquor makers are constantly crying out, "Let us alone. We are satisfied." As long as evil men want peace, righteous men must be warriors. Because every individual life is different, each in some degree must learn to recognize his own enemies, devise his own strategy, establish his own beachheads and bring to pass his own VJ days. But every seeker after truth and everyone in quest of freedom and everyone in search of justice, and every scholar, and every teacher, and every thinker, and every prophet must be a warrior.

Before the Son of God was the Prince of Peace he was

Jehovah the warrior, the leader of the armies of heaven who fought against evil and compulsion. While truth by itself may on some occasions silence its enemies, yet in most cases even truth must be defended and championed and fought for.

Some time ago I attended a church meeting where the leaders spent an abnormal share of the time saying how much they loved each other and how much they enjoyed being together. But that was about all there was to their program. The activities reflecting their leadership score, were drifting slowly along on a very low level. It is not love in leaders, that allows spirituality to fall and blessings to be lost. True love does not manifest itself in inactivity and mere verbal declarations. Rather, it shows a vital concern for those led, and is identified by a willingness to fight in their interests. The best warrior is usually the one who makes the best preparation for the battle. And effective preparation must be mental, physical, emotional, and spiritual. No one is ever quite so unsuccessful as when he is trying to carry on the important battle of life mentally and spiritually unprepared and unconcerned about results.

A successful warrior should have a "cause," and he should know what it is. He should have a plan of attack. He should have zeal enough to win. When one is mentally prepared and emotionally determined, he works with great power. It is the unprepared and the unfit that are always being laid low by the attacks of discouragement and despair.

The moment that we relax our effort, we are in danger. In his novel *The Citadel*, A. J. Cronin has the faithful young wife say to her slipping husband, "Don't you remember how you used to speak about the future, that it was an attack upon the unknown, that it was an assault up the hill as though you must take the castle upon the hilltop?" The weakening husband replied, "I was young and foolish then." When the spirit quits fighting, it is not long before the mind is taken captive. As soon as people let go of their enthusiasm for the fight, they soon lose the battle of the mind, and begin a long slide into the world of failure and defeat.

What a thrilling thing to contemplate a truly great fighter, one who has his blood filled with power and his brain supercharged with victory, one who counts it a pleasure to be on his feet and going the second mile. A fighter must have the ability to make long marches, and if necessary on short rations. The fighter is able to hold his ground in the face of difficulty. Someone once prayed, "If trouble comes, let it be in my day." That is the spirit of the warrior. He prays, "If there are difficult problems to solve, let me solve them." That is also the spirit that makes men strong.

Too frequently we become what Emerson calls "parlor soldiers." We like to dine nicely and sleep warm, but shun the vigorous battle of life where strength is born. We pray for ease and peace and prosperity. We think of comfort and enjoyment, and sometimes in the process we become sluggish, soft, and lethargic, we lose the spirit of success, and the blessings of those for whom we have leadership responsibility.

Three medical students in their laboratory were once trying to stand a cadaver up on his feet against the wall for study. Each time they thought that they had him perfectly balanced he would slump down to the floor again. One of the students said, "I know what is the matter, he hasn't any spirit in him." That is where most of us lose out. We lose the spirit of the warrior. We fail to respond to the challenge of great opportunities.

Everyone should be fighting for a cause which is greater than he is, one that he can enthusiastically give his life to. One of the greatest Christian warriors was the Apostle Paul. Think of him as he sits in his prison cell in Rome awaiting his execution. He is now an old man. For some thirty years he had turned neither to the right nor to the left, but had said, "This one thing I do." There were no sidelines, no excuses, no needless startings and stoppings—just that sure and steady quality of always being dependable, of always going forward, of always keeping in focus the one great aim and purpose of his life.

How different his actual career had been from what might have been expected over thirty years before when he was a young and influential member of the Sanhedrin with everything to make his career promising and happy—friends, position, influence, and education. And then had come that great day on the road to Damascus when suddenly there shined round him a light from heaven. And after he had fallen to the earth, he heard a voice saying unto him, "Saul, Saul, why persecutest thou me?" And Saul said, "Who art thou, Lord!" And the Lord said, "I am Jesus whom thou persecutest; It is hard for thee to kick against the pricks." And he trembling and astonished said, "Lord, what wilt thou have me do?"

For three days Paul was without sight, without food, without drink. But the Lord had said, "He is a chosen vessel unto me, to bear my name before the Gentiles and kings and the children of Israel, For I will show him how great things he must suffer for my name's sake." From that day onward, Paul ceased not to carry forward with his utmost vigor his assigned task. Then after these many years of ministry he recounted his manner of life thus:

> In labours more abundant, in stripes above measure, in prisons more frequent, in deaths oft, Of the Jews five times received I forty stripes save one: Thrice was I beaten with rods; once was I stoned, thrice I suffered shipwreck; a night and a day I have been in the deep; In journeyings often, in perils of waters, in perils of robbers, in perils of mine own countrymen, in perils by the heathen, in perils in the city, in perils in the wilderness, in perils in the sea, in perils among false brethren; in weariness and painfulness, in watchings often, in hunger and thirst, in fastings often, in cold and nakedness. Besides those things that are without, that which cometh upon me daily, the care of all the churches. (II Cor. 11:23-28.)

Of all of his experiences, this last must have been the most wearisome—the care that comes from within the church. People sometimes get tired and want to quit, or they lack the enthusiasm to supply their own initiative and must be encouraged and helped and coaxed. It is easy to fight the battles from without, but the real heartbreak comes when the wavering is from within.

But there was no wavering for Paul. He would go on and on and on and on, alone if need be and on his own power. When we consider the ability which Paul had developed for sustained, continuous effort in one direction, it is small wonder that the Lord had said, "He is a chosen vessel unto me."

That same thing might also be said of us if we could learn to stick to our convictions and our assignments as energetically and as long. Paul's bodily presence was weak; his speech contemptible; (II Cor. 10:10) he mentions his thorn in the flesh. (II Cor. 12:7) But men can get along without money, without name, without influence, without education; your appearance may be poor, your speech may be faulty. All that will amount to little if you are a fighter and know where you are going. You have never heard of Paul taking a vacation or being afraid of wearing out. He was on fire with his determination and never lost sight of his goal. He never gave up, he never relaxed his effort, he never quit. He said, "I fight on, lest I myself should be a castaway." (I Cor. 9:27)

Just before the end of his ministry Paul wrote a letter to Timothy, a young man whom he calls his son in the gospel. Inasmuch as Paul may not have had any sons of his own, he may have imagined for himself a sort of continued mortality through Timothy. But even in his death his determination never faltered, and the fervor of his admonition to Timothy shows no signs of any decrease from that first day when blinded and stunned he had said, "Lord, what wilt thou have me do?" After exhorting Timothy to the utmost of diligence, Paul expressed the realization that his own mission had almost been completed. He said, "For I am now ready to be offered, and the time for my departure is at hand. I have fought a good fight; I have finished my course; I have kept the faith:" (II Tim. 4:6-7) What a thrilling expression to come at the end of a long life of faithful, capable service. He said, "Finally, my brethren, be strong in the Lord, and in the power of his might. Put on the whole armour of God, that ye may be able to stand against the wiles of the devil." (Eph. 6:10-11)

Paul was soon to go to Rome to be beheaded, and I like to think of him on that day when the axe of the executioner granted him final release from his earthly labors, that he might go to stand a second time before Jesus of Nazareth. And I imagine that there will be few, if any, men who will ever come before their maker with greater cause to rejoice than he.

And when we come to that point in our own lives, and have cause to reflect on the fight we have fought and the course we have run, how meaningless will be the money we have made or the ease we have enjoyed, or the affluence we have attained. Life was never intended to be merely a pleasure trip; it is also a mission, a conquest, a testing. How bitter must be the final remorse of a lifetime of wasted opportunity.

Sometimes through our thoughtlessness or our sloth we lose our appetite for the struggle. Consequently we do not prepare ourselves for accomplishment, and we waste our powers sleeping the sleep of failure. "There are certain kinds of peace that belong only to the cemetery."

May our Heavenly Father help us to develop the courage, the industry, and the devotion to be good fighters in his name, and not only to say, "Lord, what wilt thou have me do?" But to get up on our feet, and without excuses or alibis stay there until the job is done.

Edward Roland Sill gives us something of the spirit of
a great warrior in his poem entitled

OPPORTUNITY

This I beheld, or dreamed it in a dream:—
There spread a cloud of dust along a plain;
And underneath the cloud, or in it, raged
A furious battle, and men yelled, and swords
Shocked upon swords and shields. A prince's banner
Wavered, then staggered backward, hemmed by foes.

A craven hung along the battle's edge,
And thought, "Had I a sword of keener steel—
That blue blade that the king's son bears—but this
Blunt thing!"—he snapped and flung it from his hand,
And lowering crept away and left the field.

Then came the king's son, wounded, sore bestead,
And weaponless, and saw the broken sword,
Hilt-buried in the dry and trodden sand,
And ran and snatched it, and with battle-shout
Lifted afresh he hewed his enemy down,
And saved a great cause that heroic day.

What a thrilling thing that if we choose we can present
ourselves before God as a generation of fighters, not fighters
against anyone, but fighters for everyone, fighters who will
dream the dreams and see the visions of eternal righteous
accomplishment, and then wage an effective war against the
empires of ignorance, sloth, lethargy, and sin.

In our own day a thrilling commandment has come from
the Lord himself asking us to be good fighters. He said:
"Therefore, O ye that embark in the service of God, see that
ye serve him with all your heart, might, mind and strength,
that ye may stand blameless before God at the last day."
(D & C 4:2)

What Is Man?

THE QUESTION that serves as our present title is taken from the 8th Psalm. The psalms, collectively, are in Hebrew called by a word meaning praises. Some of the psalms were compositions set to music. In the 8th Psalm David sang:

"O Lord our Lord, how excellent is thy name in all the earth! . . . When I consider thy heavens, the work of thy fingers, the moon and the stars, which thou hast ordained; What is man, that thou art mindful of him? and the son of man, that thou visitest him? For thou hast made him a little lower than the angels, and hast crowned him with glory and honour. Thou madest him to have dominion over the works of thy hands; thou hast put all things under his feet: . . . O Lord our Lord, how excellent is thy name in all the earth! . . ."

The great scriptures are frequently as stimulating in their questions as they are helpful in their answers. What an interesting bit of information it would be if we had the Lord's full answer to the psalmist's question, "What is man that thou art mindful of him, and the son of man that thou visitest him?" It is a very interesting thought to remember that the one thing that we probably know less about than almost any other thing in the world is our own individual selves. You can ask a man questions about science, invention or history, and he will answer you. But if you ask him to write out an analysis of himself and tell you about his mind and soul qualities, you may not get a very good answer. Suppose you ask him where he came from, or what his purpose, or destiny is? Probably the most startling part of this situation is that we don't really think about this important question very much either one way or the other, and yet no question could be more important to us than, "What is man? what is his past? what is his purpose? what is his future?"

When we make the most ordinary appraisal of someone, we always like to know something about his background, who his parents are, what his training has been, and what his aptitudes are? David's question was directed to the Lord, and that is the source from which the answer must also come. The scriptures tell us many things about ourselves including an account of our two creations. One was a spiritual creation, the other was a much later earthly creation. The Lord tells of the first creation in the first chapter of Genesis. Then in beginning the second chapter he says, "Thus the heavens and the earth were finished, and all the host of them. . . .

"And every plant of the field before it was in the earth, and every herb of the field before it grew: for the Lord God hath not caused it to rain upon the earth, and there was not a man to till the ground." (Gen. 2:1, 5)

In a modern revelation of this same scripture, the Lord says,
" . . . for in heaven created I them; and there was not yet flesh upon the earth, . . . " (Moses 3:5)

And then God formed the mortal body out of the dust of the ground, and when the spirit and the body were joined together, man became a living soul.

A very important part of our background is that our mortal birth was not the beginning of our lives. Christ is our example and nothing is more clearly taught in the scripture than that the life of Christ did not begin at Bethlehem, nor did it end at Calvary. He himself said, "I come forth from the Father, and am come into the world: again, I leave the world, and go to the Father." (John 16:28) Just before his crucifixion he prayed to his father and said, "I have glorified thee on the earth: I have finished the work which thou gavest me to do. And now, O Father, glorify thou me with thine own

self with the glory that I had with thee before the world was."
John said that Jesus " . . . was in the beginning with God. All
things were made by him; and without him was not any thing
made that was made." (John 1:2-3)

The scripture is clear in declaring Jesus the first begotten
son of God in the spirit. (Heb. 1:6) (Rev. 1:5) And the only
begotten in the flesh. (John 1:14, 18, 3:16, I John 4:9)
Throughout the Old Testament the Son is known as Jehovah,
and until his mortal birth in Bethlehem he was a personage
of spirit. Because we are also the spirit children of God we
learn much about ourselves from what we know of the pre-
mortal life of Christ.

Some ancient scripture which was revealed anew in modern times tells us of an interesting revelation of the person of
the ante-mortal Christ—given some 2200 years B.C. to a great
prophet known as the Brother of Jared. Because of this
prophet's great faith the Lord revealed himself and said,
"Seest thou that ye are created after my own image. Yea,
even all men were created in the beginning after mine own
image." Then he said, "Behold, this boy, which ye now behold, is the body of my spirit; and man have I created after
the body of my spirit; and even as I appear unto thee to be
in the spirit will I appear to my people in the flesh." (Ether
3:15-16)

In form and being the Lord was so like man that the
Brother of Jared could not understand the difference and he
said to the Lord, "I knew not that the Lord had flesh and
blood." The Lord explained that his body was spirit. However he told the Brother of Jared that at a later date he should
take upon himself a body of flesh and blood even as the plan
of God designs for all men.

One of the most wonderful of all revelations was given
by the Lord to Abraham showing the pre-existence, where
we all lived together in the presence of God even before this
earth was formed. Recording this great event Abraham said,

"Now the Lord had shown unto me, Abraham, the intelligences that were organized before the world was; and among all these were many of the noble and great ones; And God saw these souls that they were good, and he stood in the midst of them, and he said, These I will make my rulers; for he stood among those that were spirits . . . and he said unto me: Abraham, thou art one of them; Thou wast chosen before thou wast born. And there stood one among them that was like unto God, and he said unto those who were with him: We will go down, for there is space there, and we will take of these materials, and we will make an earth whereon these may dwell; And we will prove them herewith, to see if they will do all things whatsoever the Lord their God shall command them; And they who keep their first estate shall be added upon; and they who keep not their first estate shall not have glory in the same kingdom with those who keep their first estate; and they who keep their second estate shall have glory added upon their heads for ever and ever." (Abr. 3:22-26)

In our long pre-existence antedating the earth itself, some of the children of God distinguished themselves and thereby earned certain advantages for this life. But the Lord had said that all who "kept their first estate" would be added upon. We would be given this wonderful, beautiful body of flesh and bones without which we could never attain a fulness of joy. For the first time we would enjoy this miraculous power of procreation with the privilege of organizing families and having them sealed together in the temple provided for that purpose. Then we were given the promise that if we kept our second estate we would have glory added upon our heads forever and ever. For a long period we looked forward to this great privilege of mortality. And when we saw the foundations of this earth being laid and knew that we would have the privilege of living upon it, we were so delighted that "all of the sons of God shouted for joy." (Job 37:1-8)

We don't always understand these important things. For that matter we don't even understand our own birth or how our body is formed. We can't understand how our minds work or how the body and spirit are joined together.

We do know something about the love we feel for our own children. Many parents would give their lives at any time to promote the welfare of their own offspring. That should help us to understand our own importance in God's sight and his desire to help us. He has said, " . . . this is my work and my glory, to bring to pass the immortality and eternal life of man." (Moses 1:39) God desires that his children should become as he is. Jesus said, "Be ye therefore perfect, even as your Father which is in heaven is perfect." (Matt. 5:48) And that is our possible future destiny. And what could be more natural or desirable than for the off-spring to sometime become like the parent? Who can think of a more thrilling idea in the world than our own possibility of eternal progress?

The following quotation from B. H. Roberts gives us a stimulating insight into our own future. Brother Roberts said, "Think for a moment what progress a man makes within the narrow limits of this life. Regard him as he lies in the lap of his mother . . . a new born babe. There are eyes that may see, but cannot discern objects, ears that may hear, but cannot distinguish sounds. Hands as perfectly fashioned as yours and mine, but helpless. Feet and limbs, but they are unable to bear the weight of his body, much less walk. . . . And yet within the span of three score years and ten, by the marvelous working of that wondrous power within . . . what a change may be wrought. From that helpless babe may arise one like unto Demosthenes or Cicero, or Pitt, or Burke, or Fox, or Webster, who shall compel listening senates to hear him, and by his master-mind dominate their intelligence and their will, and compel them to think in channels that he shall mark out for them. Or, from such a babe may come a Nebuchadnezzar or an Alexander or a Napoleon who shall found empires or give direction to the course of history. From such a beginning may come a Lycurgus, a Solon, a Moses, or a Justinian who shall give constitutions and laws to kingdoms, empires and republics, blessing happy millions unborn in their day, and direct the course of nations along the paths of orderly peace and virtuous liberty.

"From that helpless babe may come a Michaelangelo who from some crude mass of stone from the mountainside, shall work out a heaven born vision that shall hold the attention of man for generations, and make them wonder at the God-like powers of man that have created an all but living and breathing statue. Or a Mozart, a Beethoven or a Handel may come from such a babe and call forth from the silence those richer harmonies that lift the soul out of its present narrow prison house and give it fellowship for a season with the Gods. Or from this helpless babe may arise a master-mind who shall seize the helm of the ship of state, and give to a nation course and direction through troublesome times, and anchor it at last in a haven of peace, prosperity and liberty. Crown it with honor too and give it a proud standing among the nations of the earth while he, the Savior of his country is followed by the benedictions of his countrymen."

And all this may be done by a man in this life, nay, it has been done between the cradle and the grave. Then what may not be done in the eternity by one of these God-men? Remove from his path the incident of death, or better yet, contemplate him as raised from the dead, and give to him in the full splendor of manhood's estate, immortality, endless existence. What may we not hope that he will then accomplish? What limits can you venture to fix as marking the boundary of his development and progress? Are there any limits that can be conceived? Why should there be any limits thought of? Grant immortality to man, and God for his guide. What is there in the way of intellectual, moral, or spiritual development that he may not aspire to, if within the short space of mortal life there are men who rise up out of infancy and become masters of the elements of fire and water and earth and air so that they will nigh rule them as Gods. What may it not be possible for them to do in a few hundred or thousands of millions of years?

The story is told of a great king who when his son was born, took him to a far corner of the kingdom and handed him over to a young peasant couple with the instructions that they were to rear him as their own son and not tell him who he was until he was old enough to rule, and then the king would return and make his identity known. The king didn't want his son to know of his great power before he had learned how to use it. He wanted him to know the value of great wealth before he had it placed in his hands.

That is also about what our situation is except that we are not merely the children of a great king, we are the children of the great God who created the earth. We are traveling through mortality incognito. The heavens and the earth, the moon and the stars are the handiwork of God, but man is his son.

Someone once said to his friend, "Who do you think you are?" And he whispered quietly to himself, "I wish I knew." Some day we will discover who we are, then we will know the full answer to David's question, "what is man, that thou art mindful of him, or the son of man that thou visitest him!" Then I suppose the world itself will hardly be able to contain our enthusiasm. In the meantime we should pray that God will give us a clear vision of our great destiny.

What Shall I Do with Jesus?

DURING THAT LONG, awful night of betrayal and trial, Jesus was brought before Pilate. Pilate believed Jesus to be innocent of any wrong and made a weak attempt to try and save his life by taking advantage of one of his privileges as Roman governor to release one prisoner to the Jews at the time of the Passover.

Pilate had in his custody a noted insurrectionist and murderer by the name of Barabbas and probably relying upon the sense of fairness of those accusing Jesus that certainly they would not consent to the release of a notorious criminal and punish an innocent man, Pilate said to them, "Whom will ye that I release unto you, Barabbas or Jesus which is called Christ?" (Matt. 27:17) Pilate must have been startled to hear them say, "Barabbas." He said, "Then what shall I do with Jesus?" and they replied, "Let him be crucified." Pilate said, "Shall I crucify your king?" And they answered, "We have no king, but Caesar." Then Pilate took water and washed his hands before the multitude saying, "I am innocent of the blood of this just man. See ye to it." And they said, "His blood be on us and on our children." Then Barabbas was released, and Jesus was delivered to be crucified.

We might safely assume that both Pilate and the Jews felt that they had permanently settled any question which may have arisen in connection with the life of Christ. Pilate by merely washing his hands, and the Jews by putting to death the very Son of God. But there is a peculiar relationship which exists between the life of Jesus Christ and every other person born into the world. What Pilate and the Jews did that night did not in the slightest alter that relation-

ship—either for them or for us. Inasmuch as Jesus also bore
our sins we are also a party to his death and cannot escape
our share of guilt. That is, it was our sins as well as those of
his contemporaries that made it necessary for Jesus to volun-
teer his own death. In addition, we are assured by Peter that
". . . there is none other name under heaven given among
men, whereby we must be saved." (Acts 4:12)

Our salvation is determined by the way we decide certain
important questions. James Russell Lowell spoke of this responsibility under the title of "The Present Crisis." He said:

> Once to every man and nation
> Comes a moment to decide,
> In the strife of truth and falsehood,
> For the good or evil side.

> Some great cause, God's new Messiah
> Offering each the bloom or blight;
> Parts the goats upon the left hand
> And the sheep upon the right.

> And the choice goes on forever,
> 'Twixt the darkness and the light.

Certainly the greatest question to be decided by anyone in the world is the question asked by Pilate when he said,
"What shall I do with Jesus?" The Jews made their decision
by saying, "His blood be upon us and our children." And so
it has been, and so it may be with us, because the question
is still before us, and each must answer for himself.

> For Jesus is standing on trial still,
> You may be false to him if you will;
> Or, you may serve him through good or ill
> What will *you* do with Jesus?

> You may evade him as Pilate tried
> Or you may serve him whate'er betide;
> Vainly you'll struggle from him to hide;
> What will you do with Jesus?

> What will you do with Jesus?
> Neutral you cannot be.
> And someday your soul may be asking,
> What will he do with me?

One of the best methods for solving any problem is to carefully weigh each of the alternatives. In this particular case there seem to be three possibilities. The first method for solving this problem is to follow the example set 1900 years ago and reject Jesus. As Apostle Paul points out, we may thereby "crucify the Son of God afresh." Such a course deliberately taken is unthinkable. But much of what the Jews did, they did in ignorance. Upon the cross Jesus said, "Father forgive them, for they know not what they do." Those who crucified Jesus didn't really understand the awfulness of their deeds. Pilate did not even know who Jesus was. But why didn't he know? There is only one possible answer and that is that he had not invested the time and the effort and the thought necessary to find the truth. Pilate could have found out who Jesus was just as any one of us can find out who Jesus is if we are only willing to make the necessary effort.

Pilate indicated a common technique for evading decisions when he said to Jesus, "What is truth?" And then without waiting for the answer he turned and walked out of the room. That is about the way we sometimes investigate the gospel. We may know the truth if we search for it diligently enough. For only those who fail to seek, fail to find. But the religion of Jesus has always suffered more at the hands of those who didn't understand than from those who have deliberately opposed. This is also our greatest source of personal danger.

That is, almost all of the sins of our world are the sins of ignorance. Most of those who violate the commandments of God don't really know the importance of what they are doing. When we fill our minds with evil thoughts, we seldom understand until it is too late that these ideas will determine our eternal destiny. Even the highly educated Saul of Tarsus was guilty of this great sin of ignorance. He referred to himself by saying, "Who was before a blasphemer and a persecutor, and injurious: but I obtained mercy, because I did it ignorantly in unbelief." (I Tim. 1:13) When Paul went to Athens he found many people ignorantly worshipping before the unknown God. (Acts 17:23) That sin is still common among us. We should beware of the sin of ignorance. It is the basic problem even in our world of education and enlightenment.

The second alternative for the proposition of "What shall I do with Jesus?" is that we may try to be neutral. That is, we may try to be neither one thing nor the other. Of course, that is impossible, for either God is or God is not. There is no middle ground. It is all or nothing. If we don't accept him by design, we reject him by default. When we fail to decide a question one way, we automatically decide it the other way, just as when we fail to decide to get on the train, we automatically decide to stay off the train.

A man who does not openly declare his loyalty to Christ is probably no better than a mere onlooker or what someone has described as an "inquiring neutral." There is a large group of people who say that they *do not believe*, but they also say that they do not disbelieve. It has been pointed out that there is one folly greater than that of the fool who says in his heart, "There is no God," and that is the folly of him who says he doesn't know whether there is a God or not. The skepticism of one who does not believe is not so hopeless as the skepticism of one who does not care. Unbelief is often a mere confession of lack of interest and the unwillingness to investigate. When we are unwilling to fight for a thing, we may frequently soon find ourselves fighting against it. Neutrality in faith always means defeat in accomplishment. It is frequently our faint hearts rather than our sinful minds that stand between us and our eternal exaltation. Nor can we merely brush the question of Jesus aside in unconcern. One of the most destructive sins of our world is the spiritual inertia of otherwise good people. It is so easy and so dangerous to assume rather than to investigate.

If one should err in believing the gospel of Jesus Christ to be true, he could not possibly be the loser by the mistake, but how irreparable is his loss who should err in assuming the revelations of God to be false. There are a great many people who try to dispose of this question, "What shall I do with Jesus?" by saying that he is merely a great teacher. This is also a very unsatisfactory substitute for a personal testimony of the truth.

Someone has said:

Suppose there is a Christ, but that I should be Christless,
Suppose there is a cleansing, but that I should remain unclean;
Suppose there is a Heavenly Father's love, but that I should remain an alien.
Suppose there is a Heaven, but that I should be cast down to Hell.

"No man can be saved in ignorance," but neither can one be saved in indecision.

Our third alternative for the question, "What shall I do with Jesus?" is that we may accept him for what he claimed to be, the Son of God and the Saviour of the world. On the occasion of his baptism, then on the Mount of Transfiguration, then during his visit to the Nephites and again in our own day, the voice of God the Father has been heard saying, "This is my beloved Son in whom I am well pleased." Hear ye him. (Matt. 3:17, 17:5; III Nephi 11:7; Joseph Smith 2:17) What greater authority could we have to accept Jesus eagerly and serve him enthusiastically. What a great privilege we have to fill our minds with the commandments of God and consecrate our lives to his service.

Ralph Waldo Emerson once indicated our problem when he said, "On the brink of the ocean of life and truth we are miserably dying. Sometimes we are furthest away when we are closest by. We stand on the brink of an ocean of power but each must take the steps that would bring him there." So frequently we are furthest away when we are closest by. Those who lived contemporaneously with Jesus were so near. Jesus lived among them. They saw him pass along the street; they heard him speak; they knew of his miracles; but in their lack of sufficient investigation they pronounced sentence upon themselves by rejecting their Redeemer. Now we are so near. We live in the greatest age of enlightenment ever known in the world. We see the wonders of God on every hand. We have what the Jews had, but in addition, we have the judgment of time shining upon the life of Christ. We have the testimony of the apostles who gave their lives to put it in force. But in addition, in our own day the gospel has been restored in a fulness and clarity never before known in the world.

Fervent and convincing testimony has been borne to us that in the early spring of 1820 God the Father and his Son Jesus Christ reappeared upon the earth to re-establish among men a belief in the God of Genesis, the God of Calvary, and the God of the dispensation of the fulness of times. And we are given the means whereby we may acquire a personal testimony for ourselves. There are now available for our study three great volumes of new scripture outlining in every detail the simple principles of the gospel. They give God's answer to the greatest question of our lives which will determine our eternal destiny. Pilate's question has come before us anew. "What shall I do with Jesus?" "We stand on the brink of an ocean of power, but each must take the steps that would bring him there." If these steps are not taken, it may mean that we are also so far away.

In 1932 Walter Pitkin wrote a book entitled, *Life Begins at Forty.* But life begins every morning. Life begins when we begin, and our eternal life begins when we accept God's answer to the greatest question of our lives, "What shall I do with Jesus?" May God help us to solve our problems by accepting him fully and enthusiastically.

What Think Ye of Christ?

O N ONE occasion Jesus was discussing the importance of the ministry of John the Baptist with some Pharisees, lawyers and others who had been out in the desert to hear John's message. He said to them, "What went ye out into the desert for to see?" That is a very good question because we usually find about what we are looking for.

Jesus bore a strong testimony to these people about the divinity of John's mission. He said, "Among those that are born of women there is not a greater prophet, than John the Baptist: . . . (Luke 7:28)

Although the message of John, supported as it was by the testimony of Jesus, was of the greatest possible importance, and although the Pharisees and lawyers were fully capable of understanding it, yet the message didn't help them very much because that was not what they were looking for. The way any person looks at a thing is about the most important thing about him. Sometimes we do ourselves great damage by allowing our judgment to be warped by wrong attitudes, false prejudices and evil desires. When that is so, we do not always see with minds that are open and able to accept truth.

The Pharisees and lawyers rejected the counsel of God against themselves, not because the counsel was unwise, but because they were unwise. We ought to use this important question of Jesus to find out if we also are preconditioning our minds to see the wrong things. For example, how do the important issues of life appear to us? What do we conceive our duty to be? How do we look at religion? What is the purpose to which our lives are being devoted? Do we get what we should from the great scriptures?

Jesus asked another lawyer an interesting question in which he said, ". . .how readest thou?" (Luke 10:26) Jesus was not trying to find out what the words meant, he merely wanted to know what they meant to the lawyer. Certainly we should find out what they mean to us. The teachings of Jesus are not only constructive in their answers, but they can also be very stimulating in their questions.

On one occasion Jesus asked his followers, "Whom do men say that I the Son of man am?" The disciples reported that the people had many different opinions. Some thought that Jesus was John the Baptist, returned to life. Some thought he was Elias, others Jeremias, or one of the prophets. Then he said unto them, "But whom say ye that I am? And Simon Peter answered and said, Thou art the Christ, the Son of the living God." (Matt. 16:13-16) Peter had the right answer, and what a tremendous accomplishment it would be if we could all do as well. But there are many like the Pharisees and lawyers who get the *wrong* answers.

Now suppose that we require ourselves to answer some of these important questions. How good would our answers be? Our answers would probably tell more about *us* than they would tell about the questions themselves. One of the most important of the questions of Jesus was asked of another group of Pharisees. Jesus said to them, "What think ye of Christ? whose son is he?" (Matt. 22:42) The Pharisees didn't have any very good answers. We feel sorry for the Pharisees with all of their mistakes, but how much better can we do?

In answer to the question, "What think ye of Christ?" Mr. J. A. Francis made the following very interesting estimate of his life when he said,

"Here is a man who grew up in an obscure village. The child of a poor peasant woman. He worked in a carpenter shop until he was 30, and then for three years he was an itinerant preacher.

"He never wrote a book. He never held an office. He never owned a home. He never had a family. He never went to college. He never put his foot inside a big city. He never traveled 200 miles from the place he was born.

"While still a young man, the tide of popular opinion turned against him. His friends ran away. One of them denied him. Another betrayed him. He was turned over to his enemies. He went through the mockery of a trial. He was nailed upon the cross between two thieves. His executioners gambled for the only thing he owned, while he was dying, and that was his cloak. When he was dead, he was laid in a borrowed grave, through the pity of a friend.

"But since then, 19 wide centuries have come and gone and today he is the very center of the human race. I am well within the mark when I say that all of the armies that ever marched, and all of the navies that were ever built, and all of the parliaments that ever sat, and all of the kings that ever reigned, put together, have not affected the life of man upon this earth as powerfully as has this one solitary life."

Mr. Francis makes a thrilling and accurate appraisal of the influence of the life of Christ in the world, and yet there are a large number of individuals in the world whose lives are not being greatly affected. There are a great many who do not hold the same opinion as Mr. Francis, certainly many do not share the conviction of Peter. But probably the answer that is most important is our own answer when we ask ourselves, What think ye of Christ? Whose son is he? After all that is a question that all of us must answer either with our voices or our lives. Sometimes our voices indicate that we know the right answers, but the way we live indicates that we do *not* know them. Some would answer the question, what think ye of Christ? by saying that he is a very great man. Some would say that the life of Christ had no significance for them one way or the other. Some would think of him as a great teacher. Some would say that he was the actual Son of God who was put to death on Mount Calvary over 19 centuries ago.

Many people think of him almost entirely in the past as though his account had now been closed. At Christmas time we think of Jesus as the child in the manger. Then we see him as a twelve year old boy teaching the wise men in the temple. At age thirty he began his official ministry which continued for the short period of about three years. Then he was put to death. We are very conscious of him during the trial and crucifixion. We are greatly disturbed about the injustice of his death, and we mourn for him during his suffering; but at the ninth hour from the cross came his words, "It is finished," and for some the life of Christ ended at that point. The present Christian world is filled with the crucifix. It is more than an emblem. A great number worship a dead Christ who has been left upon the cross. But the Savior of the world did not remain upon the cross. His last words were not spoken at the ninth hour of that particular Friday afternoon. For three days his body lay in the tomb of Joseph of Arimathea. But as Christ did not remain upon the cross, neither did he stay in the tomb.

Very early in the morning of the third day, two heavenly messengers sent from God rolled away the stone from the door of the sepulcher and Jesus came forth from the tomb, resurrected and immortal. When he confronted the Roman soldiers who had been placed there by Pilate to maintain the security of the tomb, they became as dead men. Yet these were not timid, easily frightened men, they were hard, bold, courageous, seasoned soldiers of Rome who had been taught to stand in the presence of death without ever a quiver of emotion. But now that they stood in the presence of a resurrected, glorified life they became as dead men.

Most of the people in that day could not understand and

did not believe in the resurrection of Jesus. But Jesus said to Thomas, "Reach hither thy finger, and behold my hands; and reach hither thy hand, and thrust it into my side: and be not faithless, but believing." (John 20:27)

Then after forty days of showing himself to his followers and teaching them many things, including the conditions under which he would come again to the earth, he concluded his post-mortal ministry and took some of his disciples out to Mount Olivet which is about a Sabbath Day's journey from Jerusalem, and there he said to them. "Ye shall be witnesses unto me both in Jerusalem, and in all Judea, and in Samaria, and unto the uttermost part of the earth." And the record says, "And when he had spoken these things, while they beheld, he was taken up; and a cloud received him out of their sight. And while they looked stedfastly toward heaven as he went up, behold, two men stood by him in white apparel; Which also said, Ye men of Galilee, why stand ye gazing up into heaven? this same Jesus, which is taken up from you into heaven, shall so come in like manner as ye have seen him go into heaven." (Acts 1:9-11)

Certainly the resurrected Christ was not trying to give the impression that he was going out of business or that he had lost interest in the world he had come to redeem. He had organized his church at Jerusalem but he had been appointed in heaven to be the Savior of all mankind in all lands, and in all ages.

Some time after his resurrection, in fulfillment of his promise recorded in the tenth chapter and sixteenth verse of John, the resurrected Jesus appeared upon the western hemisphere (III Nephi 15:17) where a great civilization flourished unknown to those who lived in Jerusalem. He also organized his church on this continent and established his truth among the people. A tremendously instructive eyewitness account of his western ministry is recorded for our benefit in the Book of Mormon, III Nephi, chapters 8 to 28. But between the time of Christ's ministry and the present, a great apostasy or falling away from the truth took place both in the east and in the west. The civilization that once flourished in the west destroyed itself, though the traditions of their descendants, the American Indians, indicate that a great white God had visited them, established his work among them, and had promised them that he would return at some future date.

When Jesus ascended from Mount Olivet, the angels had said that "this same Jesus" that was taken up would come again as they had seen him go. That is, Jesus did not lose his resurrected body of flesh and bones. (D & C 130:22) His body was not dissolved, nor did it expand to fill the immensity of space. At the resurrection his body and spirit were inseparably joined together. (D & C 93:33) And he will have his body when he comes again in this glorious second coming.

But some new developments have taken place in our own day that everyone should be aware of. In the early spring of 1820 "this same Jesus" accompanied by God, the Father, appeared to the Prophet Joseph Smith in the state of New York. At a later date under the direction of heavenly messengers, the Church was organized upon the earth for the last time. Jesus also appeared to Joseph Smith in the Kirtland Temple on April 3, 1836. From these appearances and from other latter-day revelation we have learned many things to help us with the question, What think ye of Christ? Some are that Christ has not lost his identity nor his body, nor his interest in us, nor his authority as the Savior of men and the Redeemer of the world.

In our troubled times many good Christian people are clinging desperately to the hope that God lives and still rules in the affairs of men, that Jesus is divine, that he is the "same Jesus" that promised us eternal life on condition of our righteousness. Then what a thrilling situation is brought about for someone to stand forth in our own day as the Prophet

Joseph Smith has done, and verify our belief in Christ by bearing personal testimony that he lives, that he has seen him with his own eyes. Joseph Smith said, "I had actually seen a light, and in the midst of that light I saw two Personages, and they did in reality speak to me." (Joseph Smith 2:25) The resurrected Jesus was also seen by the Nephites on this continent and they have left us their solemn testimony. (III Nephi 8:28) Jesus was seen by Oliver Cowdery in our day (D & C 110:) He was seen by Sidney Rigdon (D & C 76: 22-24) All have left their written detailed account for our study and benefit.

In addition, the Lord has given us three great volumes of new scripture making crystal clear all of the simple gospel truths taught 1900 years ago in Jerusalem, many of which were lost during the long dark ages of apostasy. One of these modern volumes of scripture is called The Doctrine and Covenants. It contains over a hundred revelations given in this dispensation indicating that the life of Christ is not all in the past, that he is presently preparing to come again to the earth. In his second coming Jesus will not be the man of sorrows to be spit upon, crowned with thorns or crucified, but he will come in clouds of glory to judge the world. The Old Testament Prophet Zechariah foretold that at *that* time one would say unto him, "What are these wounds in thine hands?" Then Jesus will answer, "Those with which I was wounded in the house of my friends." (Zechariah 13:6)

But before that time comes, great calamities and destruction are to be poured out upon the earth because of the wickedness of the people. Many *do* not and *will* not believe and that has always been the cause of our greatest problems.

On December 27, 1832, at Kirtland, Ohio, the Lord said to the Prophet Joseph Smith, "Behold, I sent you out to testify and warn the people, and it becometh every man who hath been warned to warn his neighbor. Therefore, they are left without excuse, and their sins are upon their own heads. He that seeketh me early shall find me, and shall not be forsaken. Therefore, tarry ye, and labor diligently, that you may be perfected in your ministry to go forth among the Gentiles for the last time . . . to bind up the law and seal up the testimony, and to prepare the saints for the hour of judgment which is to come." (D & C 88:81-84)

But now is the time to ask ourselves this important question, what think ye of Christ? and we should do everything possible to make sure that before it is too late we get the right answer. May God bless us so to do, I pray in Jesus' name.

A Wonder of Our Day

IT SHOULD be of the greatest possible interest to all of us that we are permitted to live in this great age of wonders and enlightenment. In many ways this is the greatest age since creation. We are a part of the greatest nation that has ever been known in the history of the world. We have the highest standard of living ever enjoyed by any people. In material things we live better than any king lived just a hundred years ago.

We live in a day when the knowledge of medicine enables us to have strong bodies and clear minds. We live in a time when physical pain is almost unknown among us. We live under conditions where we may have all of the education that we desire. In fact, one of the most distinguishing characteristics of our civilization is the great flood of new knowledge that has recently been miraculously spread across the earth.

In many ways more progress has been made in the last few years than in all of the previous generations of the world combined. The transportation, communication, invention, comforts and conveniences that are commonplace to us, would have been unbelievable miracles to our forefathers. Our voices may now be heard around the earth. We may sit in our living rooms, and see events happen on the other side of the world. We may fly through the air at the speed of sound or be guided by a radio beam under the polar icecap.

In May 1960 the atomic submarine Triton completed the first underwater voyage around the earth. Members of the crew lived comfortably and safely in the depths of the sea for the entire journey. The crew returned from this 84 day miracle, happy and in good health. They followed substantially the route taken by Magellan 400 years ago when with five ships and 270 men he started on that first trip around the world. The journey was finished three years later with a loss of 80% of his ships and 88% of his men. The progress made in navigation between the days of Magellan and those of Captain Beach who commanded the Triton has been duplicated in many fields, but the end is not yet. We may look forward expectantly to other wonders as unbelievable to us now, as those of our day would appear to the ancients of one hundred years ago. But all of the wonders of our age are not in the field of material things. And many of the most exciting of the marvels yet to come will be in the realm of the spiritual.

Anyone reading a book on science written in 1930 may find it hopelessly out of date. The methods of warfare known in either world war are now relegated to the scrap heap of the horse and buggy days. But interestingly enough, one of the most reliable sources of information concerning what might be expected in our own futures is a book written in the days when the camel was the most common means of transportation. This book is our own Holy Bible. Isn't it interesting that the Bible is still the world's first book of religion. It is still the first book of philosophy. It is still the first book of righteousness. It is still the first book of knowledge. It tells of the future of the earth itself and many things about the possible destiny of those who live upon it.

For example, as Jesus was departing from the temple in Jerusalem on the last day of his public ministry, he began his walk across the Mount of Olives. In the process, he stopped to rest, and as his disciples gathered around him, he foretold to them his own glorious second coming to the earth and enumerated some of the signs that should immediately precede it. He said, "For nation shall rise against nation, and kingdom against kingdom: and there shall be famines, and pestilence, and earthquakes, in divers places. All these are the beginning of sorrows." (Matt. 24:7-8) Then he foretold the many perplexities that would be sent upon the nations in consequence of their wickedness. And as one of the signs to precede his coming, he said, "And this gospel of the kingdom shall be preached in all the world for a witness unto all nations; and then shall the end come." (Matt. 24:14)

Then Jesus said, "Now learn a parable of the fig tree; When his branch is yet tender, and putteth forth leaves, ye know that summer is nigh: So likewise ye, when ye shall see all these things, know that it is near, even at the doors." (Matt. 24:32-33) And then as if to give them reassurance and also to fortify us who would live in these latter days of trouble and disbelief he said, "Heaven and earth shall pass away, but my words shall not pass away." (Matt. 24:35) This we can count on. We can also count on the fact that these latter days will be days of the most severe tribulation. Jesus made a comparison of our day to the days of Noah by saying "But as the days of Noe were, so shall also the coming of the Son of man be. For as in the days that were before the flood they were eating and drinking, marrying and giving in marriage, until the day that Noe entered into the ark, And knew not until the flood came, and took them all away; So shall also the coming of the Son of man be." (Matt. 24:37-39) That is going to be an exciting day for us, for no matter what the condition of our material or scientific lives may be, we, like those of Noah's day, must be responsible to God for our unrighteousness.

Our world is now moving rapidly toward great events for which we are not very well prepared. It has been the misfortune of every age that because men have disobeyed God they have lost their blessings. It was disobedience and disbelief that brought destruction upon the people of Noah's day. The people who lived in Jerusalem 1900 years ago were also unprepared. We seem to be closely following in the footsteps of the past and as a result, we live constantly under the shadow of our own possible destruction.

As if holding themselves in readiness to fulfill the prophecy of Jesus, the great nations of our world are pitted against each other in an explosive cold war, where the slightest incident could trigger a gigantic and terrible destruction. The nations are using the knowledge God has given them in a vigorous competition to see who can outdo the other in producing the most deadly instruments of destruction. Each nation also wants to be the first to reach the moon for reasons of military expedience and propaganda advantage. With all of its enlightenment and ambition, our civilization might very well find a higher aim than to put a man on the moon which is so completely unsuited for human occupancy.

An important thought for our space age is to remember that beyond the moon, there is God, who is still the highest power in the universe. From the time the very first man was placed upon this earth, Deity has been sending messengers to instruct us. Many of the people to whom the message has been sent have closed their ears.

Before the gospel could be preached in these latter days "as a witness to all nations" before the end comes, the authority to do so had to be restored to men. It is one of the greatest events of our age, from any point of view, even including that of space travel.

May 15th of each year is set apart to commemorate the restoration to the earth of the Aaronic Priesthood. One hundred thirty-one years ago [1829] in Harmony, Pennsylvania, John the Baptist appeared to Joseph Smith and Oliver Cowdery. Eighteen hundred years previously this same John the Baptist had been appointed to baptize the Savior of the world. Later, Jesus said of him that of all the prophets, none were greater than John the Baptist. (Luke 7:28) Like his master he was put to death, but like his master he rose again, and in 1829 he was sent to the earth again because he held certain authority that must be restored in establishing this, the greatest of all of the dispensations, when all things should be brought together before the glorious second coming of Christ. This ancient messenger said that he was acting under the direction of Peter, James and John who held the keys of the Higher Priesthood. Laying his hands upon the heads of Joseph and Oliver he said, "Upon you my fellow servants, in the name of Messiah I confer the Priesthood of Aaron, which holds the keys of the ministering of angels, and of the gospel of repentance. and of baptism by immersion for the remission of sins; and this shall never be taken again from the earth, until the sons of Levi do offer again an offering unto the Lord in righteousness." (D&C 13)

What a tremendous message! And what a tremendous messenger! What modern scientific wonder can match this event in importance? What a thrilling fact that God chose this great free land of America in which to restore the priesthood. How wonderful if everyone of us could understand what this restoration means to us personally and to the world as a whole, and then live by its message. The heavens are not sealed as so many suppose. Who could imagine that all of these wonders are being poured out upon the world without God having a hand in them? Or who would say that God has lost interest in men's souls, and is now only concerned with progress in material things?

The fact that some have difficulty in believing in divine messengers has always been our biggest difficulty and the cause of most of our troubles. But we cannot escape individual responsibility for our disbelief.

Think how difficult it must have been for some to have believed Zacharias when he announced that the Angel Gabriel, who had lived upon the earth centuries earlier as Noah (*Teachings of the Prophet Joseph Smith,* page 157) had appeared to him and told him that he and his barren wife, Elizabeth, would be the parents of John the Baptist. (Luke 1:5-24) Is it any more difficult to believe that John the Baptist, who was held in such high regard by Jesus Christ should in turn also be chosen to serve as God's messenger?

The fact that some disbelieve proves nothing, except that we are following the tragic pattern of the past. Most of the antediluvians did not believe that Noah had received divine messages. It has always seemed much easier to believe in the messengers who have come from God in the past than those that come in the present. Our age is the greatest age of wonders ever known in the world, but the most important of these wonders is not that we can build more atomic submarines, television sets or pop-up toasters than the Soviets, nor will our national greatness be determined by who has the largest number of earth satellites in orbit. In many ways we are making the mistake of trying to meet the Communists on their own ground. What will it profit us to "outmaterialize" this great atheistic nation? Our comparative greatness will be determined by who listens most obediently to the messages that come from God, and who are able to put his commandments in orbit most successfully.

Isn't it interesting that our response to this great upsurge in knowledge and power from God, has been a corresponding upsurge in our own crime and human delinquency rate? With all of the eleventh hour enlightenment and wonders of our day—ungodliness is still rampant among us. Certainly our doom is sealed if we outdo the Communists in unrighteousness and atheism. The leaders of communism have already abandoned religion. We must not try to match them in this field.

But certainly the most important event among all of the wonders of our days is that God has not left us completely to our disbelief and materialism but has again spoken from heaven. Not only has he sent his messengers, but in the early spring of 1820 at the beginning of this great increase in wonders, he also came to earth in person. In addition, he has caused his message to us to be written down in three great volumes of new scripture, outlining in every detail the simple principles of the gospel. What could supersede that in importance, and what could be more appropriate to our age of wonders?

Under divine direction the Aaronic Priesthood was restored, including "the gospel of repentance" and of "baptism by immersion for the remission of sins." How tremendously important this should be to us. It is the best base on which to establish our individual or national greatness. It is also a part of God's program for saving our civilization from itself.

Think how eagerly we seek and try to decipher any new records from the past such as the Dead Sea Scrolls, yet how reluctant we are even to read an authentic document of the greatest importance, put into our hands by an angel of God. Moses tells us that in the very beginning as God tried to teach his children properly, ". . . Satan came among them saying: Believe it not; and they believed it not, and they loved Satan more than God." (Moses 5:13) In our day Satan is still among us and is still saying, "Believe it not." He now goes further and says, "Don't even read it or think about it." With many people he is having a terrible and deadly success. Our eternal lives do not depend upon the number of our inventions nor the activity of the stock market. Our eternal life depends upon how we accept the messengers of God, and how well we live the messages that they bring.

I would like to close by reading to you the thrilling personal testimony of Oliver Cowdery concerning the restoration of the Aaronic Priesthood. He was one of the two who received the heavenly visitor, heard the message and had this priesthood conferred upon him.

Oliver said, "The Lord who is rich in mercy and everwilling to answer the prayer of the humble, after we had called upon him in a fervent manner, aside from the abodes of men, condescended to manifest to us his will. On a sudden, as from the midst of eternity, the voice of the Redeemer spake peace to us, while the veil was parted, and the angel of God came down clothed with glory and delivered the anxiously looked—for message, and the keys of the gospel of repentance. What joy. What wonder! What amazement!

"While the world was racked and distracted, while millions were groping as the blind for the wall, and while all men were resting upon uncertainty, our eyes beheld, our ears heard. As in the blaze of day; yes, more above the glitter of the May sunbeam, which then shed its brilliancy over the face of nature! Then his voice, though mild, pierced to the center, and his words, I am thy fellow servant, dispelled every fear.

"We listened, we gazed, we admired. 'Twas the voice of an angel from glory. 'Twas a message from the most high, and as we heard we rejoiced, while his love enkindled upon our souls, and we were rapt in the vision of the Almighty. Where was room for doubt? Nowhere; uncertainty had fled, doubt had sunk, no more to rise, while fiction and deception had fled forever. I shall not attempt to paint to you the feelings of my heart, nor the majestic beauty that surrounded us on that occasion. The assurance that we were in the presence of an angel; the certainty that we heard the voice of Jesus, and the truth unsullied as it flowed from a pure personage, dictated by the will of God, is to me *past* description, and I shall ever look upon this expression of the Savior's goodness with wonder and thanksgiving while I am permitted to tarry, and in those mansions where perfection dwells and sin never comes, I hope to adore in that day which shall never cease." (Roberts, *Comprehensive History of the Church,* Volume I—Restoration of the Priesthood.) We are all invited to join in the truth and blessings of this wonderful event and may God help us to understand and appreciate the importance of his thrilling message while there is yet time.

The World Is Planned for Good

ONE OF THE most meaningful lines of the great scriptures is Paul's declaration to the Romans in which he said, ". . . all things work together for good to them that love God, . . . (Romans 8:28) Of course, that does not mean that every experience is exclusively good in itself, but when we love God, then we have the right attitude. We follow the right course. Then we take the good and leave the evil; just as the bee gets honey from the same flower that the spider gets poison from. The key is, we must love God; we must do right.

For example, one of the finest men I know, as a young man had a father who was a drunkard. But the son became a total abstainer. He took the honey from the situation and left the poison. Because this young man loved God and thought right, no one could have been to him a more potent teacher of righteousness than his unrighteous father.

It is a pretty good procedure, in every situation, to say to ourselves "What good am I supposed to get from this experience?" "What is God trying to teach me?" "How can I use this idea, good or bad, to improve my situation and make me better?" We may be certain that every experience has something good in it if we will only distil out the good and leave the bad untouched. If we love God the world is ordered for our good.

Emerson said, "Men often live their entire lives under the foolish delusion that life can cheat them. So many people allow some blessing in disguise to get them discouraged and they throw up their hands and fail." But Mr. Emerson points out that, "We can no more do a good thing without at some time in some way receiving a reward than we can do an evil thing without suffering a penalty. If we have the right attitude, if we love God, if we do right, even our own weakness gives us a benefit."

Strength frequently grows out of weakness. It has been said that wherever life expects you to excel she gives you a weakness. When life wanted to make an orator out of Demosthenes she gave him a speech impediment. When life wanted to make a great president out of Abraham Lincoln, she gave him birth in a backwoods hut with the hardest kind of problems to solve. When life wants to make a man of wealth and power, she often starves him and taunts him and torments him and takes away comfort, laughter, sleep and friends. "Life hammers him and hurts him and with mighty blows converts him." Thereby, life builds up within him a hunger for success which cannot be denied, and eventually the accumulated power sweeps everything before it.

The key point to keep in mind is that everything has good in it. Night is as necessary as day. Labor is as important as ease. Sickness and death serve us quite as well as health and life. Into every life some rain must fall. If we had *all* sunshine we would soon live on a Sahara desert. Even evil can be our ally if we love God. In fact, it was planned that Satan himself should work for our good. That is, God could destroy Satan in an instant if he so desired. Then why doesn't he? He himself has given us the answer. He has said, "And it must needs be that the devil should tempt the children of men or they could not be agents unto themselves; for if they never should have the bitter, they could not know the sweet." (D & C 29:39)

In our own interest God desires for us to have the privilege to choose between good and evil as we see them, side by side. But God never forces us to do good, and Satan has no power to force us to do evil, except as we ourselves may give it to him. As has been said:

All the water in the world,
However hard it tried;
Can never sink the smallest ship,
Unless it gets inside.

And all the evil in the world,
The blackest kind of sin;
Can never hurt you the least bit,
Unless you let it in.

We are made stronger by every difficulty that we overcome. And if we love God, we will come from every field victorious, just as Jesus triumphed over his temptations in the desert.

Sometimes we allow ourselves to become confused because so frequently our blessings come in disguise. Mostly our greatest blessings come disguised in work clothes. But hard work and tribulations are two of the instruments by which God fashions us for better things. The fire that proves the steel also hardens it. There is a great hymn that says:

When through fiery trials thy pathway may lie,
My grace all sufficient shall be thy supply
The flames shall not hurt thee, I only design,
Thy dross to consume and thy gold to refine.

When a founder casts a bell he does not immediately hang it in the steeple but hits it with his hammer and beats it on every side to find out if there are any flaws in it. Just so God allows us to be beaten upon by temptations, the temptations of ease, the temptations of sin, the temptations of irresponsibility. But by this process we may find and eliminate the flaws from our characters.

Sometimes we blame God when our every wish is not immediately granted. But Oscar Wilde once said, that "If God wanted to punish us, all he would need to do would be to answer our prayers." If all of our requests were granted, no one would ever be sick, no one would ever suffer, no one would ever die. We would always have our own way, there would be no poverty, no opposition, no struggle, and consequently there would be no strength, for

> Good timber does not grow in ease,
> The stronger wiⅬds, the stronger trees.
> The farther sky, the greater length.
> The more the storm the more the strength.

Most of our power to succeed is developed during our trials. The Apostle Paul's success was partly due to his "thorn in the flesh." He said he had "the messenger of Satan to buffet me." Paul says, "For this thing I besought the Lord thrice, that it might depart from me. And he said unto me, My grace is sufficient for thee: for my strength it made perfect weakness. Most gladly therefore, will I rather glory in my infirmities, . . . for when I am weak, then am I strong." (II Cor. 12: 7-10) One of our greatest opportunities is to change our weaknesses into strengths.

The 32nd chapter of Genesis gives an account of a very interesting experience wherein Jacob is credited as wrestling with an angel. Who it actually was that Jacob wrestled with is not the point here. The fact is that whoever the personage was, he had the power to bless. He said to Jacob, "Let me go for the day breaketh." But Jacob had a better idea. He said, "I will not let thee go except thou bless me." And the messenger finally did as Jacob requested. It was in this particular blessing that Jacob's name was changed to Israel, meaning the father of nations. Then this messenger of the Lord paid a great tribute to Jacob saying, "as a prince hast thou power with God and with men, and hast prevailed." We can also develop the power to prevail if we understand that every experience has a blessing for us if we will only hang on long enough. Not only does every experience carry a blessing with it, but every person has something to teach us. Some experiences teach us what to think, some what to do, and some what to be. Others teach us what we should carefully avoid.

The boy with the drunken father, like Jacob wrestling with the Lord's messenger at Peniel, did not let the experience go without learning its lesson, and each received a blessing as a consequence. We may be certain that every experience has something good in it if we only know how to distil it out. The world is planned for good. Nothing can hurt us but ourselves. The main point is that we ourselves must do the distilling.

Jesus wrestled with temptations during the interchange with Satan in the desert. Jesus came away with the victory and a blessing. One of the important reasons why we left our pre-existent home in the presence of God was to be able to get a closer look at good and evil side by side. God wanted us to wrestle with problems and learn to come off victorious. For only as we have the opportunity to choose freely and overcome, can we develop the strength of a Godlike character.

However, the one thing that we should be sure of is that we do not get the poison instead of the honey. The choice is left strictly up to us, and we must also accept the responsibility. We sometimes give Satan much more credit than he actually deserves. We tell ourselves what he has done to injure our lives. We blame him for many things that we are personally responsible for. Someone has said, "The Lord always votes for us, and Satan always votes against us, and then we are asked to cast our vote to break the tie." The only time we get into trouble is when we cast our vote on the wrong side or fail to vote altogether. But if we desire strength we must not allow ourselves to be discouraged by thinking that life is picking on us, or that evil is being forced upon us. Rather, everything is for our good. Demosthenes did not become an orator in spite of his speech defect. He became an orator because of his speech defect. The classmates of Demosthenes who got "A's" in their speech courses have never been heard of because they were not sufficiently strengthened by struggle. They let their opportunities go without getting their blessings, even from the most obvious advantages. If we would get the blessing we ourselves must distil it out.

Recently a worker was released from a prominent position in the Church after ten years in office. At the time of his release he was called upon to speak. In his remarks he said that he was just as frightened and just as weak and just as unprepared as he had been ten years previously. Everyone in the audience could feel his lack of preparation. He breathed out weakness and the evidence of a negative attitude all the time he was on his feet. Life had given him ten years of the richest of all opportunities, but he had distilled out only sloth and wasted privilege, leaving himself as poor and miserable as before. His opportunities had given him no blessings. He seemed not even to have recognized any blessings.

This is not an isolated case. There are many called but few are chosen. There are a surprising number of otherwise good people who turn their backs on their blessings. This is particularly true of those blessings that come disguised in work clothes with decisions to be made and problems to be solved. These seem to be the forms of disguise that makes recognition the most difficult for many people. Yet work, responsibility, and even tribulations are loaded with blessings if we love God.

During the winter of 1838-39 the Prophet Joseph Smith with five companions spent several months in Liberty Jail, confined to a very small room under almost unbearable circumstances. Finally the Prophet cried out, "O, God, where art thou? . . . How long shall thy hand be stayed and thine eye, yea thy pure eye, behold from the eternal heavens the wrongs of thy people. . . ." (D & C 121:1-2) Then the Lord made a wonderful statement about distilling blessings out of difficulties. He said, "My son, peace be unto thy soul; thine adversity and thine afflictions shall be but a small moment; And then, if thou endure it well, God shall exalt thee on high. . . .If thou shouldst be cast into the pit, or into the hands of murders, and the sentence of death passed upon thee; if thou be cast into the deep; if the billowing surge conspire against thee; if fierce winds become thine enemy; if the heavens gather blackness, and all the elements combine to hedge up the way; and above all, if the very jaws of hell shall gape open the mouth wide after thee, know thou, my son, that all these things shall give thee experience, and shall be for thy good. The Son of Man hath descended below them all. Art thou greater than he?" (D & C 121:7-8; 122:7-8)

The strength of the difficulty that we overcome becomes a part of us. We distil strength out of all the temptations, hardships, and problems that we prove superior to. We can get power with God and with everyone else if we gain something every day and say to every experience, "I will not let thee go except thou bless me." A careful inventory of all of our past experiences may disclose the startling fact that if we have loved God, everything that has happened has been for the best. And one of the lessons that will serve us best in the future is to develop a solid faith, that "all things work together for good to them that love God."

May we develop within ourselves the determination and the ability to always be able to take the good and leave the evil that we may thereby fulfill the purposes of creation.

Your Crown Jewels

FROM THE beginning of time men have put crowns on the heads of others as symbols of power and royalty. Originally these crowns were fashioned from laurel leaves, or wreaths of flowers. Crowns were also used to adorn the heads of the winners of battles, or the victors of athletic games, or to honor those of outstanding beauty and other significant accomplishment. Later these crowns were made of gold and other precious metals. Finally wealthy rulers added luster and brilliance to their crowns by ornamenting them with precious gems and beautiful jewels.

Because the five most precious of all gems were rubies, sapphires, emeralds, pearls and diamonds, these were the most frequently used in the crowns of royalty. In addition to serving as the insignia of office for kings and queens, the crown jewels have also served as the substantial part of the treasury of empires. There was a time when the crown jewels of some nations composed most of their wealth and largely determined their influence abroad.

To this day the crown jewels of many countries are very important. The crown jewels of England are of tremendous value. They are displayed in the Tower of London and are one of the greatest tourist attractions in the world. Among the very beautiful crowns in this collection is the Imperial State Crown made for Queen Victoria in 1838. It contains 2783 diamonds, 277 pearls, 16 sapphires, 11 emeralds and 4 rubies. Many of these gems are of great historical importance and are priceless in value. In this collection is the Black Prince ruby which dates back to 1367, and the great sapphire worn by Edward the Confessor over 900 years ago. It also includes a magnificent diamond called the Star of Africa. This is the second largest diamond in the world, the largest being the Cullinan diamond now set in the royal scepter. Probably the most valuable diamond in the world is the Kohinoor. It is thought to have a history of some 3000 years. Before it was cut this diamond was the cause of many wars as it was believed that whatever nation owned it would dominate the world.

But crowns serve more than a political use—they are given great significance throughout the scriptures. When Joash was made king of ancient Israel, the records said, ". . .and put the crown upon him, and gave him the testimony; and they made him king, and anointed him; and they clapped their hands, and said, God save the king." (II Kings 11:12) In the days of Moses the Lord gave direction for the crowning of Aaron for his priestly work in the temple. Aaron was anointed with oil and given a blessing. Then the Lord said, "And thou shalt put the mitre upon his head, and put the holy crown upon the mitre." (Exodus 29:6-7) Other valuable and meaningful jewels adorned Aaron's person and gave meaning to his office.

The use of crowns have not yet lost their religious significance, as in his vision of the future, John the revelator saw a door opened in heaven and he beheld a throne, and him that sat thereon and he said, "And round about the throne were four and twenty seats: and upon the seats I saw four and twenty elders sitting, clothed in white raiment; and they had on their heads crowns of gold." (Rev. 4:4)

But there is other adornment for crowns that are even more valuable than precious gems. Peter said, "Faith is more precious than gold." (I Peter 1:7) Paul had something pretty valuable in mind when he said to Timothy, "Henceforth there is laid up for me a crown of righteousness, which the Lord, the righteous judge, shall give me at that day: and not

to me only, but unto all of them also that love his appearing."
(II Tim. 4:8)

It has always been exciting to see a great king sitting on
his throne wearing the emblems of his office and the kingly
qualities that entitle him to it. But in our minds we see
everyone as dressed in certain identifying insignia and wearing a particular crown corresponding to his accomplishment.
Isaiah mentions "the crown of pride." We see some people
dressed in arrogance and wickedness. On the other hand, the
Lord has said, ". . . be thou faithful unto death, and I will give
thee a crown of life." (Rev. 2:10) David was thinking of man
at his best when he sang to the Lord, "For thou hast made
him a little lower than the angels, and hast crowned him with
honor and glory." (Psalm 8:5, Heb. 2:7) We may clothe
ourselves with great ability and power by properly adorning
our lives with virtues. Recently a friend was telling me of a
dream in which he was greatly embarrassed by finding himself improperly dressed and lacking a vital part of his clothing
at a very important function. It is always very satisfying to
be properly dressed for the occasion. There is an old saying
that a king inspires no awe when dressed in his nightgown.
Any king would suffer a severe loss in prestige if he always
appeared before his people dressed in rags or lacking the
crown, scepter and the royal robes of his office. And the
Lord has said to us, which seems to mean about the same
thing, "Behold I come quickly: hold that fast which thou hast,
that no man take thy crown." (Rev. 3:11) We must be properly dressed when the Lord comes.

There is an old song that says, "Shall I have many stars
in my crown?" When I was younger I used to look into the
sky at night and wonder if some day I would have a star
in my crown, and I wondered which star it would be. Now
I know that we will each have as many stars as we deserve,
and they will be of our own choosing. We can also ornament
our crowns with the most precious jewels.

I am grateful for this interesting symbolism which gives us a helpful vehicle to which we may attach our thoughts and ambitions. Crowns and jewels might represent character qualities in our thinking as the parables represent ideas. In speaking to Malachi the Lord talked about the day when he would make up his jewels. (Mal. 3:17) We are all given that important privilege and responsibility, and inasmuch as we may make our own selection, what jewels should we choose?

I suppose that everyone would want to include some rubies. The ruby is the symbol of courage and valor. The blood-red ruby from Burma is prized by some as the rarest of all stones. It is thought by some as being more valuable than the diamond, but it has an additional value because of the helpful imagery of its symbolism. In more ancient times the East Indian warriors would often cut an incision in their flesh and insert a ruby with the thought that it would give them greater strength in battle. They believed that the paradise of a brave soldier was lined with beautiful, luminous blood-red rubies.

In making up our jewels we should have a good supply of the gems of courage. For lacking adequate courage, no significant accomplishment is possible. With enough rubies in our crowns almost every miracle of achievement is placed within our easy reach. This wonderful quality is the very foundation of success; it banishes fear; it overcomes discouragement and annihilates some of the most serious enemies of success. Think how our lives will sparkle with a few precious blood-red rubies in our crown.

Second, our crown jewels should include some sapphires. The sapphire is the gem of truth, sincerity, and loyalty. It is also one of the most prized of all stones for its own value. Some of the ancient peoples believed that the earth rested on a giant sapphire which gave the sky its blue color. The sapphire has been called the "celestial" stone. It is the sapphire that prompts us to refer to someone as "true blue."

What could make one more kingly in his life or more loved of the Lord than to be true blue and have in his crown the diadem of truth and hold in his hand the scepter of righteousness.

According to one legend, Moses received the Ten Commandments written on tablets of sapphire. A star sapphire is especially prized. Its three cross bars remind us of these qualities of sincerity, loyalty and truth. But when these cross bars shine in human character, they are even more prized for even the most clever person must fail if he lacks the sapphire qualities. No near truths or half-truths can substitute for the genuine gems of truth. These sapphire qualities may not only be worn in the crown, they sparkle in the eyes and shine from the face. They may also live in the heart and in the conscience.

Out of the east comes the story of a great prince who wore a ring set with a beautiful star sapphire. In addition to the value of the priceless gem itself, this ring had another special quality. Whenever its wearer entertained an evil thought or contemplated an unworthy action, the ring always gave its warning by a sudden contracting process that pinched painfully on the wearer's finger, reminding him of his wrongdoing. The star sapphire set in the conscience also notifies its owner whenever evil is present in the mind. This helps us to always maintain ourselves as true blue.

The third of our precious gems is the emerald, the jewel of friendship. The ancient monarchs wore emeralds in token of their love for their people. The life of Deity himself might very fittingly be represented by the emerald, "For God so loved the world, that he gave his only begotten Son, that whosoever believeth in him should not perish, but have everlasting life." (John 3:16)

Someone was once asked what was the religious commandment next in importance to love. He replied that he didn't know that there were any others. If we have real love we have about everything. The gospel is the gospel of love. The scripture says that "God is love."

Caesar and Napoleon carried emeralds because they believed that emeralds also possessed certain physical curative powers. Certainly love would cure most of the diseases of our sick world as well as the sickness that gets into our individual lives. When *we* make up *our* jewels we should include a generous supply of emeralds.

The fourth of the major gems is the pearl. The pearl is the symbol of wisdom, the jewel of purity. The beautiful shimmering, lustrous pearl is formed by an oyster while trying to protect itself from irritating pieces of sand or grit that may have got inside the shell. When any foreign matter is introduced, the oyster proceeds to encase it, wrapping it like an onion with alternating layers of nacren and lime. The irritation is wrapped in beauty and becomes a lovely gem. Wise *people* follow that same procedure, and no matter what the experience, they wrap it up in such a way that something beautiful is always produced.

Pearls are said to be the first gems that were prized by people. From the most ancient times pearls have been the favorites of queens and ladies of nobility, and how appropriate for the pearl is the gem of purity, modesty and wisdom.

Jesus used "The Pearl of Great Price" to indicate the most important of all values. He said, "The kingdom of heaven is like unto a merchant man, seeking goodly pearls: Who, when he had found one pearl of great price, went and sold all that he had, and bought it." (Matt. 13:45-46)

Then we come to the last of the precious stones—the diamond. The diamond is the king of gems. It is the hardest susbtance known. Nothing can cut a diamond except another diamond. The diamond is the gem of constancy and skill. It stands for industry and utility. It is prized for its hardness, its clear beauty and its unusual ability to flash beautiful colors when light strikes it. When some person shows great possibility we say he is a diamond in the rough. Queen Victoria loved diamonds and had the Kohinoor recut and set in her crown.

No crown would be complete without the symbolism, beauty and utility of some brilliant diamonds.

In Paris in 1804 Napoleon crowned himself emperor and in a little different way everyone crowns himself. The writer of Proverbs says, "The hoary head is a crown of glory if it be found in the way of righteousness." (Prov. 16:31) And while some of us may never wear a crown because of being born in a palace, yet each of us wears a crown just the same, and each will determine the number of the stars of accomplishment that it contains, and the kind of jewels by which it will be adorned. Certainly the great character qualities symbolized by the precious gems are far more valuable than the jewels in the tower of London.

The enemies of Jesus placed a crown of thorns upon his head, but God crowned him with eternal glory. We also come of a royal lineage. God is our Father. He desires that our robes will be beautiful and that we will be magnificently crowned. For if we possess the right qualities, then like the nation that owned the Kohinoor, our lives can never be defeated.

May God give direction to our lives as we make up our jewels is my humble prayer.

INDEX